THE ENGLISH MIDDLE-CLASS NOVEL

THE ENGLISH
MIDDLE-CLASS NOVEL

T. B. Tomlinson

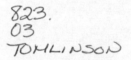

BARNES & NOBLE

BOOKS

10 East 53d St., New York 10022
(a division of Harper & Row Publishers, Inc.)

First published 1976 by
THE MACMILLAN PRESS LTD
London and Basingstoke

Published in the U.S.A. 1976 by
HARPER & ROW PUBLISHERS, INC.
BARNES & NOBLE IMPORT DIVISION

ISBN 0-06-496932-0

Printed in Great Britain

Contents

1 The Novel and Middle-Class England

Without Contraries is no progression

In the course of thinking about modern English literature and society, and the range of people who have written about it (including, that is, people as different as Arnold, Lawrence, Eliot, Leavis, Raymond Williams, Hoggart, Georg Lukács), at some point or other, it seems to me, one has to decide between two mutually exclusive ideas: you can see English language and literature *either* as the nodal point of society, the focus of all that is creative in it; *or* as one of several key influences, not all of which are, or should be, at all times either consonant or equally important.

I would argue the second view myself, for two reasons. In the first place, it is surely a simple matter of fact that in the last century as in this there has been such a large number of people so slightly touched by any literary influence, written or oral, that any notion of literature as either controlling or even reflecting the whole of English 'society' must be idealistic almost to vanishing point. You could argue, as I imagine Dr and Mrs Leavis both would, that the ways in which people read or listen to the great writers these days are cruder than they were in, say, Dickens's time, before the Education Acts of the 1870s and early 1900s had started massed schooling in a planned and organised way. And D. H. Lawrence, were he alive today, would certainly agree with such an indictment of state education systems. But even if this accusation is true (and personally I don't think it is, though I recognise that most of the great novelists and poets side with Lawrence and with Dr and Mrs Leavis in this matter), any reading of, say, Mayhew or of the reports sent in to Chadwick before the mid-century must show a nation only a small proportion of which was in a position either to read, or to be significantly influenced by, a passage of Shakespeare or Dickens. Indeed, if one thinks in terms of either Dickens's own bricklayer in *Bleak House*, or a good many of the people towards the bottom end of Booth's scale right at the end of the century, there must have been many who had not heard of any major writer, or who, if they had, regarded the names even of Shakespeare, Dickens, Tennyson simply as talismans waved around by a class of beings totally alien and impossibly remote. In such circumstances, neither readings from popular literature, the ballads, nor even from the Bible could possibly help much.[1]

For these reasons it has always seemed to me that any view that depends on the primacy of literature, or indeed of *any* single element in society, is unrealistic. I do not think that literature's comparative isolation from major portions of the community is any new, or growing, phenomenon. Statistics on these matters are hard to come by, and difficult to interpret even when you can get hold of them; but I would guess that, granted all the differences in class structure, Shakespeare's England, and Chaucer's, must have been marked by an ignorance about literature on the part of the majority even greater and more unfortunate than that which characterises the much better-documented nineteenth century. The great writers before the later seventeenth century do seem to have been lucky in that they were often in closer touch than most have been later with the life and vigour of ordinary spoken English; but even they were (or if they weren't originally they quickly became) literary men in some sense or other, and so to that extent were out of touch with, and beyond the range of, ordinary working men and women. And closer to our own day, D. H. Lawrence's life and works are almost paradigmatic: even a man who starts off life as a miner's son, and who continues to draw on this experience later on, must move towards the life 'beyond' (as the women in the opening part of *The Rainbow* have it), and therefore to a literature read by few, if any, working men. Leaving Stratford behind (or not having been born in it) is a constant literary experience.

My second reason for arguing a pluralist position, or one in which there are competing and warring elements, involves a shift of ground from stressing what was in fact the case, to stressing what *ought*, in any society, to be the case. That is, I think that a society in which there are warring elements – even one in which certain important elements are disjunct altogether – is likely to be healthier than one in which any single element (whether literature, or art, or religion, or science) is dominant. That is why Blake's position, as summarised in the epigraph to this chapter, is crucial. Or perhaps I should have said Blake's *positions* are crucial; because he is often undecided, even within the limits of a single work like *The Marriage of Heaven and Hell* (1790), whether to back one or both of the eternal opposites to which his imagination constantly recurs. He is undecided, that is, whether to back the primacy of Energy ('Energy is eternal delight') and so, presumably, of poetry; or whether to back a condition in which energy and poetry are continually opposed by their opposites (in Blakian terms, 'Urizen', reason, God). Personally, I think he is at his best, at least in works like *The Marriage*, when thinking in terms of this second position, quite unlike some of his cloudier statements in the late prose-poems, and most concisely summarised by his sentence, 'Without Contraries is no progression'. In context, this leads him to denounce the supremacy of religion; though it is clear that he is prepared also to oppose the supremacy of any other of the terms and impulses he mentions. So, from two different sections of the poem, come these two quotations:

Without Contraries is no progression. Attraction and Repulsion, Reason and Energy, Love and Hate, are necessary to human existence.

These two classes of men [roughly, poets and reasoners] are always upon earth, & they should be enemies: whoever tries to reconcile them seeks to destroy existence.
Religion is an endeavour to reconcile the two.

These are splendidly true statements, and ones to which one constantly has recourse in thinking about the life and literature that followed after Blake. It is the more important to bear them in mind because not merely Romantic and post-Romantic poetry, but even some sections of the novel too, are tempted from time to time to take refuge from the obstinate contradictions of life in a transcendentalist nirvana in which all difficulties shall be reconciled. Among minor novelists, Disraeli comes to mind, with his vision of a new feudalism in which all have and know their place, so that a future clouded by peasants' revolts is unthinkable. Later on, and the more dangerously as the position of the artist as reconciler and artificer gains still more prominence, there is of course George Eliot's own St Theresa dream, and in this century there are various sections of Lawrence in which he lays by his own livelier and more specific prose in favour of the lyrical apocalypse of, for instance, the worst sections of 'Excurse'. In many works of art there is a lurking irritation at the difficulties that have been raised by the very conception and working out of the works themselves, and in some cases this can all too easily lead to an assumption by the author of a kind of absolutism and autocracy which, however defiantly put, is virtually a denial of Blake's 'contraries'. And the tendency can gain further ground in any age in which poets begin to see themselves as bards, or as 'the un-acknowledged legislators of mankind', and to think that criticisms of their own work may be refuted by rejoinders such as this of Wordsworth's, in a letter to Sir George Beaumont:

... In short, in your Friend's Letter, I am condemned for the very thing for which I ought to have been praised; viz., that I have not written down to the level of superficial observers & unthinking minds. —Every great Poet is a Teacher: I wish either to be considered as a Teacher, or as nothing. [From an undated letter, *c.* 20 February 1808.]

Actually, the nineteenth-century novel, with its broadly based dramatisation of conflicts between a multiplicity of different people, temperaments, and outlooks generally, is only rarely in danger from an incipient authoritarianism of this kind. At the same time, however, it is clear that the novel cannot avoid such dangers simply by taking over unmodified that balancing of equal opposites ('Reason and Energy, Love and Hate') recommended, quite properly in the context of his own poem, by the early Blake. The position is complicated in any extended work because in the first place, as I imagine Blake himself would have acknowledged, conflicts of this kind, however necessary they are to the kinds of life and living most novelists are talking about, do not necessarily produce unalloyed good (in fact they virtually never do); and in the second place, the novel must embrace all kinds and facts of life – the obstinate day-to-day realities of working and living conditions, class differences, personal affinities and antagonisms from all walks of life – that would be distorted by any attempt to fit them into a work of art governed at all points by opposing terms like reason and energy, or religion and science, or art and life. 'If you try to nail anything down, in the novel, either it kills the novel, or the novel gets up and walks away with the nail.' The fact that Lawrence himself, in some places, tries to nail things down too much does not disprove either the truth of this statement, or the truth of his own writing in by far the greater part of his essays and novels.

There is a famous statement of J. S. Mill's, diagnosing the condition of 'human affairs' in nineteenth-century England a little after Blake, that deserves comment in this connection:

> Coleridge used to say that everyone is born either a Platonist or an Aristotelian: it may similarly be affirmed, that every Englishman of the present day is by implication either a Benthamite or a Coleridgian; holds views of human affairs which can only be proved true on the principles either of Bentham or of Coleridge.

That statement, first published in 1840 in *The Westminster Review*, has indeed the strength of a true and (for all Mill's later disclaimers that he was no more than an 'interpreter' of other people's thoughts) original insight into nineteenth-century England. The difficulty is, it cannot possibly be the *whole* truth. We can take for granted the fact that Mill is clearly talking in terms that would limit his diagnosis to views held by every *educated* Englishman (a very small percentage, that is, of England's population, which rose from just over ten million in 1811 to nearly eighteen million at the 1851 census). Even so, the kind of extensions or modifications that must be made, both to his diagnosis and to Blake's still more commanding equations, becomes clear when once we use them to illuminate – as indeed they often can illuminate – the work of any of the great novelists. Many of the novelists do have their affiliations with one or other 'camp' (as George Eliot, for instance, does with the German philosophers, Comte, Coleridge); but equally clearly none of them can possibly be seen simply as 'Benthamite' or 'Coleridgian', or whatever. They see life differently from any of the philosophers, and very much in their own terms. This means not simply that Jane Austen, for instance, has not been in the least influenced by either Bentham or Coleridge, but that her novels fall completely outside their range of mind. If you try to read Jane Austen on any of their principles, you will miss almost everything she has to say that is valuable and interesting.

In the spirit of Blake's own 'Marriage', then, and rather than trying to read literature as following in the wake of, or 'dramatising', what the leading philosophers have originated; or philosophy as, however interesting, a mere background to the work of the truly original spirits of the age, the poets and creative artists; rather than thinking about the period in either of these ways, it seems to me much better to allow both literature and philosophy, together indeed with quite other and different impulses, *its* own truth, but at the same time to count them *all* as competing, often indeed conflicting, truths. Thus, for instance, Mill's statement (within which, indeed, Benthamites and Coleridgians clearly compete, much as characters and impulses within a drama or novel do) offers a clear and true insight into the period, and one which, therefore, may be used as a critique of certain novels, poems, plays; but by the same token the best novels, poems and plays, both from within the period and from outside it, must be allowed to act also as a critique of the philosophers.

And it is essential to recognise that, in this period as in any other, a term like 'critique' must be read as implying criticism, and indeed 'enmity', rather than just mutually helpful correction. There is not, and never has been, any single 'culture' in England (or even two cultures) with all the constituent parts subtly interwoven to work for, and meet in, a common end. Within the nineteenth century, one does not need the (often very true) diagnoses given by Marx, Engels and their followers, but merely common sense to realise that there was no community of living embracing the whole, or even any majority, of the inhabitants; and so for this reason alone there could have been no common culture either, even were any such desirable in the first place.

Personally, as I have said, I do not think it is desirable to have either any agreed unity of aims and objectives covering the whole of society, or a unity imposed by circumstances which give any single element (such as literature, religion, science) a virtually unchallenged leadership. A large part of nineteenth-century life presents a grim picture indeed, particularly if we look at those areas of living only barely touched on by novelists and poets but amply documented in reports by sanitary officials, royal commissions on conditions in factories, children's employment, and so on. Even so, and even if it is granted that the reforms since then, which, incidentally, have been brought about largely by people outside the literary field altogether) have been partial; nevertheless

I still think that any alternative based on 'agreement' between the conflicting parties would have been either so unreal as to be totally ineffective, or, much more likely, an outward form of agreement only that was in fact masking an unhealthy, because insufficiently challenged, leadership.

'To generalise is to be an Ideot.' Blake was right again, and it is time to look a bit more specifically at the novel's part in nineteenth-century life.

In a society which, though in the upshot more peaceful than most parts of the Europe that led up to and continued from 1848, was still torn by class-conflict and the developing industrial revolution, the English novel emerges as broadly speaking a middle-class, and very stable, enterprise. Taken over any longish spell of time, it is of course divided within itself. Lawrence's deliberately provocative repudiations of the work of some of his predecessors are well known; and changes of intention and enterprise within individual works by various writers complicate the issue further. But some general, descriptive terms are essential, and personally I think that, granted all exceptions, the term 'middle-class', with all the stability and vigour that implies in nineteenth-century England, is a fit and proper one for the novel up to and including Lawrence.

To put it with more historical accuracy: what seems to me to have happened was that writers from Jane Austen onwards picked up leads developed in the main by Richardson, whose heroines grasp, unconsciously perhaps but very accurately, the mixture of personal and economic factors surrounding them, and then went on to develop the middle-class and bourgeois interests that he had distilled as one at least of the novel's main concerns. There are breaks in the history of the novel between Jane Austen's death in 1817 and the early Dickens (most of the concerns in Scott's novels are rather different from those in the English novel), but certainly by the mid-century a hundred years after Richardson, there is no doubt about the status and function of the English novel: it is very much a middle-class enterprise.

And so, indeed, it ought to be, at least as long as the middle class continues to dominate English life. Whether you see 'the middle class' as, to use Georg Lukács' terms, sick and 'dehumanizing';[2] or whether you see it, as I myself do, in much more hopeful and positive terms, it quite obviously has been, in the England and indeed Europe since Napoleon's day, both an increasingly distinct 'class', *and* the class that has focused the most powerful and intelligent impulses in society. I think it still does, though admittedly a good many commentators on contemporary life – creative writers included – more and more doubt this.

Lukács himself, as a practising Marxist, would of course have put the emphasis very differently. The novelists he singles out include Sir Walter Scott and, a hundred years later, Thomas Mann. His argument for both Scott and Mann is that they write about individuals, but individuals who focus, and in varying ways act as a critique of, broadly representative trends in modern life. The characters in Scott and Mann are not just symbols: they live the life their personalities and circumstances demand. But they are also part of novels that diagnose – very truly, according to Lukács – the weaknesses of and in the dominant culture. Lukács notes that Scott 'very seldom speaks of the present. He does not raise the social questions of contemporary England in his novels, the class struggle between bourgeoisie and proletariat which was then beginning to sharpen.'[3] Despite this, Scott has a very sure historical sense, and one that enables him to pit the virtues of a decent, 'more or less mediocre, average English gentleman' against the extravagant and eccentric behaviour of many Romantic, 'Byronic' heroes. One might quarrel a bit with Lukács' notion of an average English gentleman in relation to Scott, but his general account of the English and European novel has a lot of truth in it. As against what he calls the 'epic' novels of Scott, Mann and others, Lukács sets what he sees as the *really* decadent trend in 'modernism': that is, the tendency in many twentieth-century writers in particular (he names Virginia Woolf, Joyce and others) to discount the broader movements of society, to see these as unimportant or unreal; and to record, therefore, merely the moment-to-moment reflections of discrete individuals. In other words, a good deal of modern literature is, in Lukács' view, solipsistic and self-regarding.

I agree very much with Lukács' argument about the self-regarding and subjectivist tendencies of a lot of twentieth-century literature, as indeed I do with D. H. Lawrence's still more pungent attack in 'Surgery for the Novel – Or a Bomb'. Clearly Lawrence would part company with Lukács on a number of issues (the future of working-class culture, for instance!); but on 'modernism' ('Did I feel a twinge in my little toe, or didn't I?') they are often very close, and personally I think very right:

> And there's the serious novel: senile-precocious. Absorbedly, childishly concerned with *what I am.* 'I am this, I am that, I am the other. My reactions are such, and such, and such. And, oh, Lord, if I liked to watch myself closely enough, if I liked to analyse my feelings minutely, as I unbutton my gloves, instead of saying crudely I unbuttoned them, then I could go on to a million pages instead of a thousand. In fact, the more I come to think of it, it is gross, it is uncivilized bluntly to say: I unbuttoned my gloves. After all, the absorbing adventure of it! Which button did I begin with?' etc.[4]

Where I disagree with both Lawrence and Lukács is in what I take to be their evaluation of bourgeois, middle-class living as reflected in nineteenth- and twentieth-century novels. Lukács' argument (and again one is reminded of Lawrence in some of his essays, and in his letters during the war period) is that the best novelists diagnose what the worst merely exemplify, namely a radical and irreversible sickness or decline in middle-class life (Lawrence would say in all modern life, at least in Western Europe). Obviously there is at least a partial truth in this; but personally I would want to stress in addition the ways in which the novelists concentrate the *best* things in the dominant culture: that is, in the bourgeois, middle-class life that their characters respond to, react against, or even, in some cases, reject entirely. Clearly many novelists are strongly, and rightly, critical of the society they see developing around them. In the end, however, the best of them (Lawrence himself included, I think) support it. I think that they are right to do so; and that it is precisely this involvement in both the failures and the achievements of middle-class life that makes the novel the most broadly based of all the literary forms in England since the virtual collapse of drama after the 1620s.[5]

On the other hand, and even granted this status for the novel, some consequences follow that are less fortunate, or at any rate less easy to evaluate. One of these, closely relevant to the chapters that follow on Jane Austen, Dickens and George Eliot in particular, is that the nature of the middle class, from pre-1832 days onwards, has been in part that of a defensive alliance. It is an alliance of conflicting interests (for example, of county families, shopkeepers, some upper working-class people, factory owners, bureaucrats, and so on), not so much against Tory landowners or the big industrialists, as against the working class. The results of the 1831 election, and of the passing of the First Reform Bill that followed in May 1832, were in part a closing of the ranks in the face of what some historians at least describe as pressure from below. In other words, if the £10 householders had to be admitted to the vote, this was done in order to enlist their support as new members of the incipient middle class, and so help prevent further outbreaks of the Luddite and Peterloo kinds. In retrospect, this seems to have worked, though a lot of people at the time, and some of Mrs Gaskell's working-class characters a bit later on, saw it as an act of betrayal by some of the Radical leaders.[6]

How far the 1832 settlement was politically and morally justifiable in the long term is of course debatable. What does seem clear is that the nature of the middle-class alliance, particularly in the years before 1832 itself, was in part defensive, and that this may well have had its consequences for literature at that time and later. In Jane Austen's day, for instance, and without placing any blame either on her or on other writers for not having given us major works specifically about Napoleon, the Luddites, Sidmouth, Castlereagh, Wellington, there is perhaps something guardedly self-contained about the literature of the period as a whole, including the novel. Admittedly, the best poems and novels are deeply involved with many aspects of England's life and culture (though it is perhaps worth recording that, despite attempts by some of the Romantic poets, there is no drama worth mentioning in the period); but there is at least one commanding fact about this period that literature hardly registers at all, and that is the surely very general and deep-seated impulse to violence, not merely on the Continent but also at home. In England, the years from about 1811 to 1820 seem to have outweighed even the Reform periods and the 1840s in outbreaks of public violence, and though historians stress that the outbreaks up to and including Peterloo (1819) showed no sign of any national or foreign-based *organisation* linking them together, many of them do seem to have been so violent, so rapid, indeed so unexplained by any overt programme or organisation that their existence must surely point to some very deep-seated potential for violence in England, war-weary though the country must have been then.

Compared with, for instance, Shakespeare's history plays (which, though set back in time, are quite clearly involved with both the life and the politics of Tudor England), or even some of the earlier Romantic poems, such as *The Prelude*, it is perhaps one of the less fortunate aspects of the dawning middle-class consciousness that, as far as literature goes, it stands aloof from currents of this kind in the community. This is the more disappointing, and certainly the more surprising, since there are several of the writers of the time who do comment on the contemporary situation as a matter of urgency, but who keep these comments outside their major published works. Thus we have Wordsworth, for instance, writing to the Prime Minister, Lord Liverpool, from Keswick in the Lake District, and warning him about sedition 'even among these mountains';[7] and Sir Walter Scott writing to Southey in 1812: 'The country is mined below our feet'.[8] If Wordsworth here sounds rather needlessly panic-stricken about the Lake District itself, he is nevertheless clearly very alarmed, and his comment to Liverpool is perhaps one pointer to the fact that, with the exception of some political satire (very uneven in quality) by Byron and Shelley, and perhaps some of Wordsworth's own political poems (by this time both increasingly conservative and increasingly dull), writers seem to have concentrated their feelings in private, rather than in public, discourse.

More generally, and thinking of the later years of the century, which were troubled more by economic and industrial unrest than by incipient revolutionary movements, this hiving-off of middle-class interests in literature from many of the more popular disturbances means that even the novel will continue to leave large areas of English life either untouched, or insufficiently incorporated into its broadly social concerns (see Chapters 5 and 6 below on political novels from the 1840s on). The slightly alarmist and defensive nature of many middle-class reactions does decrease a bit as the century goes on. At least one historian finds the early 1830s (particularly the 'Days of May', 1832, when for a time it was thought that the Duke of Wellington might intervene to stop the Reform Bill) more unsettled politically than any subsequent period, including the Chartist 1840s or the period of the Hyde Park riots just before the passing of the Second Reform Bill.[9] On the other hand, the passing of the Second Reform Bill in 1867 itself provoked at least some defensive reaction (often unpleasant, as in Robert Lowe's bitter comment, 'We must educate our masters'); and in addition, by this time 'the workshop of the world', which England had indeed become with the railway age and the vast increase in manufacturing consequent on this, led also to an upper middle-class prosperity which, though not of course shared by many literary people, and severely criticised by most, had its due effect. With the possible exception of Dickens, anybody brought up in, or living in, middle-class literary circles during the second half of the century must have had to make a huge and deliberate effort to get into any sort of direct and immediate contact with the working classes (still, of course, by far the majority of England's population, and still, despite the efforts of private organisations and the passing of the acts on primary schooling in the 1870s, basically uneducated). And to have to make any such deliberate effort naturally inhibits the writing of literature. In any case, Beatrice Webb's attempt to pose as a working woman and live for a while in a working-class family would hardly have been open to a George Eliot or a Henry James.[10]

The other side of precisely the same coin, however, is that middle-class England was far from being *merely* complacent or defensive, but on the contrary, in a good many of the matters that closely concerned it, extremely vigorous and enterprising. The facts about England's prosperity, especially in the twenty years from the mid-century to at least the beginnings of the Great Depression in the mid-seventies, are well known; and although trade declined periodically after this (ironically, in part because of England's very success in exporting skills and manufactured goods like railways to her competitors), the sheer energy of the early years of Victoria's reign continued, to the point indeed where even Charles Booth, writing mainly about the very poor in London, could conclude of the nation as a whole, 'We thus have the general impression of a well-to-do energetic people . . .'[11]

In saying this about the England whose extremes of poverty he himself documented so thoroughly, Booth is clearly being a little naïve or, perhaps, partial (he is of course committed to backing Victorian ideals of individual initiative in men and masters alike). But his confidence in England is there, and is clearly a directing influence in the huge scope of the work he undertook; moreover, it seems to have been shared by more sophisticated commentators, even though their over-all conclusions are different from his. Thus in the following extract, Beatrice Webb herself remembers the end of the century as producing what must clearly have been, not Charles Booth's simple-minded confidence in the future, but a whole series of much more interesting and lively debates on the question of poverty and what, if anything, the government should do about it. The confidence Mrs Webb records here is one which, though solving no problems, and though leaving the bleak facts about London's poor exactly where they stand at the end of Booth's series (completed early in this century), is a better testimony than any trade figures alone could be to the continuing vigour and enterprise even of the *fin de siècle* of Victoria's reign:

> There were, in fact, in the 'eighties' and 'nineties' two controversies raging in periodicals and books, and giving rise to perpetual argument within my own circle of relations and acquaintances: on the one hand, the meaning of the poverty of masses of men; and, on the other, the practicability and desirability of political and industrial democracy as a set-off to, perhaps as a means of redressing, the grievances of the majority of the people. Was the poverty of the many a necessary condition of the wealth of the nation and of its progress in civilisation? And if the bulk of the people were to remain poor and uneducated, was it . . . safe to entrust them with the weapon of trade unionism, and with making and controlling the Government of Great Britain . . .?[12]

This is rather staid prose (a far cry from Carlyle, for instance, on similar topics) but, if we remember that discussion of many of these questions had begun fifty years or more before the period Mrs Webb is describing here, and that much of it had been as lively and controversial as she implies, the conventional picture of a staid, dully respectable Victorian England governed by purely business and material interests must surely fade, almost to vanishing point. And most of the novelists, I think, though obviously they do not act merely as servants or by-products of the driving 'material interest' that so strongly informs Conrad's *Nostromo*, for instance, share something of the spirit of the class from which they themselves all come. In particular, they share many of the worries that middle-class intellectuals, reformers and politicians had (thus, for instance, it is Conrad's Mrs Gould who gives such prominence to the stultifying effects of the 'material interest' that her husband, though for thoroughly idealistic reasons, virtually lives for); but they also share a good deal of the energy and spirit of enquiry that in fact dominates much of Victorian England. And certainly the novel's foundation in, and community of interest with, such a broadly based movement as the rising middle class of the nineteenth century must have helped prevent any great indulgence in the sort of in-turned, solipsistic writing that Lukács complains of.

By the end of the nineteenth century and the beginning of this, the English novel, though clearly the dominant, because the most widely based, literary form, is still partial. That is to say, not merely does it leave out of account large tracts of English life at the time (there is scarcely a mention, for instance, of the effects on the working class of the long depression that lasted, with intervals, from the mid-seventies to the end of the nineties); but, partly in consequence of this, its most interesting and rewarding enquiries are directed towards the achievements and frustrations of life in the England that the novelists – George Eliot, James, Conrad, Lawrence – know best: the very powerful and commanding middle class to which, though in many ways its most searching critics, they all belong, immigrants like Conrad and James very much included here. Personally I think the novelists were wise in choosing (though instinctively rather than deliberately) to limit the sphere of their enquiries in this way. Any attempt to cover the life of all classes of people in England, let alone in the American and continental areas that James, for instance, often moves in, could only have ended in a surface presentation that would have brushed aside the very controversies and difficulties that the novel, at its best, thrives on.

Finally in this introductory chapter I should like to notice briefly one interest that many of the novelists have that falls outside the range of a term like 'middle class', and indeed outside the range of any terms that have to do with men and women living, as of course the characters we will be considering all do live, in one or other social group or community. None of these novels is limited to the merely private or personal (even though some of the characters within them are). And each does have, as part of its main concern, an attempt at seeing the relations – or disrelations – between people and their society. Nevertheless there are in most of the novels, and so in some of the characters within the novels, impulses that are not so much anti-social, as quite disrelated, at least by origin, from any concerns either fostered or hindered by society. Two examples of the sort of thing I will have in mind here are, in Jane Austen, the impulse towards what D. W. Harding calls 'regulated hatred'; and in George Eliot, the kind of impulse she portrays in Gwendolen's unaccountable fits of despair. I say 'unaccountable' because these impulses, together with the ones Harding notes in Jane Austen, seem to me to represent chronic strains of behaviour that the novelists see as so deeply embedded, not just in the particular characters concerned, but in human nature itself, that no change of circumstances, and no improvement in social conditions, could affect them radically. The feeling is most extreme perhaps, and most interesting, in Hardy; as in those scenes for instance where he pictures, not just people, but parts of the natural world and even man-made machinery like the reaper in Chapter XIV of *Tess*, as driven by a kind of automatism. These are not the moments in Hardy where he despairs about the 'Fates', but much more naturalistic scenes in which he seems to be proposing a world – a universe, indeed – in which some impulses and actions fit together and make perfect sense, and some do not and never will.

Conrad has related feelings about the nature of the world we live in, and so have other novelists of the period. In their weaker moments, the novelists allow such insights (if one may beg the question and call them that for the moment) to result in a dislocation of the novel itself; and this is generally caused, not by any technical fault on their part, but by fits of despair that they simply cannot, or have not managed to, control. But at their best such writers give a view of life which, without being in any sense concerned with religion or mysticism or the occult, brings society itself sharply up against certain vital natural forces that affect all our lives but that are, in part at least, finally beyond either our control, or any 'control' detectable in the universe itself.

In practice (that is, in the terms put by the actual novels) this seems to me related to, but in the end rather different from, any 'tragic' view of life, at least as that is conventionally conceived. Certainly there is no matter here simply of a tragic loss of potential, or of man as a heroic figure pitted against the Gods or against a meaningless universe. And even if we take the very unconventional notions of tragedy that emerge variously in Shakespeare's plays, none even of these is quite the same as the views (equally various in fact) put by the English novelists. The reason for this is partly to do with Shakespeare's own unique abilities, but partly too that the novels are concerned at once with natural forces and impulses, *and* with a solid and relatively predictable middle-class society. The result is a series of books posing both fairly large social groups which it is increasingly more difficult, though still possible, for human agencies to change; and, mixed inextricably with these, forces which we can sometimes use and come to terms with, but which have also their own quite unpredictable, and not always mutually consistent, impulses and origins. As in many tragedies, the authors recognise that it is misleading to seek to comprehend these or any other matters in or by any holistic design; their enterprise is generally the much more interesting and rewarding one of exploring this world in which, though the pieces (at least those of extra-human origin) will probably never make complete sense, the mixture may be seen as one that is both destructive of human life and potential, and also almost endlessly productive.

The chapters that follow are mostly on single texts or pairs of novels. I have chosen this method because otherwise, given the extraordinary wealth of material available, one might have had to try to cover too much too quickly and so beg the essential question of how far certain themes and interests are maintained over the length of a whole book. There are also some chapters on general issues such as the ones I have noted here, and the position of the English political novel around the mid-century.

The term 'middle class' I will continue to use pretty much as George Eliot envisages it in *Middlemarch*: as including, that is, a wide range of people and ocupations, from the bottom end of her scale (some of the more prosperous of the 'parcel-tying' shopkeepers, plus people like

Toller and Wrench), to families intent on climbing the social ladder (the Vincys, the Bulstrodes), 'intellectuals' and clergy like Lydgate and Fare-brother, and established 'county' families like the Chettams and the Brookes. Other writers, like Trollope, of course add different occupa-tions (for example, from the growing army of clerks and parliamentarians), but without changing the over-all picture radically. There is only one kind of radical extension of the term that perhaps needs forecasting here, and that is the extending of the novel's frontiers to include areas and experience beyond England itself, as James and Conrad in particular did towards the end of the nineteenth and during the beginning of the twentieth century. For instance, I take James's Strether to have a lot in common with, say, Farebrother, Lydgate himself, Trollope's Plantagenet Palliser; but to bring also distinctively American characteristics, *and* distinctively American strengths, to the European and English scene.

2 Jane Austen's Originality: *Emma*

If Jane Austen belonged, as I believe she did, to a literary age and class that had to be rather guarded as far as politics, at least, were concerned, there are lots of other ways in which her writing, particularly in *Emma*, is the reverse of 'guarded'. I once began a lecture to second-year students: 'Whatever you may have heard to the contrary in First Year, the English novel begins with Jane Austen.' With some regrets, I no longer begin lectures this way: partly because the habit of dragging first-year students through a lot of eighteenth-century novels is happily declining, but mainly because phrases like 'the first modern novelist', or 'the first great novelist', are clearly too simple-minded to do justice either to what went before Jane Austen or to what came after her. If and when such phrases are relevant at all, it must be in a spirit very different from simply asking, Who came first in such-and-such a tradition or *genre*?

Nevertheless I do have some regrets in giving up or even modifying very much the phrase 'the English novel begins with Jane Austen'. It goes without saying that there is something absurd in such a claim, but still I wonder whether there isn't a greater disjunction between Jane Austen and the eighteenth-century novelists than is usually allowed; or even than Dr Leavis (and he is surely *very* unusual here) allows when he discusses her position in Chapter 1 of *The Great Tradition*. Clearly there are links between Jane Austen and her predecessors (Leavis himself insists on this, particularly in the case of Richardson, better than anybody else I know); but the more one thinks of the English novel to the present day, the more it seems to start, almost *ab initio*, with Jane Austen. In terms of simple 'likeness', Fanny Burney is I suppose her nearest neighbour, but personally I would find the simplest of comparisons and contrasts between Jane Austen and modern novelists more profitable than almost any that one can think of with the eighteenth century. What is it, for instance, that yokes together Jane Austen's clear tendency to shun a really frank discussion of sex (except when safely distanced by irony) with Lawrence's insistence (which becomes at times a completely un-ironic over-insistence) that an openness in these matters must be at the very heart of novel writing? By contrast even the triumphs of the eighteenth-century novel seem isolated phenomena, only marginally necessary or preparatory to the novel as we know it now.

Of course, to say that they are not necessary to the modern novel is not to say that they are bad or merely illusory. Leaving Richardson aside for the moment, Fielding is an obvious difficulty. I like Fielding's sense of fun, and recognise that no later novelist – not even Dickens – can match it. It is not just a question of there being no more Fieldings: we simply do not know how to live as relaxedly as this any more. But by the same token Fielding's ebullience and his sense of fun go with a laxness – a too willing suspension of moral belief – that punishes seduction in ordinary people (Nightingale), but is happy to allow the child of nature, Tom, to go scot-free. The moral basis of *Tom Jones* is confused, and though this in itself would not damn a novel – obviously in certain cases a partial confusion of motive and outlook can be the heart of a novel's progression – taken together with the over-all, fairly unthinking optimism of Fielding's tone it makes for irrelevance rather than any really challenging comedy. Fielding's irony or humour is not of the kind that can bring together (at any rate in *Tom Jones*) the two terms of his enquiry: natural impulses – the picaresque and sympathetic 'Tom' story – on the one hand, and social pressures, social needs and engagements on the other.

The great bulk of eighteenth-century fiction is remoter still from Jane Austen and modern considerations. If one can forget for the moment the wordiness of Fielding's unfortunate addresses to 'the reader', his more characteristic tone is much more humane, and therefore much more aware of rights, claims, pressures that may be exerted by a whole variety of people than is the characteristic tone of most novelists in the amoral, picaresque *genre*. Certainly Fielding is a nicer man, and also a livelier one, than one imagines Defoe to have been; and he could neither have imagined nor entertained the boldly uncommitted tone of this, for instance, from Smollett's *Roderick Random* (Roderick is chained to the deck during a sea-battle):

... however I concealed my agitation as well as I could, till the head of the officer of marines who stood near me, being shot off, bounced from the deck athwart my face, leaving me well nigh blinded with brains. I could contain myself no longer, but began to bellow with all the strength of my lungs: when a drummer coming towards me, asked if I was wounded, and before I could answer, received a great shot in his belly, which tore out his entrails, and he fell flat on my breast. This accident entirely bereft me of all discretion ...

This calmly 'precise' language, applied to such material, looks nowadays like a strange parody of Jane Austen; in fact, of course, it is merely the staple of much of what preceded her. The dubious advantage of the eighteenth-century picaresque tale is that, like the continental and Elizabethan novels from which it derives, it leaves the hero or prostitute-heroine free from any ties of society, family or even common feeling. Moll, Roderick, Gil Blas, Lazarillo de Tormes – they all wander with complete freedom up and down the social scale, uncommitted to any particular class or group of people. They don't even make lasting enemies; thus Roderick Random, meeting by chance a woman who had previously deceived him, instantly offers to share his room with her and cure her of the pox, provided only that she will share expenses and nurse him through the same disease.

Some feeling for picaresque independence, and for the armour-plated toughness of mind this induces, will always be with us. Any reader of Evelyn Waugh's early tales will surely recognise in the tone of these a distant echo of the same bold un-morality, and the kind of wit that this can certainly generate. Today 'Theatre of the Absurd' and 'Theatre of Cruelty' are clearly different, but related, phenomena. And indeed this kind of writing, at its best, does work to question any too cosy assumption that men *can* live together in a community. But even in the hands of an Evelyn Waugh – and he is much funnier than either Defoe or Smollett – or in its American versions, the picaresque novel simply does not bulk very large these days. For one thing, its slim possibilities were pretty thoroughly written-out by the end of the eighteenth century; more importantly, there is the tremendous and radical change in the total outlook of the English novel initiated by Jane Austen.

When I say that the change was 'initiated' by Jane Austen, I mean that it was very largely thought out, and 'felt out', by her; but also that it was her originality that made it part of the common coin of life and literature. Before her a few others had begun to think in similar ways, and of these the main one, because the best, was Richardson. Clearly Richardson adumbrates a good many of the interests and qualities of nineteenth-century and later English fiction. He is also, at his best, distinctively and robustly eighteenth-century:

> My mother's hand was kindly put into his, with a simpering altogether bridal; and with another How do you now, Sir? – All his plump muscles were in motion, and a double charge of care and obsequiousness fidgetted up his whole form, when he offered me his officious palm. My mother, when I was a girl, always bid me hold up my head. I just then remembered her commands, and was dutiful – I never held up my head so high. With an averted supercilious eye, and a rejecting hand, half-flourishing – I have no need of help, Sir! You are in my way.
> He ran back, as if on wheels . . .

That seems to me splendid writing, at once solider and also more imaginative than anything in Fielding, but also distinctively eighteenth-century in its confident physicality: certainly beyond the means of any later writer. In addition, Richardson's insight (especially in *Clarissa*) into the lets and hindrances (psychological, moral, financial) to marriage is much more mature than anything possible in either the picaresque or the purely sentimental vogue.

On the other hand it is still Jane Austen who, losing something of the imaginatively physical in Richardson ('all his plump muscles were in motion, and a double charge of care and obsequiousness fidgetted up his whole form . . .'), transforms his other qualities into something more readily and generally available. *Clarissa* is an extraordinary book, but it is, quite simply, too long, and Richardson's talents are spread correspondingly thin. After Richardson some other, crucial step had to be taken.

The 'step' that Jane Austen took involved first of all writing books short enough to be commanded by (and in) a reasonable span of attention, but also re-forming and broadening Richardson's notions about the stresses and strains of marriage and family situations. It all looks simple enough in retrospect, especially if one thinks of her picaresque predecessors, or of Sterne, rather than of Richardson himself; but in fact Jane Austen's realisation of what living in society can mean is more like a literary revolution than a step in developing the novel. The corpus of her work affects the whole of English literature, not just the novel, and it does so by restoring to it a social dimension that had been pretty much lost with the eclipse of serious drama after Middleton in the 1620s. It goes without saying that there are exceptions to this sweeping generalisation – Pope, at any rate in his best poetry, almost upsets it entirely. But Pope, like Johnson, is exceptional, rather than merely 'representative', in the eighteenth century; and both Pope and Johnson are the more exceptional because their grasp of forces at work in the community was not extended by anything at all in contemporary drama, and only minimally, if at all, by the poetry of the later eighteenth century. Certainly this is true of poetry up to Blake, and probably of most poetry between his early poems and the publication of Jane Austen's major novels. If there are excellent passages in, say, Cowper, they still do not touch society in any very general way; and most of the other pre-Romantics are simply weakly ineffectual. The first-generation Romantics themselves, on the other hand, are major figures; yet none of them has written a work about how men and women live together which has anything of the staying-power of *Sense and Sensibility*, *Pride and Prejudice*, *Mansfield Park*, *Emma*, *Persuasion*. If their imaginations range – as they certainly can do – beyond Jane Austen's, their effective span of attention is generally less than hers.

What Jane Austen added to literature, on the other hand, was not what the Elizabethan dramatists had added; nor was it something that could ever properly be described in sociological terms, though it has to do with society. Jane Austen's 'sociology', if this could ever be extracted from the novels, would look, and be, conservative to the point of supporting as some kind of ideal a society that had already ceased to exist (if indeed it ever did exist with that completeness and self-sufficiency). Reading her novels (at least those before *Persuasion* and the unfinished *Sanditon*) one can sense that she is struggling to perpetuate something like the Darcy and Knightley way of living, and struggling to do this in the face of history and, more immediately, of her own biting comments on the pride and snobbishness this sort of living can engender. Her admiration of Pemberley, for instance, and Donwell Abbey, is undisguised. It would not need a Marxist historian but only a simple realist to point out that she depicts these estates and others like them from the owners' point of view (fallible though this is shown to be) and not that of the tenants, or families casually dependent on the tenants.

More interestingly, it is hardly even a real 'owner', in the historian's sense, who is given us in Knightley or Darcy. To take either of these men as representing the likeness of actual historical figures would be to convict Jane Austen of naïvety. Her originality does not lie at all in that direction. What she gives us, rather, is a kind of construct or myth which includes a strong infusion of the real. Pemberley, for instance, is in a sense overtly an ideal, certainly not a reality that we can depend on in the sense that we depend on Elizabeth Bennet's common sense. But Elizabeth's common sense falls overboard for Pemberley and Darcy, almost – as she ironically accuses herself – in that order. In the end it is needless to distinguish what is actual 'historical' fact from what is ideal. One is only conscious of a strong impulse to think Pemberley a wonderful place, nicely tempered by the actual Elizabeth – her irony, her impossible mother, her worries about Darcy, and so on.

For these reasons Jane Austen's work is misjudged, I think, by those who see her as representing her times, or expressing more clearly what others also then felt or saw. For all its settled and at points rather too cosy atmosphere, it is much more creative, more unforeseen, than that. To change the emphasis from places to people: the ease with which Jane Austen imagines people – as Knightley, Emma, Elizabeth Bennet, Mr Woodhouse – who are also and at the same time much more than just individual 'characters', is practically unrivalled in English literature before the nineteenth century. Shakespeare can do this and a great deal more besides; so perhaps, in a very different way, can Pope. But these are exceptions, and would be so in any age. Jane Austen's own originality is best described as an extraordinary turn of mind that can make Emma, say, or Elizabeth Bennet, at once a person to be reckoned with, manifestly alive and real throughout the length of the novel, and at the same time an issue, a generalising tendency, a habit of thought and action, an idea. With her, the people in a drama and the ideas in it are indistinguishable. In the same way her various and varying country estates are at the same time real and also notions, hypotheses, possibilities in the mind.

At one point late on in *Northanger Abbey* Jane Austen says: '... there are some situations of the human mind in which good sense has very little power.' This is a simple statement of what I would claim to be one of her main, but largely unrecognised, interests, and it points to the source of her freshness and individuality. She is always, of course, a novelist who pins a great deal of faith on the actual, the sensible, the rational; and the sense of her delight in intelligently and precisely *ordering* her world so predominates as to give that impression by which she is commonly known of backing unequivocally the common sense of an Elizabeth Bennet, an Elinor Dashwood or an Anne Elliot. And in *Emma*, though the heroine is deluded, the book for the most part is not.

There is of course a good deal of truth in this general feeling about Jane Austen. She is less venturesome, or at any rate less willing to uncover the depths of emotional states than, for instance, the George Eliot who portrays Gwendolen Harleth's horrified repulsion at Rex's proposal, or the 'sick motivelessness' of Gwendolen's own spiritual desolation and boredom. (Later English and Continental novelists would clearly offer more striking contrasts.) Nevertheless it is possible, and usual, to stress too much or too exclusively Jane Austen's dependence on a sort of sensitive rationalism. The significance of that sentence from *Northanger Abbey* is that it is said with no feeling of regret or impatience at the powerlessness of good sense in 'some situations of the human mind'. A clearer case still – in some ways too clear – is *Sense and Sensibility* where, despite the many accounts of the novel that take the sensible Elinor Dashwood as clearly and unambiguously her sister's superior, Marianne's impulsiveness (and indeed Mrs Jennings's) is obviously essential to the book. Where Elinor's 'sense' is sceptical, they show an ability to commit themselves fully, immediately and single-mindedly to a person or situation or event. The social blunders and thoughtlessnesses, and the disaster that follows with Willoughby, are far from a simple condemnation of such an outlook and personality. Jane Austen is prepared to *trust* emotion here, for all the risks involved.

Emma, however, is the most interesting case of all and the one on which I would like to concentrate. In *Emma*, Jane Austen is finding the merely or purely 'sensible' much more elusive, and therefore still less trustworthy, or less self-sufficient, than when she has it focused mainly in the one figure of Elinor Dashwood. Curiously enough this results, not in any uncertainty or hesitation in the prose, but in an evident and generous interest in the phenomena of an Emma, a Mr Woodhouse advising a little thin gruel and lightly boiled eggs, or even a Miss Bates chattering mindlessly. Except for the Eltons and their barouche-landau relations,

Jane Austen is immediately and actively involved in almost everything she contemplates in this novel.

This is why one's first impressions, on reading those famous opening pages of *Emma*, are of an assured, well-placed confidence. The book is tinged from the first line with an irony expectant of delusion and uncertainty in Emma's future; but to read this prose as predominantly ironic or critical or conservative would surely be to misread the tone of the whole book: 'Emma Woodhouse, handsome, clever, and rich, with a comfortable home and happy disposition, seemed to unite some of the best blessings of existence; and had lived nearly twenty-one years in the world with very little to distress or vex her....' (Vol. I, ch. I)

The impulse here is forward-looking. The precision and ease of the writing obviously owe a lot to the eighteenth century (though not specifically to any of the well-known novelists except possibly Richardson), but what seems to me far more striking than any debt to the past is a sense of discovery and newness. The wandering bachelordom of Moll Flanders, Roderick Random, Humphrey Clinker, Tom Jones, adventurous though this might seem in theory, is here outdated in a few paragraphs and replaced by an entirely different, and far more interesting, sense of discovery.

Immediately, and most simply, the confidence is a confidence in the heroine herself. Jane Austen begins the novel by mixing her own account with a generous and open sharing of Emma's content and happiness: 'Emma Woodhouse, handsome, clever, and rich ...' This is, as it were, 'Jane Austen' governed at this point by something that is almost 'Emma's' own confident tone and outlook. The second and third paragraphs then move into a tone of more precise, sharply factual, summary ('She was the youngest of two daughters of a most affectionate, indulgent father ...'); but in a sentence this can change again to an alertly ironic indulgence (itself different in tone from the opening sentence) of Emma's outlook. It is almost Emma herself speaking in the special-pleading that follows the account of Miss Taylor's fondness for her: 'Between *them* it was more the intimacy of sisters...' The quick, assured changes of voice and outlook here are themselves a most important local sign of Jane Austen's having discovered a fresh and substantial interest that enlivens and transforms what would otherwise be a stiffly conventional social outlook. Another is the risks she is prepared and willing to take in backing – much more fully and wholeheartedly than most of her critics seem prepared to allow – her deluded heroine.

It therefore does Jane Austen no service to see *Emma* as a book that is 'perfect of its kind'. For one thing it isn't perfect; more importantly, this very common approach fails completely to capture the note in the prose that welcomes difficulties and disturbances. Her main endeavour, I take it, is to re-form and establish imaginatively a certain stability in social norms and personal relationships like marriage. In the act of doing this, however (of showing for instance how and why Knightley must marry Emma, and could not possibly marry Jane Fairfax, let alone Harriet), she discovers fresh instabilities in her 'society', her vision of things generally. Some of these unsettling difficulties she obviously fails to meet, or fails to meet fully. Most, however, are not merely 'met', or subjugated, or distanced by irony, but actively welcomed as a staple of the book's interest.

In this connection there is one very interesting, but I think in the end crucially misleading, account of *Emma*: that in Marvin Mudrick's book, *Jane Austen: Irony as Defense and Discovery*. Mudrick does demonstrate, as nobody else I know has, Jane Austen's tendency to use irony not only as a means of criticising and shaping her 'social' world, but also of warding off the impact of deeper and more unsettling 'discoveries' in love and marriage. In the particular case of *Emma*, however, Mudrick thinks that she has solved these difficulties ('. . . the sense of strain and anxiety is purged altogether'). I would myself dispute this sort of perfection as at all applicable to *Emma*: even the surface seems much more disturbed than Mudrick allows. More interestingly, however, I think Mudrick has distorted his own very important insight into the book by attempting to subsume it under the notion of a perfection of form.

'Irony as Form' is the title of his chapter, and its bearing is to see Jane Austen as very calmly, precisely, 'noncommittally' evaluating this apparently charming girl as having no other real qualities – a certain 'very circumscribed honesty' apart – than surface charm. Mudrick charts the very complex ways in which, for him, Emma's true companions are finally seen to be Frank Churchill and Mrs Elton. Mrs Elton is 'too transparently vulgar to be effective' socially, but the other two seduce everybody, even Mr Knightley, by their charm; only the reader, through Jane Austen's poised art, remains immune:

> Emma's and Frank Churchill's society, which makes so much of surface, guarantees the triumph of surface. Even Mr Knightley and Jane Fairfax succumb. Jane Austen, however, does not ask us to concern ourselves beyond the happy ending: she merely presents the evidence noncommittally. (p. 206)

Well, in the first place there seems to me a clear and obvious distinction between Emma's charm, which Jane Austen (for all the criticisms that Mudrick rightly shows her to be making of it) obviously admires, and Frank Churchill's, which by comparison she sees as indeed frivolous and, despite some elements of genuineness, finally untrustworthy. There is also the simple fact that Frank Churchill's deceptions are largely deliberate, Emma's hardly ever so. As for Mrs Elton, it would seem to me more relevant to see Jane Austen's portrayal as on the edge of uncontrolled hatred than to see parallels, which are hardly more than casual, with Emma. I am myself very much more indebted to Mudrick's study than this account indicates. In particular I think he is absolutely right about the significance of the Emma–Harriet relationship, and I do not know anybody else who has seen this: 'Harriet begins to seem a kind of proxy for Emma, a means by which Emma – too reluctant, too fearful of involvement, to consider the attempt herself – may discover what marriage is like.' (p. 203)

But Mudrick has failed to read the book accurately; *Emma* is more imperfect, and Jane Austen more adventurous, than he sees. Certainly there is no sense that I can see in which she could be said to be 'noncommittal'.

In the place of any attempt to subsume the book under a notion of poised or noncommittal irony, I would suggest, first of all, looking at Jane Austen's active interest in situations such as those where John Knightley, having struggled to contain it at Hartfield, openly betrays his irritability at being expected to conform socially. This is more than the irritation at Mr Woodhouse's hypochondria that Mudrick, over-stressing the emptiness of Emma's world and Emma's father, notes. It is often sparked off by that, but by other things as well, for instance by Mr Elton and the need to dine away from home: 'I know nothing of the large parties of London, sir – I never dine with anybody.' His irritability is, in fact, an expression of something ungovernable in, probably, both the Knightleys, and Jane Austen's attention is on what this quality may do to hypotheses of containment, order, propriety.

Bulking larger in the novel is the case where chance and some curiously submerged facets of character make the sensible and elegantly accomplished Jane Fairfax fall in love with Frank Churchill, and furthermore return to him despite her evident distress at his public flirting with Emma, and his equally public tormenting of her over that wretched piano. Mr Knightley's condemnation of Churchill – 'His letters disgust me' – is surprisingly vehement in context, and of course obviously partial since he senses Churchill as a rival for Emma; but it is also very largely right; and if one merely took Jane Austen as intent on illustrating decorum and proportion in marriage, or (which is closer to Mudrick's position) maintaining a poised irony about it, one would surely expect her to condemn this marriage of Frank and Jane as offending against every notion of judgement and good sense. Knightley is right about it, and Jane Austen herself clearly knows that there is indeed an instability in a union that must depend so much on the oddness of Jane's attraction to a shallow, irresponsible man. But Jane Austen does not condemn the marriage, or even remain uncommitted about it: we are left with the clear sense that it is more likely to succeed than fail. I think we must conclude that, for all her firmness and decision in these matters, Jane Austen takes a greater interest in deviations from rational behaviour than any simple moralist would, or any simple ironist; the possibility of instability in the Jane Fairfax–Frank Churchill marriage is not merely real to her, but as fruitful an interest as the certainty of stability and good sense (for all the struggles between them) in Knightley's marriage with Emma.

To put the same point differently: she is as interested in and as stimulated by the aberrations – I am tempted to say the suppressed turbulence – in Emma and in Mr Knightley himself as she is in their resolve and firmness of character. Mr Knightley's bluntness of manner and his irritability, particularly when these are stimulated by opposition and intransigence in Emma, are rather like the qualities of a minor Dr Johnson. He is eminently a man of sense, certainly a leader, and Emma's charmingly unguarded praise of him to Mrs Weston over the gift of the piano is thoroughly just: 'I do not think it at all a likely thing for him to do. Mr Knightley does nothing mysteriously.' But he is also a man whose forcefulness goes even deeper than his reasonableness: 'A degradation to illegitimacy and ignorance, to be married to a respectable, intelligent, gentleman-farmer?' 'Vanity working on a weak head produces every sort of mischief. ... Men of sense, whatever you may choose to say, do not want silly wives.' This is indeed close to the accents and mode of Johnson himself, and includes something of his unconforming energies. The outline of the long argument between Knightley and Emma from which the last two quotations come (Chapter VIII) accords entirely and predictably with Jane Austen's sense of propriety, with Knightley clearly in the right about Harriet and Robert Martin, and Emma disastrously in the wrong; but its reverberations go beyond that rational good sense of Knightley's and link him with Emma's own intransigence. Sensible though he clearly is, he is depending here on a blunt forcefulness whose roots are not entirely in the reasoning mind.

As the novel progresses, it becomes unmistakably clear that both Emma and Knightley unexpectedly diverge from the usual and the conventional, at least as much as they agree in support of it. There is one very interesting passage of hectic special-pleading from Emma where she attempts to prove to Mrs Weston that Mr Knightley is like herself in that he is a man who does not want to marry. Hearing Mrs Weston's conjecture ('In sort, I have made a match between Mr Knightley and Jane Fairfax. See the consequence of keeping you company! ...') she bursts out:

'Mr Knightley and Jane Fairfax! ... Dear Mrs Weston, how could you think of such a thing? – Mr Knightley! – Mr Knightley must not marry! – You would not have little Henry cut out from Donwell? – Oh, no, no, Henry must have Donwell. I cannot at all consent to Mr Knightley's marrying; and I am sure it is not at all likely. ...' (Vol. II, ch. VIII)

She is of course saying this far more for her own sake (though perfectly unconscious of any selfish motive) than for little Henry, whose claims are largely forgotten when, much later, Knightley proposes to her; and she is forced, by Mrs Weston's sensible logic ('I am not speaking of its prudence; merely its probability'), to rationalise helplessly: 'But Mr Knightley does not want to marry. I am sure he has not the least idea of it. Do not put it into his head. Why should he marry? . . .' (Vol. II, ch. VIII)

But the interesting thing is that, for all the obvious self-justification and rationalising here, Emma is not altogether off the mark about Knightley. There is something odd about a man of his stamp seeming so placidly content to live at Donwell and allow William Larkins and Mrs Hodges to regulate his domestic life for him – even down to details like the number of apples he may keep for his own use or give to a friend! ('William Larkins let me keep a larger quantity than usual this year.') The strong sense of principle that makes Knightley a leader in society and public affairs could not be half as strong as it is if it weren't at odds with – indeed partly suppressing and constricting – an almost opposite quality of impetuous and very strong feeling. Equally, there is an interesting contradiction between the strong and warm feeling he shows for Emma, and the contained bachelordom that has now lasted nearly to the age of forty. There is always a hint of some tension underlying Knightley's firm composure. It is this that makes Emma's wild comments on his not marrying partly true; and it is a related tension that underpins his qualities as a leader. In a different way, the same is true of Emma herself. For despite her extraordinary – and harmful – mistakes in judgement, she too is surely seen by Jane Austen as a leader, and this partly *because of* the impetuosity that also causes her blunders.

This is borne out by the dominance of the scene at the Box Hill picnic, and the oddness or unexpectedness of Emma's role in it. Ostensibly, and certainly to the conscious mind of Emma herself reflecting on it afterwards, this scene is a condemnation of her irresponsibility and cruelty to Miss Bates. So indeed it is; but the extraordinary thing about it, and what escapes easy summaries on the level of ethics and social conduct, is the strength of the impulse that drives Emma to act as she does in those (surely perfectly ordinary) circumstances. As Mr Knightley's dismayed condemnation makes clear, it is more than mere thoughtlessness, or mere irritation at the Eltons. To put the whole situation in more modern, and perhaps too explicit, terms: there is a high charge of emotional and sexual energies and frustrations permeating the social comedy, and these focus on Emma's role in it. The 'comedy' is not at all unlike, for instance, those scenes in the schoolroom and cottage early on in *Women in Love* where Ursula, Gudrun, Birkin, Gerald and Hermione confront each other in 'social' terms, at the same time however revealing the generative and disruptive forces beneath the merely social. In *Emma*, at Box Hill, the heroine is caught in a situation where her playful matchmaking – comparatively innocent up to now – will no longer answer, or free her from mounting pressures and annoyances. She is therefore forced to channel her considerable energies and quickness of mind into an unexpectedly vicious attack. It is not for nothing (though wholly unconscious on Emma's part and indeed on Jane Austen's) that the object of her attack is the manifestly unmarriageable and completely innocent and harmless Miss Bates.

An account like Mudrick's would put this down as a charge against Emma's ruthlessly efficient charm, aided and abetted as she is by Churchill in this scene. In fact, of course, Emma is sincerely sorry for it, and accepts the justness of Mr Knightley's rebuke. The novel itself accepts Emma's impulse, however, even more fully than Knightley in the end does. It *is* a disruptive and destructive impulse; the comedy of the scene, though much lighter in texture than Lawrence's, does not attempt to disguise this. But it is also the same impulse or set of impulses as that which generates Emma's lively intelligence and through this animates the whole book.

If the book nevertheless remains clearer and firmer in outline than any later novel in English could possibly do, the clarity does not depend on previously established, rock-bottom notions of ethics or morality. In *Emma*, Jane Austen's clarity of mind emerges from, but is still always tinged and invigorated by, all sorts of error and confusion. Confusion bred it, at least in part.

But this is to talk as if the novel were indeed perfect, flawless. I don't want to catalogue imperfections here, but merely to state that they exist and, more importantly, that they represent certain limits to Jane Austen's originality, certain points where she is forced to retreat rather than explore further. The retreat is observable in the way in which the irony of situation is kept up for so long; so that there are places where, since no further discovery about Emma's delusions is possible, the neatness of the irony draws attention to itself rather than to anything it might reveal or release. This is true not merely at the end, with Emma's mistakes about Mr Knightley, but even at Box Hill where she jumps to the conclusion (surely unlikely, even given Emma's blindnesses in match-making!) that Frank Churchill's frivolous prescriptions for a wife might perhaps point to Harriet. In these examples the irony is needlessly insistent, and this is the more disappointing because it is clearly a failure of imagination and nerve rather than of 'technique'.

Something similar might be said of the social world of *Emma* considered as a whole. There is Abbey Mill Farm – quite well done, but clearly not in any sense a full-scale treatment of issues about rural communities, and hence not a major extension of the Highbury horizons. There are also the Coles. The Coles are well and humanely treated by Jane Austen, but all the time it is clear that they are so because they keep their place. In the novel, they must assimilate themselves to Mr Knightley's world, not at all he to theirs. If the Coles keep their proper distance they may, the novel implies, grow into the neighbourhood and share some of its virtues; but clearly it never occurs to Jane Austen that such people, having made their money in trade, could possibly bring anything that might add to or challenge Highbury life. By contrast the Eltons, with their pushing vulgarity, represent a threat to Knightley's and Emma's world that Jane Austen only *just* manages to contemplate steadily. By her marriage, Emma will be saved from seeing Mrs Elton taking precedence at Highbury dinners, but this is hardly a confident facing by Jane Austen of what common knowledge would have shown to be an increasing, rather than a diminishing, threat. In sum, there are moments in the novel when one feels the presence of a slightly too easy reliance on the myth of Donwell and Hartfield as all-embracing, protective.

This is related, finally, to self-protection of a much more personal kind that spoils one crucial scene at the end: Emma's acceptance of Knightley's proposal. 'She spoke then, on being so entreated. What did she say? Just what she ought, of course. A lady always does. She said enough to show there need not be despair – and to invite him to say more himself.' (Vol. III, ch. XIII)

This is coyness taking over from confident irony. Irony alone would anyway be insufficient for this scene, but Jane Austen clearly shies away from any confident involvement in Emma's deeper feelings at this particular point. As Mudrick has very convincingly documented, this abrupt shying away from emotional involvement is typical of at any rate the earlier Jane Austen, though it is a bit unexpected if one takes *Emma* (as he does) to be much more poised and expert than earlier, or even later, novels. As I have said, I think the truer view is that *Emma* is far from the perfectly poised and distanced irony Mudrick sees in it. It is taking more risks than he supposes, and its doing so is one of the things that makes it, I think, clearly her best novel. But by the same token – Jane Austen being what she is – the novel is subject to certain fits of regression. Jane Austen doesn't actually run for cover when faced with the Eltons, but her habit in treating them is to look back to established defences, rather than forward to the unknown and (at least partly) feared. With a subject that cuts much closer to the bone still – Emma's private, emotional involvement – there is at least this one moment when she has to cover up and retreat almost out of view behind the defensive, sheltering irony that marks her letters and some of her earlier work. Knightley's actual proposal is the one moment Jane Austen really fears, partly because (*pace* Mudrick) she is indeed thoroughly involved with Emma.

Personally I am very happy to leave the novel's success as largely dependent on Emma and Knightley, and on Jane Austen's close involvement with them. In most of the book, she is as open and frank as her own very engaging heroine. ('The truth is, Harriet, that my playing is just good enough to be praised, but Jane Fairfax's is much beyond it.') From the whole book it is clear that openness and frankness of this kind are very much admired by Jane Austen. There is even a degree of self-identification (of novelist and heroine) that in most other writers would be dangerous, because likely to end in sentimentality. George Eliot is the obvious comparison here; but Jane Austen's evident liking for Emma (and through her, for Knightley) is a projection of some part of herself much wittier, much more confidently and alertly prepared for whatever blunders she or her heroine may make, than the side of George Eliot that produced Maggie Tulliver and Dorothea. To do George Eliot only common justice, her books range beyond the compass of Jane Austen's – there are simply more and greater difficulties in them for the author/heroine to meet. But Jane Austen is still doing more than prudently staying within bounds; and she is certainly doing more than regarding her foolishly adventurous heroine with a composed, ironic assurance. She is closer to admiring Emma whole-heartedly than to exposing her weaknesses from the vantage-point of a secure and traditionally established position, when she gives her, in the penultimate chapter, the coolly demanding reply to Knightley's objection:

> 'Do you dare say this?' cried Mr Knightley. 'Do you dare to suppose me so great a blockhead as not to know what a man is talking of? What do you deserve?'
> 'Oh! I always deserve the best treatment, because I never put up with any other; and, therefore, you must give me a plain, direct answer . . .' (Vol. iiii, ch. xviii)

It is obvious that, in the personality of Emma, the good and the less than good are mingled. This is a truism, and would apply to anybody, fictional or real. What is not so obvious is Jane Austen's intuition that good sense and worth may, in some way very hard to define outside the crisp, lively prose of the novel itself, actually draw strength from silliness, confusion, misjudgement. Jane Austen's claim – whether conscious or unconscious doesn't matter here – is that Emma's impulsiveness (and hence her snobbery, her mistakes with Harriet, her insults to Miss Bates) is so much a part of her engaging frankness and resolution that the two are mutually dependent: the frankness and openness spring from the same impulsiveness that constantly and at times disastrously tempts her. Indeed this is true of the book as a whole, not just of its heroine. Some narrowness and hesitation aside, Jane Austen's originality in *Emma* is to formulate, almost for the first time in English literature, the sense in which the good qualities in and of a whole society like that of Highbury may actively depend on the bad, or at least on impulses that must also result in foolishness, misjudgement, at times active cruelty.

To say this is not to say that Jane Austen's writing is at all like the Blake I quoted in Chapter 1 – an absurd proposition, obviously. She is much more interesting in her own right than any mere satellite of his could be. It might, however, point to some areas of experience, or some outlooks, that the two of them share. For instance, I should imagine that at least the earlier Blake might have welcomed the degree of 'enmity' that exists (and one is left in no doubt will continue to exist during their married lives) between Emma herself and Knightley, and also of course between Jane Fairfax and Frank Churchill. With Churchill, there will probably always be a slightly unpleasant element of 'play' or disguise in it all – it is hard to see Jane Austen envisaging this young man as ever, finally, growing up – but this is a perfectly proper extension of the spirit of Blake's own recommendation of 'contraries', and in no way invalidates the novel. On the contrary, all of the major novels after Jane Austen will include, as part of the very texture of the life they render, some of the rather grating elements that she, too, sees. Not all of them, however, will manage the kind of crisp confidence with which, in *Emma* at least, she treats such difficulties.

3 Doubts and Reticence: *Sense and Sensibility* to *Persuasion*

Yet to leave that as the final note about Jane Austen – the kind of confidence she does indeed achieve in *Emma* – would be to leave a slightly distorted picture, both of Jane Austen herself and of her position in relation to later novelists. Because in the first place it doesn't sufficiently stress the fact that, in the England of her day, confidence of this crisp, alert and intelligent kind was so unusual that it must have been hard won. The state of England at the end of the Napoleonic wars cannot have been much better (and in some ways must have been much worse) than it is today. Indeed, most other writers (the second-generation Romantic poets, in particular) have moods in which they reflect, however indirectly, a feeling of disillusionment, or a collapse of energy, that is clearly more widely spread than just their own personal feelings of the moment. Bliss *was* it in that dawn to be alive . . . In such a context, the appearance of a novel like *Emma* must have been almost as unexpected as it would have been at any later date.

In the second place, and thinking more particularly within the compass of Jane Austen's own works, any attempt to 'place' her various novels side by side, as part of an unbroken and continuous development, must fail. Thus in *Emma* Jane Austen's whole enterprise is both venturesome, and remarkably stable. But to say that is also to remind oneself how very different *Emma* is, in spirit, conception and therefore 'style', from *Mansfield Park*, which appeared about a year earlier (1814); and also how very different *that* is from either *Pride and Prejudice* (begun 1796, published 1813), or *Sense and Sensibility* (begun 1797, published 1811). Not that any of these books is *unstable* (or gloomily Byronic, or in any state of withdrawal from the world in general); but each is indeed a 'fresh raid on the inarticulate', and in certain ways almost disjunct from the preceding ones. Of all of these, even if we include the posthumous *Persuasion* (published, with *Northanger Abbey*, in 1818), I suppose *Mansfield Park* is the one Jane Austen herself might have picked as the novel most clearly and unambiguously enshrining the virtues of stability, decorum and decency she placed such reliance on throughout her writing career.

The trouble here, however, is that, though most people find *Mansfield Park* an interesting book to read, and indeed a very rewarding one, a good part of the interest that the book arouses stems from the fact that Jane Austen's intentions do not by any means coincide with her achievements. There are points where her left hand really does not acknowledge what her right hand is doing (or rather, writing). Thus for instance very few readers can believe in Sir Thomas Bertram as the figure of authority that Jane Austen, for all the criticisms of him she makes, seems to want him to be; and practically nobody can see Fanny as interesting enough to enliven the pretty sedentary Mansfield virtues in the way an Emma might have done, or an Elizabeth Bennet, or either of the Dashwood sisters. Mary Crawford might have, if she had been allowed to stay; Tom Bertram might have, if he hadn't been subdued beyond recognition by a convenient (gratuitously imposed?) illness. As it is, Fanny is left in command, with Edmund as consort. But it is almost impossible to *like* Fanny, except perhaps during the momentary fits of jealousy she is allowed over Mary Crawford. And often enough Jane Austen herself comes dangerously close to satirising her headaches, and her tiresome protestations about being of no importance whatsoever.

If this is so, the general picture of Jane Austen's work is different from any that would show *Emma* and *Persuasion* as, in their different ways, the natural progression from earlier novels. If there is a 'progression' at all, it is much more jagged than this, and I think it shows Jane Austen as rather more jolted by the failures, and by the sheer nastiness, that human nature is capable of than a consideration of *Emma* alone would do. It is important not to darken the picture too much, because, even beyond the confines of *Emma* considered alone, Jane Austen remains by far the most buoyantly confident writer of her age (or of any later one), and also the writer most immediately interested in whatever is going on around her. The alert, crisp writing that every reader knows and welcomes is clearly not a matter of any 'style' or 'technique' of a kind that another writer of comparable abilities might have managed. In Jane Austen, the style is indeed the woman; or rather, the woman responding to the things that she likes as readily, or almost as readily, as to the things that she hates.

Almost, but perhaps not quite. In this connection, I would like to draw attention to what still seems to me one of the best articles on Jane Austen published so far, and indeed to distinguish it from the majority of what has followed. This is Professor D. W. Harding's essay in *Scrutiny*, VIII (1940), 'Regulated Hatred: An Aspect of the Work of Jane Austen'. In part, of course, Professor Harding was concerned simply to reveal the inadequacy of the 'gentle Jane' readings then prevalent, and he himself stresses that his article is, in consequence, 'deliberately lop-sided'. Well, there may be a lot to be said for lop-sidedness, particularly when, as in this case, one considers what has followed. The more positive side of Professor Harding's attempt, like that of Arnold Kettle a bit later, was to reveal Jane Austen as a writer who must be taken seriously, rather than just as a pleasant relief from deeper literary concerns. The trouble since has been that Harding and Kettle have succeeded all too well. Jane Austen is indeed now taken seriously – solemnly, in fact – and to the point where the majority of essays on her from the 1950s onwards are so loaded with impertinent complexities and abstractions that some of the best insights of earlier writers have been muffled, and in consequence her own novels smoothed over, her career made to seem far less interesting and significant than it was. And though, for the most part, the verbal and structural intricacies that have been loaded on to perfectly straightforward novels by critics like Mark Schorer and Reuben A. Brower are now simply ignored ('. . . what looks most diverse is really most similar, and ironies are linked by vibrant reference to basic certainties'),[1] I am not so sure that Jane Austen is safe, yet, from more menacing solemnities:

> She is the first novelist to represent society, the general culture, as playing a part in the moral life, generating the concepts of 'sincerity' and 'vulgarity' which no earlier time would have understood the meaning of, and which for us are so subtle that they defy definition, and so powerful that none can escape their sovereignty . . .

Would Richardson, one wonders, have been as helplessly puzzled as we are by these notions? Would the barbarism or the religious dominance of Shakespeare's age have ruled him out completely? The passage continues:

> She is the first to be aware of the Terror which rules our moral situation, the ubiquitous anonymous judgment to which we respond, the necessity we feel to demonstrate the purity of our secular spirituality . . . to put our lives and styles to the question, making sure that not only in deeds but in *décor* they exhibit the signs of our belonging to the number of the secular-spiritual elect.[2]

What the self-importance of this sort of prose misses, first of all, is the openness, the absolute lack of modern pretentiousness, in Jane Austen's own writing. What it also misses, or misrepresents, are some of the best insights in D. W. Harding's earlier essay. In outline, Harding's essay might seem to resemble Professor Trilling's chapter on *Mansfield Park*. He does not talk in terms of 'the Terror which rules our moral situation', or 'the ubiquitous anonymous judgment to which we respond . . .'; but he is concerned to draw attention to certain fears Jane Austen has about the society she lives in and about people she knows. Where he differs most from later essayists like Trilling, who also see Jane Austen as in some sense embattled or worried, is in his ability to pinpoint these worries in very simple, direct terms that do not obscure or muffle the crispness and buoyancy of her writing. Thus he begins by quoting Henry Tilney's remonstrance to Catherine for having imagined that General Tilney has behaved like a villain from one of Mrs Radcliffe's novels, and either murdered his wife or kept her prisoner in some dungeon in the abbey Catherine is exploring: 'Dear Miss Morland, consider the dreadful nature of these suspicions you have entertained. What have you been judging from? Remember the country and the age in which we live. . . . Does our education prepare us for such atrocities? Do our laws connive at them?'

So much, as Harding points out, is relatively easy going for any novelist or essayist of reasonable common sense. Indeed, these things do not, and never did, happen. What is unusual, though perhaps only partly comprehended by Jane Austen at this early stage, is the quietly unobtrusive clause that Harding deliberately leaves out the first time he quotes the passage from Henry Tilney and then re-inserts (my italics): 'Could they be perpetrated without being known, in a country like this, where social and literary intercourse is on such a footing, *where every man is surrounded by a neighbourhood of voluntary spies*, and where roads and newspapers lay everything open?'

This sort of 'unexpected astringency', in the middle of perfectly genuine praise of the social class in England that her readers and friends are part of, becomes much more important and much better handled in later novels. Part of its importance – a large part, in fact – lies simply in the direction in which such barbs are aimed. They are aimed (though not necessarily consciously) at Jane Austen's own readers, at people she knew, and at us. Harding uses terms as strong as 'fear and hatred' to describe some of the impulses in her novels; and he claims that, though there are clear and strong counterbalancing impulses there too, the presence of these makes impossible, not just any sentimental 'gentle Jane' reading, but also any easy assumption that Jane Austen's virtues stem from her being a writer on good and intimate terms with her public and with the society she lived in. This is one reason why terms like 'satire' and 'caricature' are inadequate for her work. A satirist can remain on perfectly happy terms with his readers, and with his friends, simply by inviting them to laugh at behaviour far in excess of any they themselves would commit. Jane Austen does invite such laughter, of course (Mr Collins and Lady Catherine are two examples among many); but this is only one part of a more comprehensive range of writing that must, at certain key points, cut much closer to the bone than satire, as the term is ordinarily understood, can possibly do. Harding puts it this way:

To her the first necessity was to keep on reasonably good terms with the associates of her everyday life; she had a deep need of their affection and a genuine respect for the ordered, decent civilisation that they upheld. And yet she was sensitive to their crudenesses and complacencies and knew that her real existence depended on resisting many of the values they implied.

And it is essential, I think, to stress that the values resisted here are not those of a Mr Collins when he is caught out in his ridiculous proposal to Elizabeth, but ones that permit, perhaps even encourage, much more ordinary and familiar nastiness. Harding continues:

> Hence one of Jane Austen's most successful methods is to offer her readers every excuse for regarding as rather exaggerated figures of fun people whom she herself detests and fears. Mrs Bennet, according to the Austen tradition, is one of 'our' richly comic characters about whom we can feel superior, condescending, perhaps a trifle sympathetic, and above all heartily amused and free from care. Everything conspires to make this the natural interpretation once you are willing to over-look Jane Austen's bald and brief statement of her own attitude to her: 'She was a woman of mean understanding, little information, and uncertain temper.' How many women amongst Jane Austen's acquaintance and amongst her most complacent readers to the present day that phrase must describe!

'She was a woman of mean understanding, little information, and uncertain temper.' Everybody remembers sentences of this kind from Jane Austen; there are Mrs Musgrave's 'large fat sighings' over Dick 'whom alive nobody had cared for'; Anne Elliot's reflection that her sister Mary was 'not so repulsive and unsisterly as Elizabeth'; Elinor Dashwood's comment that Lucy Steele, mean though she is, is nevertheless 'a woman superior in person and understanding to half her sex'; and the reflection from Elizabeth Bennet (very like many of her father's) about the nice Mr Bingley's having such extremely nasty sisters ('. . . their indifference towards Jane when not immediately before them, restored Elizabeth to the enjoyment of all her original dislike.').

Two things in particular seem to me to stand out about these sharply comic, but also pretty acid, comments. One is that though a good many arise, as Harding points out, fairly unobtrusively from the dialogue without changing the tone of it at all towards misanthropy or despair, there are occasions when whole scenes, though still lightly toned, endorse the particular comments. In *Pride and Prejudice*, for instance, Chapter 18, the Netherfield Ball, is only the most concentrated of many occasions on which Elizabeth, with nothing more than her father's amusement at people's folly to fall back on, has to blush for her family and for others close to them. Her mother chatters endlessly, and very audibly, to Lady Lucas about Bingley; Mr Collins fawns on Darcy; and Mary sings. During most of this, Darcy continues 'impenetrably grave', and the ball draws to an end with Jane Austen's summarising reflection: 'To Elizabeth it appeared that had her family made an agreement to expose themselves as much as they could during the evening, it would have been impossible for them to play their parts with more spirit, or finer success . . .'

The second of the things that stand out in this connection – though admittedly, in this case, only very occasionally indeed – is that sometimes Jane Austen is not in perfect control of her feelings of dislike, or as Harding puts it, 'hatred'. The notorious case here is, of course, her comments in Chapter VIII of *Persuasion* on the 'unbecoming conjunction' between Mrs Musgrove's genuinely bulky figure and the insincerity of her equally bulky regrets for her dead son Richard. To add to this, two chapters earlier, we have had Jane Austen's comments on what really happened to 'thick-headed, unfeeling, unprofitable Dick Musgrove':

> The real circumstances of this pathetic piece of family history were, that the Musgroves had had the ill fortune of a very troublesome, hopeless son; and the good fortune to lose him before he reached his twentieth year; that he had been sent to sea, because he was stupid and unmanageable on shore; that he had been very little cared for at any time by his family, though quite as much as he deserved; seldom heard of, and scarcely at all regretted, when the intelligence of his death abroad had worked its way to Uppercross, two years before.

Personally, I have no criticisms at all to make of this paragraph in itself. There seems to me no reason on earth why novelists shouldn't tell the truth, and since truth includes the fact there are some people whose death is no cause for regret even to their closest relations, it should be welcomed, not deplored as if it were some lack of taste or feeling. In this case, however, the difficulty is that the comments come so unexpectedly, and at least in part so needlessly, that the run of the story as a whole does not quite justify the strength of the feeling (obviously perfectly genuine) that Jane Austen shows. Mrs Musgrove we know, and her selfishness and hypochondria are a part of the book. Richard Musgrove, however, is no part of the story – by definition, almost, he can affect nobody in it – and so the viciousness of the attack is surprising, to say the least.

But what is striking in Jane Austen is the combination of this (very occasional) lack of control over such impulses *and* their presence, not only in incidental remarks throughout the novels, but in whole scenes like that of the Netherfield Ball. This is a good scene, I think, and not in the least out of control. On the contrary, the sheer nastiness of people like Miss Bingley or Mr Collins gives a charge to the atmosphere of an evening that might otherwise have been merely flaccid. Jane Austen is here very much in command of virtually the same impulses that, in the Dick Musgrove incident, seem to take her by surprise. What holds our interest at Netherfield is the very sharp juxtaposition of, for instance, the embarrassing silliness of Sir William Lucas's compliments to Darcy

('Such very superior dancing is not often seen. It is evident that you belong to the first circles.') and, with absolutely no break in tone to mark Sir William's arrival, the liveliness – appropriately barbed – of Elizabeth to Darcy just before this:

> After a pause of some minutes, she addressed him a second time with – 'It is *your* turn to say something now, Mr Darcy – *I* talked about the dance, and *you* ought to make some kind of remark on the size of the room, or the number of couples.'
>
> He smiled, and assured her that whatever she wished him to say should be said.
>
> 'Very well. – That reply will do for the present. – Perhaps by and bye I may observe that private balls are much pleasanter than public ones. – But *now* we may be silent.'
>
> 'Do you talk by rule then, while you are dancing?'
>
> 'Sometimes. One must speak a little, you know. It would look odd to be entirely silent for half an hour together, and yet for the advantage of *some*, conversation ought to be so arranged as that they may have the trouble of saying as little as possible.'

Elizabeth's part in the whole scene concentrates what Reuben Brower calls 'the poetry of wit' in Jane Austen's writing; but his turn of phrase omits almost entirely the lightly underscored, but very telling, discordance of people like Sir William just after this, along with the very pointedly enquiring nature of Elizabeth's comments on Darcy's character and his relations with Wickham. If we put this kind of succcess in juxtaposing the attractions in human nature and the slight (or in some cases marked) notes of menace in it, together with occasional failures of the kind most marked in the Dick Musgrove scene, the conclusion must indeed be that, even if D. W. Harding is slightly wrong to talk about an impulse of 'hatred' somewhere in Jane Austen's nature, any description of her writing as 'the poetry of wit' is inessential, of the surface only.

What seems more essential to a reading of Jane Austen is that the impulses Harding notes, even if he does exaggerate them slightly (or, as he himself says, puts the case a bit lop-sidedly), are there, *and* that they represent something Jane Austen feels to be engrained in human nature, not just excusable lapses from taste or decorum. Jane Austen is not, I think, as threatened by this possibility as some later novelists are, but it is there in her writing none the less, even though she is more confident, and more consistently 'comic', than they are. One of the most remarkable things in this connection has always seemed to me to be the amount of what, in another writer, would have to be called sheer scepticism about human nature that we note in *Sense and Sensibility*, a novel that is popularly, and in many ways rightly, acclaimed one of her lightest works. *Sense and Sensibility* is a splendid story, and a pleasure to read. From beginning to end it is obvious that the man who wears 'flannel waistcoats' (Colonel Brandon) will nevertheless marry the impulsive and beautiful Marianne; and it is equally clear that Elinor will marry Edward Ferrars, despite the schemings of Lucy Steele and the faint-heartedness of Edward himself. All this, including the element of 'difficulties' overcome, is standard stuff in story-telling, but so well and so crisply done by Jane Austen that the obvious and expected is transformed into something really interesting: what indeed *will* happen next? and how will the standard difficulties and troubles be overcome?

We read this novel in particular, and others of Jane Austen's, for familiar, and indeed standard, reasons of this kind. What interests me is that, though *Sense and Sensibility* is in some ways the most clearly 'expected' story in all of Jane Austen, yet it is this novel that produces almost more of the sharply discordant notes she is capable of than any other. Because, in the first place, there are the Misses Steele; and despite the fact that Lucy at least has 'a smartness of air' and some 'distinction to her person', these young ladies are, from their first introduction in Chapter XXI, thorns in everybody's side. At first it looks as if Jane Austen is saying that their thoroughly unpleasant characteristics are merely the result of lack of education and a poor home background. And indeed of course they are in part, for it is the sensible Elinor who reflects, in Chapter XXII, that:

> Lucy was naturally clever ... but her powers had received no aid from education, she was ignorant and illiterate, and her deficiency of all mental improvement, her want of information in the most common particulars, could not be concealed from Miss Dashwood. ... Elinor saw, and pitied her for, the neglect of abilities which education might have rendered so respectable ...

This is true, and not true. Lucy Steele could indeed be improved by the sort of education that Jane Austen clearly admires and wants for all her heroines. But the crunch comes with our realisation of Jane Austen's own admission that nothing at all could change Lucy's real nature. She might learn to talk less crassly about her 'beaux', or to hide her interest in money more effectively, but her intelligence – and it *is* a formidable one – would still reside in the 'little sharp eyes full of meaning' with which she quizzes Elinor and Edward Ferrars in Chapter XXIV, where the two girls are admitted rivals for Edward's hand.

Moreover, comments of this kind are often extended to become, quite explicitly, comments about human nature and people in general. For instance there is the swiftly glancing blow I have already quoted from Elinor about Lucy being 'superior in person and understanding to half her sex'. Then there is Mr Palmer's studied rudeness to everybody, and Elinor's reflection (virtually the same in this instance, one can be sure, as Jane Austen's own) that this is in part the result of 'a wish of distinction ... the desire of appearing superior to other people'; but in part too it is connected with Mrs Palmer, whose silliness Elinor sees as a common enough phenomenon:

> Elinor was not inclined, after a little observation, to give him credit for being so genuinely and unaffectedly ill-natured or ill-bred as he wished to appear. His temper might perhaps be a little soured by finding, like many others of his sex, that through some unaccountable bias in favour of beauty, he was the husband of a very silly woman, – but she knew that this kind of blunder was too common for any sensible man to be lastingly hurt by it. (ch. xx)

The smile in this prose is easy and relaxed, preventing even the slightest touch of Romantic or post-Romantic despair about the human condition; but the adverse comments are very sharp indeed, and they clearly point to something permanently embedded in human nature, rather than to anything that could possibly stem from lack of breeding or education. And even Elinor's more favourable comments on Mrs Palmer later on, in Chapter xlii, have a deftly unemphasised sting in the tail. Here, she finds Mrs Palmer friendly, open, kind; and concludes that 'her folly, though evident, was not disgusting because it was not conceited; and Elinor could have forgiven everything but her laugh'.

Finally, in this vein, there are aspects of the novel such as Mrs John Dashwood's calculated meanness and selfishness about her father-in-law's wishes to provide for his widow and daughters, and John Dashwood's easy compliance by reducing his intended gift of three thousand pounds, first of all to half that sum; then, at his wife's further prompting, to an annuity of one hundred a year during the widow's life; then, when Mrs Dashwood points out that some widows live a long time, to 'a present of fifty pounds, now and then . . .'; and finally, on reflecting that the widow's stock of china, plate and linen is really very handsome – in some ways better than his own – to nothing at all beyond 'such kind of neighbourly acts as his own wife pointed out'. That sequence is from Chapter ii; the novel as a whole ends with this much happier, but still mildly quizzical, comment from Jane Austen:

> Between Barton and Delaford, there was that constant communication which strong family affection would naturally dictate – and among the merits and the happiness of Elinor and Marianne, let it not be ranked as the least considerable, that though sisters, and living almost within sight of each other, they could live without disagreement between themselves, or producing coolness between their husbands.

Given this sort of note present in the writing of both *Sense and Sensibility* and *Pride and Prejudice*, together with moments (especially in *Sense and Sensibility*) of rather more acerbic comment on the permanent possibility of folly, meanness, even viciousness in human nature, it is no surprise that Jane Austen's next novel should have such a very different stress and emphasis. In *Mansfield Park*, for all the obstacles the novel itself very interestingly raises, the main impulse is clearly a wish for seclusion and quiet, almost as an escape from human beings themselves. This change of direction is certainly understandable; just as it is also very much in key with the quieter passages from the late-Augustan and Romantic poets that Jane Austen, and certain of her heroines, admired. But, in the case of *Mansfield Park*, it is so very sudden – and indeed, as suddenly reversed in the much more active and outward-looking writing in *Emma* about a year later – that it would be almost impossible not to expect some degree of dislocation within the planning and organisation of the novel itself.

And personally, I am convinced that that is exactly what we find on reading and re-reading the novel: a dislocation of precisely the kind that would result from a local and temporary, but precipitate, reversal of direction. Previous novels, and *Emma* later on, look outward, expectantly and interestedly. *Mansfield Park* looks persistently, almost wilfully, inwards, placing its faith in the quiet seclusion and stability of a small and isolated circle that in fact the novel itself, at its best, has shown to be both more disrupted, and more alive, than any state of seclusion from the world (or from the Crawfords) could possibly be.

Certainly, there are criticisms of the Mansfield way of life within the novel, and some clearly have Jane Austen's backing. The most telling of these are not so much Sir Thomas's admission that, in his own plan of educating his daughters, 'Something must have been wanting within. . . . He feared that principle, active principle, had been wanting . . .' (So indeed it had, but what he really wants here, at the end of the novel, is only a more complete version of what he had hoped Mansfield always was.) More telling than this are, first of all, some moments earlier on of typically light Jane Austen comedy, such as the one in Chapter XIII when Tom catches himself out trying to pretend that putting on the play is really to help Lady Bertram through the anxieties of Sir Thomas's absence:

'And as to my father's being absent, it is so far from an objection that I consider it rather as a motive; for the expectation of his return must be a very anxious period to my mother, and if we can be the means of amusing that anxiety, and keeping up her spirits for the next few weeks, I shall think our time very well spent, and so I am sure will he. – It is a very anxious period for her.'

As he said this, each looked towards their mother. Lady Bertram, sunk back in one corner of the sofa, the picture of health, wealth, ease, and tranquillity, was just falling into a gentle doze, while Fanny was getting through the few difficulties of her work for her.

Edmund smiled and shook his head.

'By Jove! this won't do,' – cried Tom, throwing himself into a chair with a hearty laugh. 'To be sure, my dear mother, your anxiety – I was unlucky there.'

That says more than Sir Thomas ever could, not so much about a want of principle but about a want, in any version of Mansfield Park that will be dominated by even the best qualities in Fanny and Edmund, of any outside influence. Tom's advantage (though it nearly kills him in the end) is that he is of the world, worldly. Here at least, Jane Austen allows him the kind of comic sanity that the world produces, and that is very much at odds with the secluded Mansfield virtues.

But as well as glancing blows of this kind that Jane Austen allows herself, there is, almost throughout, the presence of the Crawfords. I think it says a lot for Jane Austen that she admits so much in their favour (particularly in Mary Crawford's favour). If she had reduced them to caricatures; or even if she had diminished them only slightly, as for instance by giving either of them the faintly 'romantic hero' tinge she allows Willoughby; in either of these cases the note of challenge to the Mansfield quietism espoused by Fanny and Edmund would have been lacking, and the novel far less interesting in consequence. As it is, the Crawfords, though subdued in the end, are allowed a pretty fair hearing. In particular, Mary Crawford's liveliness, sheer good health, and the openness with which she admits her self-interested motives in Edmund's worldly prospects are an absolutely essential balance to Fanny's vulnerability, physical weakness and shyness. For instance, for all the slightly brittle quality in some of Mary's conversation which Jane Austen claims is the result of her uncle's dissipation and her city environment, it is Mary who is given the novel's best and most direct questioning of Edmund's pretensions to the clergy:

'So you are to be a clergyman, Mr Bertram. This is rather a surprise to me.'

'Why should it surprise you? You must suppose me designed for some profession, and might perceive that I am neither a lawyer, nor a soldier, nor a sailor.'

'Very true; but, in short, it had not occurred to me. And you know there is generally an uncle or a grandfather to leave a fortune to the second son.'

'A very praiseworthy practice,' said Edmund, 'but not quite universal. I am one of the exceptions, and *being* one, must do something for myself.'

'But why are you to be a clergyman? I thought *that* was always the lot of the youngest, where there were many to choose before him.'

'Do you think the church itself never chosen, then?'

'*Never* is a black word. But yes, in the *never* of conversation which means *not very often*, I do think it . . . (ch. IX)

Nobody else in the novel would query Edmund in this way. Obviously it would never occur to his father, let alone to Lady Bertram. And Fanny, though she is actually very perceptive about other people's motives (particularly the Crawfords'), would shun the very notion of it. Mary, therefore, and to a lesser extent her brother, are given the absolutely essential role in the novel of people who show an intelligently open, wordly self-interest. Mary wants the man she will marry to be rich enough to support her.

So much is, in a way, familiar Jane Austen territory. She may have retired from the field of Waterloo, and from the Luddite and other disturbances of her period; but she always has her eye on public interests (of property, the rights and obligations of marriage, the interest, or lack of interest, of one's neighbourhood, and so on) rather more than on the purely personal and private interests favoured by some of the poets in her own day and, increasingly, by writers generally since then. Where she strikes difficulty in this novel is in a tendency to lurch away from her natural habits of mind towards a mode of existence that, without being intensely personal in any Romantic or post-Romantic way, backs a secluded circle of living that will be protected from the difficulties of day-to-day life that Mary Crawford and her brother, in particular, introduce. I think this sudden distaste for life of any worldly or experienced kind is indeed the result of earlier doubts of Jane Austen's, strongly and well dramatised as they are in *Sense and Sensibility* and *Pride and Prejudice*, about the bearing and tendency of certain basic impulses in human nature generally. In *Mansfield Park*, however, there are many scenes in which this kind of distrust (or 'fear' to use Harding's word) takes too easy refuge in a wholly imaginary life of seclusion, and in the delights of a natural world almost as rid of people as the one Birkin/Lawrence imagines a hundred years later in *Women in Love* ('. . . a world empty of people, just uninterrupted grass, and a hare sitting up?').

In the Jane Austen of *Mansfield Park* vintage, perhaps one scene can stand for a good many others, particularly since it includes Mary Crawford, who is interruptive in something the way Ursula is allowed to be in the relevant scenes in Lawrence. Chapter xxii includes the scene in Mrs Grant's shrubbery in which Fanny talks to Mary about nature: '"This is pretty – very pretty," said Fanny . . . "Every time I come into this shrubbery I am more struck with its growth and beauty."' A bit later she continues:

'I am so glad to see the evergreens thrive!' said Fanny . . . 'My uncle's gardener always says the soil here is better than his own, and so it appears from the growth of the laurels and evergreens in general. – The evergreen! How beautiful, how welcome, how wonderful the evergreen! – When one thinks of it, how astonishing a variety of nature! – In some countries we know the tree that sheds its leaf is the variety, but that does not make it less amazing, that the same soil and the same sun should nurture plants differing in the first rule and law of their existence. You will think me rhapsodizing . . .'

'To say the truth,' replied Miss Crawford, 'I am something like the famous Doge at the court of Lewis xiv; and may declare that I see no wonder in this shrubbery equal to seeing myself in it . . .'

But where Ursula's blows (though also, in the upshot, rather muffled) are directed fairly and squarely at Birkin, Mary's comments here, however much of a relief they may be from Fanny's silly raptures about evergreens, are glancing blows only. They put a different, worldly, point of view; but they do not demolish, as surely they ought to have been allowed to do, once and for all in the novel, banalities like 'When one thinks of it, how astonishing a variety of nature! . . .' If anything, the position is worse in the previous chapter, where 'Lovers' Vows' has been banished from the stage and Fanny reflects on Sir Thomas's return:

'I suppose I am graver than other people,' said Fanny. 'The evenings do not appear long to me. I love to hear my uncle talk of the West Indies. I could listen to him for an hour together. It entertains *me* more than many other things have done – but then I am unlike other people, I dare say.'

Mary Crawford is not present here, and so the novel gives us nothing beyond Edmund's smiling acquiescence, and the beginnings of a retreat towards his marriage to Fanny and their succession, on the convenient death of Dr Grant shortly afterwards, to the shrubberies and evergreens of the Mansfield living.

That does not render the interest of *Mansfield Park* very fairly. It is, and always will be, a contentious novel, simply because of its extraordinary bid for seclusion and quietism towards the end of what in most respects is the career of a very out-going novelist, somebody clearly interested in taking part in the general run of day-to-day living, including the potential or actual viciousness of human nature generally. Indeed, *Mansfield Park* is the more interesting if we consider the extraordinary change (or, as I would prefer to say, rejuvenation) in Jane Austen's writing in *Emma*, a year later. And this resurgence of energy – it is certainly an outgoing energy, not at all one devoted to refurbishing the gardens, plantations and woods of Mansfield – is the more remarkable still by its closeness in time to the apparently quieter, more retired virtues that centre on Anne Elliot in *Persuasion*, a year or so later again. This closeness (between *Emma* and *Persuasion*) is, quite obviously, chronologically true; but it is also, when one considers it, true also in kind. There must have been a great temptation to Jane Austen to take a step backwards in time and make Anne Elliot, despite her better connections, just such another Cinderella figure as Fanny. And indeed, they share a lot, in particular some physical weakness (though not much, in Anne's case) and a hatred of towns. Thus Anne, 'dreading the possible heats of September in all the white glare of Bath, and grieving to forego all the influence so sweet and so sad of the autumnal months in the country', is prefigured in Fanny's longings for Mansfield, and in her contrast (strongly rendered, actually, by Jane Austen in Chapter XLVI) of the influence of the sun in Portsmouth:

> Here, its power was only a glare, a stifling, sickly glare, serving but to bring forward stains and dirt that might otherwise have slept. There was neither health nor gaiety in sunshine in a town. She sat in a blaze of oppressive heat, in a cloud of moving dust; and her eyes could only wander from the walls marked by her father's head, to the table cut and notched by her brothers, where stood the tea-board never thoroughly cleaned, the cups and saucers wiped in streaks, the milk a mixture of motes floating in thin blue, and the bread and butter grow-ing every minute more greasy than even Rebecca's hands had first produced it.

That is an extraordinary passage. For one thing, the 'blaze of oppressive heat', the 'cloud of moving dust', Fanny's mildly paranoiac gaze, wander-ing about the marks on the wall, the table cut and notched by her brothers – all this is more reminiscent of some few scenes in Hardy (summer in the kitchen at Talbothays), and of a great many in twentieth-century novels, than of anything else in Jane Austen. For another, the Portsmouth scenes as a whole are indeed one of the things that make *Mansfield Park*, for all its over-proper morals and self-protective impulses of retirement and seclusion (and perhaps in part *because* of these), a very compelling book indeed. If the resilience of the tone of this particular passage is in marked contrast to some others in the same chapter ('The horror of a mind like Fanny's, as it received the conviction of such guilt . . . can hardly be described'), the resultant discordance is typical of the conflicting impulses within Jane Austen at this point in her career – impulses, that is, towards retirement and disengagement, in conflict with others that look outward, even to the 'stains and dirt' of Portsmouth.

Nevertheless, and despite the resurgence in *Emma* of the much more outward-looking, even at points aggressive, side to Jane Austen's person-ality and writing, the temptation (if I may put it that way) to make the quieter-toned *Persuasion* rest solely on some more developed version of the Mansfield seclusion that Fanny and Edmund back must have been strong. In fact, however, and if we consider Fanny Price and Anne Elliot at large, within the compass of their lives to the time when each marries the man who really loves her despite the attractions of much livelier girls, Anne must surely be by far the more attractive, just as she is also the one who gains by being much closer to the decisive, self-confident *Emma*. One clear example of this would be the quickness and decision with which Anne acts after that perhaps slightly ridiculous accident at Lyme Regis. A better one from this point of view (because more directly concerned with Anne's own life) would be Anne's behaviour at the concert in Chapter xx. At the beginning of the chapter, in the octagon room, she takes a 'gentle' initiative:

> But hardly were they so settled when the door opened again, and Captain Wentworth walked in alone. Anne was the nearest to him, and making yet a little advance, she instantly spoke. He was preparing only to bow and pass on, but her gentle 'How do you do?' brought him out of the straight line to stand near her . . .

Certainly, this sort of behaviour is a good way from Emma's habit of openly confronting people, including Mr Knightley, on any occasion where her impulse so directs. But it is also both more self-aware than are Emma's actions, right to the end, and at the same time closer to the spirit of 'Emma Woodhouse, handsome, clever, and rich . . .' than it is to Fanny's patience and reticence. In fact what we have here, close to the end of Jane Austen's writing life, is something like a slightly quieter version of Elizabeth Bennet. Anne's reflections on her own manoeuvrings to get a seat near the end of a row, so she can perhaps talk to Captain Wentworth, are typical, and in direct contrast to almost everything Fanny says and does:

> In re-settling themselves, there were now many changes, the result of which was favourable for her. . . . and by some other removals, and a little scheming of her own, Anne was enabled to place herself much nearer the end of the bench than she had been before, much more within the reach of a passer-by. She could not do so, without comparing herself with Miss Larolles, the inimitable Miss Larolles, – but still she did it . . .

Obviously, Fanny Price, Emma and Anne Elliot are different in all sorts of ways; but there is a degree of kinship between Emma and Anne, each so strongly commanding the two novels immediately after *Mansfield Park*, that shows Jane Austen much more on the attack during the last part of her writing career than we might have expected from her determination to give Fanny's marriage to Edmund the kind of predominance it has in *Mansfield Park*. Retirement, nostalgia, reticence . . . impulses of this kind are very clearly present, not merely in Jane Austen but also, and increasingly, in later nineteenth-century novelists from Dickens, through George Eliot, Conrad, Hardy, James. They are more marked still in twentieth-century novelists like Joyce, with his concentration on the artist-hero Stephen (admittedly, strongly off-set by Bloom), and Lawrence, who singles out Gerald, Gudrun, Birkin and Ursula from the threatening herd. And it is more than possible that most of these writers in some sense share Jane Austen's feeling that not merely modern society, but human nature itself, contains threatening and aggressive impulses of a kind that call for at least some relief in an answering reticence.

What singles out the novel, however, in Romantic and post-Romantic writing, is its ability to answer back once again; to say, as I think *Persuasion* in particular says very effectively indeed, that reticence and seclusion are not enough. Jane Austen's mood in *Mansfield Park* is one which makes her diminish, and finally exclude, both the worldly voice of Mary Crawford and even the strong realism of the Portsmouth scenes. *Persuasion*, while it gives perfectly fair recognition to the autumnal mood evident in some of Anne's more private recollections, allows an equal and answering voice to scenes such as the concert scene in Chapter xx, and scenes or people temperamentally quite different from her, such as the scene from the end of Chapter x in which Admiral and Mrs Croft take her up into their gig and talk, quite openly and unaware, about Captain Wentworth's intentions of marrying one or other of the Musgrove girls ("'And very nice young ladies they both are; I hardly know one from the other'"). This is also the scene in which even Mrs Croft feels she must do something about the Admiral's splendidly reckless driving: "'. . . One could not be connected with better people. My dear admiral, that post! – we shall certainly take that post.'"

In a mildly comic way, Jane Austen's grouping of Anne and the Crofts in that drive home from Anne's long and (for her) tiring walk could well stand as a signpost for the best of later English novels. So, indeed, could the concert scene in Chapter xx of *Persuasion*. In both these scenes, the impulse to indulge private emotions is pitted quite fairly against the demands of more public and open affairs. Later novels, at their best, take this tip. Though their colour and cast is changed – in some cases, deepened – by various combinations of an increase in the sheer size of urban groups, and an increasingly self-conscious awareness of how this can matter to particular individuals, they still build on a certainty, very close to Jane Austen's own in *Persuasion* and most of her earlier novels, that the public world must and should continue its demands on the private. And this is particularly the case since the 'private' world will always, as she herself has shown, include both threats and challenges that stem from permanent instabilities built into human nature itself. The social world, however much it grows and changes, can never abolish these; but neither, on the other hand, will private emotions be able to live while ignoring it.

4 Dickens: *Dombey and Son, Bleak House*

Dickens reacts – erratically, but much more vividly than Jane Austen could have done – to an almost infinite series of misjudgements, stupidities, acts of cruelty and unkindness. In a sense, this is simply a natural extension of the difference between the England of her day and the England of his: in the thirty-odd years between Jane Austen's death in 1817 and the beginning of 'late' Dickens novels, the population of England and Wales increased from just over ten million (1811 Census) to nearly eighteen million (1851); the drift to the towns accelerated; 'reform' and (a bit later) attempts at factory and health legislation got at least some official recognition; and England's industrial power increased to the point where it could claim to be indeed 'the workshop of the world'.

But obviously Dickens is not simply documenting these changes. What is interesting about him – and what has been in dispute from at least as early as Henry James's adverse review of *Our Mutual Friend* (1865) – is how far he met the challenges presented by and in what was then the world's most successful and vigorous commercial–industrial nation. This is a continuing controversy, though up to a hundred years after James's brief review, our own century had not added much to the debate that began in Dickens's own lifetime. Certainly, for twenty years or so after Edmund Wilson's symbolist essay 'The Two Scrooges' (1941), it seemed that nothing was being said or done beyond a tracing of patterns (of themes, symbols, images), or the reiteration of the still older claim that sentimentality was popular in Victorian England and therefore we must judge sentimental novels by sentimental standards. In circumstances like these, it hardly seemed necessary to reconsider any claim for Dickens as a major writer.

There is a new interest in Dickens now. The wider circulation of Dr Leavis's essays, and more particularly of his and Mrs Leavis's book, *Dickens the Novelist* (1970), has given a fresh impulse, not just to Dickens studies, but to the whole business of what he meant to Victorian England. The interest they have created is widely spread indeed, and it includes seminar discussions, theses, articles not yet in print; but if I have understood its focal point correctly, this lies in the claim that Dickens's best novels create, in the threatening atmosphere of Victorian England, new centres of individual feelings, perceptions, selves. For all his tendency at times to overvalue the individual in pathetic isolation, Dickens, it is said, correctly diagnoses the oppressive and over-systematising tendencies in utilitarian, technological England, and opposes to these his strong realisation of the individual as the true centre of creative life and of society. Dickens is a Victorian, as his obvious weaknesses (of sentimentality, melodrama, and so on) testify; but he is also a rallying point in his own age and a portent for life in our century too.

That summary of the claims now being made for Dickens is of course unfairly brief, but if I can use it simply as a reminder of the much more varied and interesting accounts available, I should like to challenge these by recurring to what still, and despite all that is now being said, seems to me a crippling weakness in Dickens: his lack of staying-power. There are passages, chapters, sections in Dickens's novels that answer brilliantly to the claim that he is a source of life and interest in what, to some people at least, seems to have been an oppressively systematised age. But is there anything like a whole novel?

As part of the argument about Dickens's staying-power at novel length, I would like to question first of all the nature even of his best sections or passages within a given novel. I don't mean that these are not good, even great; but what *exactly* do they support? What kind of individualism do they in fact envisage as significant in the mid-nineteenth century and later? My own sense of the later Dickens (that is from *Dombey and Son* in 1848 to *Our Mutual Friend* in 1864–5) is that his most interesting writing is backing a powerful egocentricity, focused more often on women than on men, but in any case of a kind that neither he himself, nor even the most intelligent of his critics and admirers, will consciously allow as a dominant and productive part of the novels.

As one example, the beginning of *Dombey and Son* seems to me as good as anything Dickens ever wrote; and one reason for its greatness is his rendering – it is unconscious rendering, but no less significant for that – of a certain power and fitness in Dombey's self-congratulatory personality here. Dickens cannot, or dare not, sustain this, and later in the novel the Dombey presence is softened and subdued by constant applications of Florence, Captain Cuttle, 'Wal'r', the melodrama of marriage to Edith, and so on. But early on, Dombey is someone to reckon with.

The prose of these opening chapters is rich (certainly beyond the means of any other nineteenth-century writer in English, whether novelist or poet), strongly idiomatic, flexible. Dickens ranges easily and surely to include in one glance of the mind, almost, the near-farce of Doctor Parker Peps, the much more acidly real portrait of Miss Tox ('Her hands had contracted a spasmodic habit of raising themselves of their own accord as in involuntary admiration. Her eyes were liable to a similar affection . . .'), a genuine impressiveness in Mr Dombey's pomposity, and a dozen other quickly changing tones of voice that would normally, even in Dickens, be hardly concordant with the simple good fun of Mr Chick's amiable ineffectuality: 'Don't you over-exert yourself, Loo,' said Mr Chick, 'or you'll be laid up with spasms, I see. Right tol loor rul! Bless my soul, I forgot! We're here one day and gone the next!' (ch. 11)

There are times in Dickens when passages like this, or like Mr Chick's eruption into the conversation about wet-nurses for Paul ('Couldn't something temporary be done with a teapot?'), seem either illustrations of a fairly obvious thesis (compare some passages about the Veneerings in *Our Mutual Friend*), or moments of brilliant comedy that look bizarre because isolated from their surroundings. But in the early chapters of Dombey, it would be quite absurd to see Mr Chick as meant to illustrate any solemnly symbolic or sociological 'point' about nineteenth-century life; on the other hand, his presence is so easily and naturally part of the quite serious comedy of 'Dom-bey and Son!' that it sticks in one's mind as essentially part also of Dickens's ranging over the possibilities (and impossibilities) of life itself. The result is that Dickens is both funnier *and* more genuinely constructive here than he is in passages where he tries more specifically to protest against or overcome the threats to living that he sees in utilitarianism, system, law, formal education of Gradgrind's or Dr Blimber's kind, government generally.

Certainly, the constructive side to this whole novel includes also, as Dr Leavis has pointed out, a specifically anti-Dombey theme: Dickens's evocation of the 'apple-faced man', Toodles, and his wife Polly. Scenes such as those on the station platform (Chapter XX), or here in Chapter 11, where Dickens quite consciously opposes the Toodles family and the Dombeys, are genuinely impressive. If there are points in which the opposition verges on the over-obvious, it remains impressive none the less, and very telling in the general run of Dickens's imaginative and diagnostic probing into nineteenth-century England. The Toodles are fertile ('Four hims and a her' at this early stage), inarticulate, much happier in their naturally uneducated state than in the dreadful attempt to improve their unfortunate son at the Charitable Grinders. The Dombeys, on the other hand, are threatened by actual and metaphorical sterility, very articulate (mainly in the person of Paul Dombey), and as highly educated as possible under the circumstances.

At first glance, the outline of this situation would seem to place Dombey himself at a hopeless disadvantage: in contrast to the unreflecting and inarticulate Toodles, he neglects his wife and he sacrifices his son simply for the sake of aggrandising the name, 'Dombey and Son'. Also, he

neglects and resents Florence because she is a daughter and therefore
cannot advance either his name or his commercial prospects. But two
things complicate and enrich this contrast between the two families. One
is simply an agility of mind in Dickens's writing here that easily avoids
the thematic obsessiveness threatening some others of his famous comic
scenes. In the following exchange, for instance, Mr Toodles is clearly
backed by Dickens as a good thing, but he is also shown as painfully
awkward and unable to cope, and the resultant comedy takes on a life
of its own, one that cannot be summarised as showing simply Miss
Tox's false gentility, or Dombey's arrogance in the arrangement of his
household.

> The apple-faced man ... stood chuckling and grinning in a front
> row.
> 'This is his wife, of course,' said Miss Tox, singling out the young
> woman with the baby. 'How do you do, Polly?'
> 'I'm pretty well, I thank you ma'am,' said Polly. ...
> 'I'm glad to hear it,' said Miss Tox. 'The other young woman is her
> unmarried sister who lives with them, and would take care of her
> children. Her name's Jemima. How do you do, Jemima?'
> 'I'm pretty well, I thank you, ma'am,' returned Jemima.
> 'I'm very glad to hear it,' said Miss Tox. 'I hope you'll keep so. ...
> The fine little boy with the blister on his nose is the eldest. The blister,
> I believe ... is not constitutional, but accidental?'
> The apple-faced man was understood to growl, 'Flat iron.'
> 'I beg your pardon, Sir,' said Miss Tox, 'did you? –'
> 'Flat iron,' he repeated.
> 'Oh yes,' said Miss Tox. 'Yes! quite true. I forgot. The little creature,
> in his mother's absence, smelt a warm flat iron. You're quite right,
> Sir. You were going to have the goodness to inform me, when we
> arrived at the door, that you were by trade a –'
> 'Stoker,' said the man.
> 'A choker!' said Miss Tox, quite aghast.
> 'Stoker,' said the man. 'Steam ingine.' (ch. 11)

This whole dialogue is in a sense about classes of society, differences in
education, income, habits; but it is lightly and agilely enough done to
keep possibilities open instead of pigeon-holed, labelled, flattened under
a weight of exhortatory rhetoric. That glancing, comic vision given to Miss
Tox – maybe there are whole trades and classes the genteel world has never
seen: chokers, perhaps! – a moment of this, lightly but surely relevant, is
worth pages of Dickensian satire or rhetoric condemning what anyone
can see at a glance are the bad sides to nineteenth-century commercialism.
    The second complicating factor is indeed Dombey himself. It is not
simply that, together with the business of opposing him to Toodles,
Dickens shows a real and genuine sympathy for Dombey. That much,

like the sympathy for Sir Leicester Dedlock wanting his wife back home, is clear, and undoubtedly a consciously directed impulse in the novel as a whole. The more interesting fact is that even the inhumanly pompous aspect of Dombey is not crushed out of existence by the irony (as Sir Leicester's less vicious pomposities in *Bleak House* pretty well are). Clearly Sir Leicester Dedlock would be a better man if he weren't so silly about Britain going to the dogs and if he weren't so stand-offish to people like Mr Rouncewell. I do not think we can quite so surely say that Mr Dombey would be, or later in the novel actually is, a better man without his gold watch-chain, his stiffness, his pronouncing of the all-powerful name, 'Dom-bey and Son!'

> Dombey, exulting in the long-looked-for event, jingled and jingled the heavy gold watch-chain that depended from below his trim blue coat, whereof the buttons sparkled phosphorescently in the feeble rays of the distant fire. Son, with his little fists curled up and clenched, seemed, in his feeble way, to be squaring at existence for having come upon him so unexpectedly.
>
> 'The house will once again, Mrs Dombey,' said Mr Dombey, 'be not only in name but in fact Dombey and Son; Dom-bey and Son!'
>
> The words had such a softening influence, that he appended a term of endearment to Mrs Dombey's name (though not without some hesitation, as being a man but little used to that form of address): and said, 'Mrs Dombey, my – my dear.'
>
> A transient flush of faint surprise overspread the sick lady's face as she raised her eyes towards him.
>
> 'He will be christened Paul, my – Mrs Dombey – of course.'
>
> She feebly echoed, 'Of course,' or rather expressed it by the motion of her lips, and closed her eyes again.
>
> 'His father's name, Mrs Dombey, and his grandfather's! I wish his grandfather were alive this day!' And again he said 'Dom-bey and Son,' in exactly the same tone as before. (ch. 1)

There is no figure quite like this, or quite so impressive, in *Bleak House* or, I think, in any other Dickens novel. Dickens's conscious mind and intention would insist that Mr Jarndyce is much more of a whole man, a human being, than Dombey can possibly be, at least up to the point where his pride is humbled and he recognises Florence as a daughter. In fact, Mr Jarndyce, for all his retreats to the 'growlery', is pallid in comparison. For this reason it is easier for Dickens to sustain him consistently throughout the book, but impossible for him to give to Jarndyce the charge and impetus he gives to Dombey in the opening chapters. In these chapters, Dickens for once allows that the powerful egocentricity of and in Victorian middle-class life can have a side to it that is very impressive indeed.

· · · · ·

There is I think a charge and impetus to parts at least of *Bleak House* too, and it springs from something very close to the half-buried impulse in Dickens that gives us the early Dombey. In the later novel, however, the impulse, though in context perhaps even more interesting, seems to be buried deeper still in Dickens's subconscious, and when it does appear in the novel it assumes more twisted and disruptive forms: in brief, those of the dominant and domineering females, amongst whom I would myself include the apparently innocent and all-virtuous Esther. These women almost all, in different and differing ways, show an interesting and compelling individuality, but in every case it is one that is even more drastically at odds than Dombey's is with the conscious intentions of the book as a whole.

Before this discrepancy comes to the surface we have, however, another justly famous Dickens opening. If one looks at this prose, one can certainly see why Leavis would claim that for all the signs of over-insistence and repetition already there in Chapter 1, it is nevertheless to Dickens we must look for strongly imaginative writing in the mid-nineteenth century:

> London. Michaelmas Term lately over, and the Lord Chancellor sitting in Lincoln's Inn Hall. Implacable November weather. As much mud in the streets, as if the waters had but newly retired from the face of the earth, and it would not be wonderful to meet a Megalosaurus, forty feet long or so, waddling like an elephantine lizard up Holborn Hill. Smoke lowering down from chimney-pots, making a soft, black drizzle, with flakes of soot in it as big as full-grown snow-flakes – gone into mourning, one might imagine, for the death of the sun. Dogs, undistinguishable in the mire. Horses, scarcely better. . . . Foot passengers, jostling one another's umbrellas, in a general infection of ill-temper, and losing their foothold at street corners . . . adding new deposits to the crust upon crust of mud, sticking at those points tenaciously to the pavement, and accumulating at compound interest. (ch. 1)

Clearly that is in the first place extraordinarily fluent language, and an extraordinarily fluent and lively mind at work *in* the language. One telling contrast might be with almost any typical passage of George Eliot speaking or describing in her own person. She has a stronger, much more self-reliant mind and personality than Dickens, but in his favour it must surely be said that George Eliot's very strength – almost always a little academic in tone and character – would prevent her from achieving this rapidly imaginative construct of the elephantine lizard 'forty feet long or so' waddling up a famous London street, or the soot like snow-flakes gone into mourning for the death of the sun.

In contrast to George Eliot's, Dickens's mind ranges freely – too freely, sometimes – and it picks up imaginative, suggestive references without his having to think consciously where they will come from or how they will be organised. And people who support Dickens are right, I think, in saying that one reason for this is his being closer to the life and liveliness of popular, spoken, everyday English than most nineteenth-century writers were. It's not so much that he can copy the accents of street-dwellers like Jo the crossing-sweeper. He can't, actually. At any rate, I remain to be convinced that even Jo's more famous turns of phrase are the thing itself. I don't believe that actual people went round saying 'He wos werry good to me, he wos.' But on the other hand, I don't think it matters much whether they did or not. The advantage Dickens has is not so much any ability to copy real speech or even real people in literal detail, as a much more generalised feeling for the life and liveliness of popular London. One doesn't even need the details of his life (visits to his father in the debtors' prison, his work as an articled clerk, his few months in the blacking factory, then later his reporting and journalism), to know that this is a Londoner writing: relatively uneducated, certainly not hampered by intellectual or academic preoccupations, and, perhaps in consequence, absolutely at home with those short, idiomatic phrases that begin *Bleak House* ('London. Michaelmas Term lately over. . . . Dogs, undistinguishable in the mire. Horses, scarcely better . . .') If Dickens hated and distrusted some of the London he knew, this hatred was clearly mingled with a trust and confidence in it and in its language.

The constructive and creative side to Dickens's confidence includes here, as indeed it does also in the best of *Dombey and Son*, a brilliantly simple gift for parody that has none of the obsessive quality that mars some of his famous set pieces ('From my Lord Boodle, through the Duke of Foodle, down to Noodle . . .'). For instance, the parodying of lawyers towards the end of the first chapter of *Bleak House* is successful for a combination of two reasons: it has something substantial to say – there's not much doubt that, for all the Chancery reforms of the 1870s, a lot of lawyers get more money than their clients get justice, even today – and *therefore* Dickens's language is at its most agile, not just copying but actively and I think creatively parodying Mr Tangle's subservience:

> 'Mr Tangle,' says the Chancellor, latterly something restless under the eloquence of that learned gentleman.
> 'Mlud,' says Mr Tangle. Mr Tangle knows more of Jarndyce and Jarndyce than anybody. He is famous for it – supposed never to have read anything else since he left school.
> 'Have you nearly concluded your argument?'
> 'Mlud, no – variety of points – feel it my duty tsubmit – ludship,' is the reply that slides out of Mr Tangle. (ch. 1)

After a bit more of this the man from Shropshire, who later dies simply because he can't stand it any longer, tries to get a word in but is ignored

completely, and the Lord Chancellor goes on to the question of the wards
in Chancery:

> 'In reference,' proceeds the Chancellor . . . 'to the young girl –'
> 'Begludship's pardon – boy,' says Mr Tangle prematurely.
> 'In reference' proceeds the Chancellor, with extra distinctness, 'to
> the young girl and the boy, the two young people,'
>   (Mr Tangle crushed)
> 'Whom I directed to be in attendance today . . . I will see them and
> satisfy myself as to the expediency of . . . their residing with their
> uncle.'
> Mr Tangle is on his legs again.
> 'Begludship's pardon – dead.'
> 'With their,' Chancellor looking through his double eyeglass at the
> papers on his desk, 'grandfather.'
> 'Begludship's pardon – victim of rash action – brains.' (ch. 1)

If only Dickens could have kept it up! But he couldn't, or not for very
long. Here, there really is an agility in language comparable to that in the
opening paragraphs of the novel. The satire is trenchantly simple, but
not in the least negative in spirit or dry in tone. Dickens's interest is
immediately aroused by the things, situations, people he so effectively
condemns: 'Mlud, no – variety of points – feel it my duty tsubmit –
ludship.' Even the telescoping of Mr Tangle's phrases, which looks so
simple now that Dickens has done it, is alive, immediate, wholly positive
in spirit. Indeed, the whole novel is a cornucopia of people, figures,
incidents that would make most Jacobean drama, for instance, look thin
by comparison. And in such circumstances it wouldn't normally matter
all that much that the author seems implicated in some of the less pleasant
features of the tale (Jarndyce's and Ada's sentimentality, for instance, or,
at the other end of the scale, the thick yellow liquor that is all that is left
of Mr Krook after his death by Spontaneous Cumbustion).

   What does seem to me to matter is that, for all Dickens's inventiveness,
the book as a whole is alarmingly repetitive. Too often there is a disproportion between what Dickens has to say, and the number of times he
goes on saying it. I think one can detect signs of this disproportion even
in an obviously good and telling chapter like the opening one. A number
even of his good points about the inhumanity of Chancery proceedings,
the illusory nature of the hopes these throw out to suitors, lawyers
wasting clients' money on purely procedural argument and so on – a
lot of these are stated, here and elsewhere in the book, more often than
they need be. More significantly, there are times when Dickens's generally
very fluent writing stiffens into heavily patterned rhetoric.

   Well may the court be dim, with wasting candles here and there;
well may the fog hang heavy in it, as if it would never get out; well

> may the stained glass windows lose their colour, and admit no light
> into the place; well may the uninitiated from the streets . . . be deterred
> from entrance by its owlish aspect . . . (ch. 1)

I think one is justified in being immediately suspicious of symbolism that
needs to be as literal-minded and specific as this. But worse is to come,
because a few lines later the rhythms of the prose get heavier still and all
the nimbleness of Dickens's mind and comic intelligence deserts him
entirely:

> This is the Court of Chancery; which has its decaying houses and its
> blighted lands in every shire; which has its worn-out lunatic in every
> madhouse, and its dead in every churchyard; which has its ruined
> suitor, with his slipshod heels and threadbare dress, borrowing and
> begging through the round of every man's acquaintance; which gives
> to monied might the means abundantly of wearying out the right . . .
> (ch. 1)

I know that Dickens doesn't *intend* this to be taken as literally true, but
the patterned exaggeration ('. . . every madhouse . . . every churchyard
. . . every man's acquaintance . . .') makes it sound almost as if he does,
for the moment, and so the edge is lost to what is elsewhere a true
condemnation of Chancery.

But more is at stake even in these opening sections than simply the
effectiveness or otherwise of Dickens's polemic against Chancery.
Unfortunately, he is as thoroughly committed to the heavy rhetoric of
parts of these as he is to his most fluently inventive passages. With a
writer as good as Dickens, the style is indeed the man, to the point where
nobody could mistake even his feebler passages for anybody else's:

> What connection can there be, between the place in Lincolnshire, the
> house in town, the Mercury in powder, and the whereabout of Jo
> the outlaw with the broom, who had that distant ray of light upon
> him when he swept the churchyard-step? What connection can there
> have been between many people in the innumerable histories of this
> world, who, from opposite sides of great gulfs, have, nevertheless,
> been very curiously brought together! (ch. 16)

Theoretically, passages like this, Dickensian though they are, could
simply be the result of a lapse in concentration on his part, a resort to
mannered writing or to worn-out mental track-habits such as must
bedevil any prolific writer from time to time. And perhaps something
of this kind is indeed in part the case here. But I am inclined to feel that
the stiffening of the sinews in the prose, and the incipient sentimentality
('that distant ray of light upon him when he swept the church-yard step'),
are so *thoroughly* characteristic, both of this book and (even more so) of
others of the late novels, that there must be some other cause or causes

operating as well. Dickens is so energetic a writer that the passages where the dead hand of sentimental rhetoric falls as heavily as it does here demand some further explanation than simply that of tiredness or habit. What happens to the figure of Dombey in the earlier novel might, obliquely, give us a hint worth pursuing in the admittedly very different territory of *Bleak House.* In *Dombey,* the main character is first of all condemned as a pompous egotist, and then, finally, purged of this completely under the influence of the gentle Florence. That is, Dickens has not dared to face the consequences of what backing individualism might really entail (such as, for instance, allowing Dombey to remain impervious to Florence's shallow sentiment). Here in *Bleak House,* though there is no figure that corresponds to Dombey, the stiffness and/or sentimentality in some passages, together with Dickens's repetitive insistence that all forms of system and government are totally bad, may I think point once again to his unwillingness to allow full rein to what he nevertheless instinctively knows, namely that any true individualism must involve something more threatening than the simple kindness he lavishes on Ada and Mr Jarndyce; as also that it should be allowed to invigorate, rather than simply draw back from, the vast and still growing world of government, bureaucracy, nineteenth-century technological and business life generally.

Admittedly, there are whole sections of *Bleak House* that show Dickens as quite openly committed to an individualism that must have been extreme even by the standards of contemporary *laissez-faire* (survival of the fittest?) philosophies. Perhaps his reliance on coincidences is part of this; compare, for instance, the factitious 'connections' Dickens feels he has to manufacture between Jo, 'Nemo', Lady Dedlock, Esther and Trooper George: it is almost as if he is declaring that people are so *radically* individual that any connections that may spring up between them must be founded on chance and coincidence. More certainly, because much more impressively, there are the eccentrics and outsiders. These are the best part of *Bleak House,* and one could not imagine the book without Mr Turveydrop's 'deportment', the horrible Mr Krook and his cat, the Snagsbys, Phil Squod tacking about the shooting gallery, or Mr Vholes, with his parent safely tucked away in the Vale of Taunton, patiently watching Richard: 'Mr Vholes, after glancing at the official cat who is patiently watching a mouse's hole, fixes his charmed gaze on his young client . . .' The trouble with the novel, and the reason for the long dead stretches of writing in it, seems to be not the existence of so many eccentrics and villains like these, or like Mr Chadband ('Mr Chadband is a large yellow man, with a fat smile, and a general appearance of having a good deal of train oil in his system'), but on the contrary Dickens's refusal to allow his 'good' characters (Jarndyce, Ada, Allan Woodcourt) even the faintest touch of the powerful self-interest or eccentricity that animates the rest. In this and most of his other books,

Dickens is trying to have his cake and eat it. He wants an individualism powerful enough to oppose Chancery, but one that is also purged of any of the impulses that make his writing about the real egotists so alive and so threateningly real. The result can only be a secluded quietism of the Jarndyce kind, almost totally ineffectual in an England as demanding and rapacious as the one Dickens himself (pretty truly, one would guess) imagines.

Over all, Dickens's view of nineteenth-century society is thoroughly atomistic. He does have a general case against Chancery and system, but in practice he puts this so heavily and so repetitiously that he leaves no room at all for government, education, or communal living of any kind more extensive than isolated pockets of goodness and charity such as the shooting gallery and Bleak House itself. And since his attempt is to purge these of any taint of either system or self-seeking, they cannot possibly affect any but a few individuals who happen to stray into them. Neither, even, can most of Dickens's villains, powerful though they are. Grandfather Smallweed's miserliness, for instance, has a clear effect on people who get in his way, but this is incidental to one's memory of him at home, throwing the cushion at his wife and undergoing 'the two operations at the hands of his granddaughter, of being shaken up like a great bottle, and poked and punched like a great bolster' until 'some indication of a neck [is] developed in him by these means'. The sensuousness of this, as of the 'thick, yellow liquor' to which Krook is melted down, has a horrible fascination for Dickens, and he is implicated in the lingering detail more than his condemnation of the Smallweed way of life, or his contrasting praise of Mr George's, will allow. At the same time, there is a vein of horror-fun running through his account of the family that ends by making their miserliness far less of a real and continuing threat than, say, the viciousness of a Rosamond Vincy or the powerful hold that is effected by Bulstrode on the lives of Lydgate and others round him. The Smallweed family is strikingly memorable, but memorable as an isolated, and in the end relatively harmless, phenomenon:

> 'You're a brimstone idiot. You're a scorpion – a brimstone scorpion! You're a sweltering toad. You're a chattering clattering broomstick witch, that ought to be burnt!' gasps the old man, prostrate in his chair. 'My dear friend, will you shake me up a little?' (ch. 21)

But Dickens's staking his all on personal, individual feeling *versus* bureaucracy, technology, educational institutions, society generally, has one of its most striking results in the kinds of women he produces, and in the ways they confront the men in his novels. In *Bleak House* there is on the one hand Ada, whose melting sentiment is not far removed from Florence's in *Dombey and Son*, and in any case is clearly identifiable as a familiar Dickensian resort in the face of the regimentation practised by Chancery and by 'inexorable moral policemen' like Mrs Pardiggle.

When Ada sees the dead child in the bricklayer's cottage, she is given this speech:

> 'O Esther!' cried Ada, sinking on her knees beside [the child].
> 'Look here! O Esther, my love, the little thing! The suffering, quiet, pretty little thing! I am so sorry for it. I am so sorry for the mother. I never saw a sight so pitiful as this before! O baby, baby!' (ch. 8)

When Dickens faces us with this as the alternative to, say, Mrs Jellyby, who scarcely remembers the names of her own children, but who is terribly concerned about natives of the Borrioboola-Gha tribe in Africa, it is Hobson's choice indeed. He is twisting what might have been a true case against nineteenth-century impersonality by focusing it on the extremes of personal sentiment on the one hand, and regimentation on the other.

Admittedly, Ada herself, typical though she is of the general run of gentle females in Dickens, is powerless and ineffectual in the world of lawyers and scoundrels that clusters around Chancery in *Bleak House*. What is much more significant is that she, together with some of the men who show pretty obviously female characteristics (Jarndyce, Mr Snagsby, Sir Leicester; even, in his chest-expanding way, Trooper George), is one side of an archetypal Dickensian coin. The other side is the plethora of dominant and domineering females in *Bleak House*. If one thinks even casually of the run of the story, these include: Lady Dedlock herself (a figure of guilt and remorse but still a far stronger personality than Sir Leicester), Mrs Jellyby, Mrs Pardiggle ('distinguished for rapacious benevolence'), Mrs Snagsby, Mrs Bayham Badger and, last but certainly not least, Hortense the French maid, who cannot bear Lady Dedlock's preferring anybody (in this case, Rosa) to herself:

> Her retaliation was the most singular I could have imagined. She remained perfectly still until the carriage had turned into the drive, and then, without the least discomposure of countenance, slipped off her shoes, left them on the ground, and walked deliberately in the same direction, through the wettest of the wet grass. . . .
>
> We passed not far from the House, a few minutes afterwards. Peaceful as it had looked when we first saw it, it looked even more so now, with a diamond spray glittering all about it, a light wind blowing, the birds no longer hushed but singing strongly, everything refreshed by the late rain, and the little carriage shining at the doorway like a fairy carriage made of silver. Still, very steadfastly and quietly walking towards it, a peaceful figure too in the landscape, went Mademoiselle Hortense, shoeless, through the wet grass. (ch. 18)

A moment of rare concentration on Dickens's part. Elsewhere, he might all too readily have pursued the agreeable fantasy of 'the little carriage shining at the doorway like a fairy carriage made of silver'. Here, this is strictly subservient to the dominant image of Hortense deliberately taking off her shoes and walking back home 'through the wettest of the wet grass'. My reason for singling out the stillness and rightness of this image is that it seems indeed a concentration of what really interests Dickens in his presentation of the monstrous regiment of women in *Bleak House*. In point of influence, action and personality it is the women who dominate; the husbands in this company, and indeed most of the single men, count for nothing. The almost archetypal case is Mr Bayham Badger, who can do little more than repeat his favourite refrain, 'You would hardly suppose that I am Mrs Bayham Badger's third!' Of the other men in the story, most are ineffectual. Mr Tulkinghorn, admittedly, isn't, but he determinedly stays a bachelor. He says, indeed, to Lady Dedlock: 'My experience teaches me, Lady Dedlock, that most of the people I know would do far better to leave marriage alone. It is at the bottom of three-fourths of their troubles.' After this, he is himself never-theless faced with the implacable demands of Hortense, who kills him when he refuses to meet these demands. Two others of the leading men in the story are also elderly bachelors. Mr Jarndyce does, at the age of about sixty, propose to Esther, but then of course willingly (and very wisely?) gives her up to Woodcourt. His friend Mr Boythorn remains determinedly an angry bachelor to the close of the novel.

A company, then, of ineffectual men and keenly rapacious women. Admittedly there are exceptions, or apparent exceptions. Miss Flite is a real exception, though in her case it is madness that has given her wit, freedom and benevolence beyond the range of other women in the book. Caddy Jellyby, if sentimentalised at points of the narrative, is another. Of the apparent exceptions Trooper George, with his stoic masculinity, is really a sentimentalist underneath; and like the stronger Tulkinghorn he stays single, as far out of women's range as he can get, though from this safe distance indulging the tenderest admiration for Esther Summer-son. Mr Boythorn, with his comic anger always at boiling point, is another whose masculinity is skin-deep only. This time, however, as the comic exaggeration of it all clearly shows, Dickens is well aware of the nature of the case. Not even Mr Boythorn's enemy and neighbour, Sir Leicester, is in much danger from him, and the best of his outbursts stress a comic impracticality as much as anything else:

'By all that is base and despicable,' cried Mr Boythorn, 'the treatment of Surgeons aboard ship is such, that I would submit the legs – both legs – of every member of the Admiralty Board to a compound frac-ture, and render it a transportable offence in any qualified practitioner to set them, if the system were not wholly changed in eight-and-forty hours!'
'Wouldn't you give them a week?' asked Mr Jarndyce.

'No!' cried Mr Boythorn firmly. 'Not on any consideration! Eight-and-forty hours! As to Corporations, Parishes, Vestry-Boards, and similar gatherings of jolter-headed clods, who assemble to exchange such speeches that, by Heaven! they ought to be worked in quicksilver mines for the short remainder of their miserable existence, if it were only to prevent their detestable English from contaminating a language spoken in the presence of the Sun – as to those fellows . . .' (ch. 13)

Dickens is indeed very funny about Mr Boythorn, but the fun is of a kind that makes it perfectly clear that he is what his name suggests, a grown-up boy. Despite his reputation for knocking two (Mr Boythorn himself claims six) of a bully's teeth out at school, he would be no match now for any of the dominating and dominant women in the book. He might frighten Ada for a few moments, but that is all he could do.

So, given a world where most men take various expedients to avoid any really close contact with women (by remaining bachelors when they can, or failing this choosing the most pliable and sentimental women to hand, or as a very last resort throwing cushions at them, as Grandfather Smallweed does), what does one make of the female lead in *Bleak House*, Esther Summerson? Partly, she figures in the novel simply as an impersonal narrator, and as such she is both innocuous and useful in the telling of the story. But what most people remember is the side to Esther that colours the very prose of the novel when her own personality is allowed full sway:

I don't know how it is, I seem to be always writing about myself. I mean all the time to write about other people, and I try to think about myself as little as possible, and I am sure, when I find myself coming into the story again, I am really vexed and say, 'Dear, dear, you tiresome little creature, I wish you wouldn't!' but it is all of no use . . . (ch. 9)

This, though not exactly honest Dickens prose, does expose the very worst side of his chosen heroine, her ghastly winsomeness. The trouble is, he also wants us to believe in this, or at least to believe it is forgivable and basically innocent. Much later on he gives us, for instance, this version of Esther trying to find out what is the matter with Ada (in fact, Ada is secretly married to Richard, and troubled by Richard's animosity towards Mr Jarndyce):

What could I do to reassure my darling . . . and show her that I had no such feelings [of disappointment]? Well! I could only be as brisk and busy as possible, and that, I had tried to be all along . . . [But] I resolved to be doubly diligent and gay. So I went about the house, humming all the tunes I knew; and I sat working and working in a desperate manner, and I talked and talked, morning, noon, and night.
And still there was the same shade between me and my darling. (ch. 50)

The wonder is that the shade didn't deepen to impenetrable gloom under this sort of treatment. Girls who try to smooth out difficulties by going around humming tunes and calling other women 'my own pet' are asking for trouble, advertising as clearly as humanly possible that their ostensible interest in other people is really the reverse of that, a covert, but demanding egotism.

Personally, I much prefer Hardy's treatment of the threat of female dominance and self-interest, particularly as this appears in the case of Sue Bridehead. Obviously, Sue herself is a twisted, or at least a thoroughly divided, personality. On the one hand there is her angelic appearance, her shrinking from the grossly physical, and even, in the end, from the scholarly Phillotson; on the other, there is the sheerly, and sexually, provocative part of her that forces Jude to go through that mock wedding-ceremony a couple of hours before she is to marry Phillotson:

> 'I like to do things like this,' she said in the delicate voice of an epicure in emotions, which left no doubt that she spoke the truth.
> 'I know you do!' said Jude.
> 'They are interesting, because they have probably never been done before. I shall walk down the church like this with my husband in about two hours, shan't I!'
> 'No doubt you will!'
> 'Was it like this when you were married?' (*Jude the Obscure*, III, vii)

But Hardy is both much clearer and more open about the implications of divided personalities like Sue's than Dickens ever is. Certainly in this passage from *Jude*, dominated as it is by Hardy's unambiguously clear comment on that 'delicate voice of an epicure in emotions', there is nothing equivalent to Dickens's frequent attempts to win us, and himself, over to Esther's side and see her as a centre of hope and light in Chancery-ridden England:

> 'Is the wind in the East to-day?' I ventured to ask him. . . . He answered, 'No!' again; and this time my dear girl confidently answered 'No,' too, and shook the lovely head which, with its blooming flowers against the golden hair, was like the very Spring. 'Much *you* know of East winds, my ugly darling,' said I, kissing her in my admiration – I couldn't help it.
> Well! It was only their love for me, I know very well, and it is a long time ago. I must write it, even if I rub it out again, because it gives me so much pleasure. They said there could be no East wind where Somebody was; they said that wherever Dame Durden went, there was sunshine and summer air. (ch. 30)

What prevents Dickens from admitting openly that the Esthers of this world have some pretty nasty streaks in them, is the same sentimentality about nineteenth-century life that makes it almost impossible for him to think a really bad thought about any of the leading characters in his books, except the villains. Dombey, until Florence melts him with sentimentality, is an obvious and powerful exception. In *Bleak House,* Esther's character has the makings in it of another and very interesting one; over all, though, and certainly in the consciously directed plan of the book, she is lumped in with the good characters, who are either victims of Chancery and oppressive circumstances generally, or bravely fighting these by opposing their own single, and therefore totally ineffectual, acts of kindness and love. Indeed, one of the nastiest results of this affects Esther herself: Dickens's insistence on scarring her face by a disease that apparently leaves Charley and even Jo unscarred seems very close to a token gesture, an uneasy admission that his heroine can't possibly remain untouched by the pervading misery of the world in which he has placed her. Esther has to have smallpox scars before she can earn the right to Allan Woodcourt and the cottage garlanded with jasmine, woodbine and honeysuckle at the end. On the other hand, the scars are indeed a token gesture because, in the last pages of the novel, we find Dickens hinting that they have mysteriously disappeared.

To have written differently, Dickens would have had to have changed his whole notion of what nineteenth-century England was about; what forces in it were really dominant; and what the significance and worth of these forces might finally be or become. What this and other novels do testify to beyond doubt is the sheer power of the ego in society – in the women who dominate most of this story, and in men, or phenomena, like Chadband, Smallweed, Guppy. What they will not allow openly is the necessary consequence of this, namely that an egocentricity as powerful as Dickens's own rendering shows it to be cannot just be smoothed out of existence, or treated as if it were simply the product of an eccentricity so extreme as to be of little or no general significance. In practice, smoothing out results only in the sentimentalising of figures like Dombey, and in twisting the self-interest clearly displayed by people like Esther into an escapist and irrelevant whimsy. Dickens is much more at home, and certainly very lively, in his rendering of eccentrics and outsiders such as those who crop up again and again in *Bleak House.* But even the villains among these are safely isolated: there is no real recognition or pondering of the possibility that Chadband's hypocrisy might be in some ways rather like Esther's, or the Smallweeds' meanness simply the reverse of Mr Jarndyce's sentimental generosity. And the likeable eccentrics are in general equally safe, in various ways either isolated or defused. Thus Mr Vholes cannot really harm Richard, because Dickens has already placed the blame squarely on an impersonal 'Chancery'; Miss Flite, whose individuality is, like Vholes's, sharpened by a telling self-interest, is safely mad:

'Oh!' said she. 'The wards in Jarndyce! Ve-ery happy, I am sure, to have the honour! It is a good omen for youth, and hope, and beauty, when they find themselves in this place, and don't know what's to come of it.'

'Mad!' whispered Richard, not thinking she could hear him.

'Right! Mad, young gentleman,' she returned so quickly that he was quite abashed. 'I was a ward myself. I was not mad at that time,' curtseying low, and smiling between every little sentence. 'I had youth and hope. I believe, beauty. It matters very little now. . . . I have the honour to attend Court regularly. With my documents. I expect a judgment. Shortly. On the Day of Judgment. . . .'

As Ada was a little frightened, I said, to humour the poor old lady, that we were very much obliged to her.

'Ye-es!' she said mincingly. 'I imagine so. And here is Conversation Kenge. With *his* documents! How does your honourable worship do?' (ch. 3)

In the end, so far from being a writer who trusts individuality, personal feeling, the creative life in a mass society, Dickens takes one expedient after another to avoid trusting these impulses except in their shielded and powerless form of sentimental or eccentric behaviour. A powerful personality himself, he seems afraid of the power of pesonality he can so vividly create, especially when this issues in the women who dominate so many of his books. It is this fear of what might underlie his sentimentalised love of individuality and humanity generally that makes him turn his best diagnoses of 'system', Chancery, government into exaggerated and repetitive rhetoric. If individuals can not be trusted, then a scapegoat must be found, even at the risk of disembodying both whole sections of the novels, and the prose in which these sections are written:

The Lord Chancellor of that Court, true to his title in his last act, has died the death of all Lord Chancellors in all Courts, and of all authorities in all places under all names soever, where false pretences are made, and where injustice is done. Call the death by any name Your Highness will . . . it is the same death eternally – inborn, inbred, engendered in the corrupted humours of the vicious body itself, and that only – Spontaneous Cumbustion, and none other of all the deaths that can be died. (ch. 32)

5 Love and Politics in the English Novel, 1840s–1860s

The title of this chapter is in a sense fraudulent: 'Small politics and less love' would be nearer the mark for Disraeli, Mrs Gaskell, and the George Eliot of *Felix Holt*. Each of the novels I want to consider here is minor, and each of them seems to me badly flawed. Compared with the best of English literature, these are not about either love or politics in any full sense of those words. They must, therefore, be very untrustworthy evidence of what love and politics might really have meant either in the period generally or, if it comes to that, in the lives of these authors.

Nevertheless, and with the possible exception of Trollope, these are the nineteenth-century novelists in English who most specifically engage with political issues. I don't myself count Trollope as a political novelist, because even the Finn/Palliser series, close though it is to the parliamentary scene, seems to me more interested in the general moral dilemma that Palliser's career, for instance, figures: for Plantagenet Palliser, to act in the world is essential and honourable; but honour cannot survive dirtying one's hands in the business of the world. Phineas Finn comes to feel much the same in the end, and I don't think it would have made very much difference to these men, or to Trollope (despite his consuming interest in the House of Commons), if the 'business of the world' had been trade and commerce instead of rigged elections and party managers. But in other novels of the period politics, political economy and trade unions loom large. There are in fact too many political novels to discuss here – nominally a list might include, for instance, Kay-Shuttleworth's dreadful effusion, *Scarsdale* – but a fair selection from among the better ones of the period would be: Mrs Gaskell's *Mary Barton* (1848) and *North and South* (which appeared in *Household Words* 1854–5); Disraeli's *Sybil* (1845); and George Eliot's *Felix Holt* (1866).

The question that interests me most about these is how and why did they fail? I do not believe it is simply that politics is intractable material for literature (it certainly wasn't for the Shakespeare of *Henry IV*, for instance). Nor do the kinds of weaknesses here seem simply weaknesses of and in the individual novelists concerned. There is a more general malaise than that operating, I think, and though it escapes final or complete diagnosis, one might approach an understanding of it by considering the persistent disjunction in these novels between politics on the one hand, and the rather unconvincing love-stories very much on the other. There is at least one other consideration that should be weighed in with this, though I don't want to do more than mention it in passing here: each of these novelists must have been cut off by the conditions of nineteenth-century middle-class life, education and aspirations from the popular movements they wrote about. If Disraeli's education, for instance, took place largely by reading in his father's library, he nevertheless had a library to read in beyond the dreams of the self-educated minority of the working class he and others describe in their fiction. The novelists' approach had to be to some degree academic, and this can only have increased their difficulties in the already difficult enough business of trying to write fiction that might make essentially personal emotions and affairs impinge on public ones.

On the other hand, I don't think that the novelists' lack of direct contact with working-class life and politics, debilitating though this must have been, was the only, or even the main, factor operating against them. Looking first at Mrs Gaskell's two novels (though they are in fact a few years later in time than Disraeli's), and thinking still in largely political and sociological terms: one thing about these that deserves notice first of all is that they seem to have stirred up more political or quasi-political controversy than they warranted. Most reviewers accepted the sentimental love-affairs for the most part uncritically, but took offence at Mrs Gaskell's interest in artisans and the working class. For instance, she was accused in *The Edinburgh Review* of April 1849, in an unsigned article in fact by W. R. Greg, of 'a sincere, though sometimes too exclusive and indiscriminating, sympathy with artisans'. Others joined in the complaint, but in fact there is no substance in it: her novels are full of doctrines of co-operation and self-help of precisely the kind advocated by the *Edinburgh* itself in its review of *Mary Barton*, and tend merely to protest against abuses, never against the wage-system itself or the existence of the employer class.

Indeed, I am inclined to think it might have helped her novels had Mrs Gaskell been a shade less conventional, a shade more outrageous in her political and sociological thinking. There are interesting and convincing sections in both novels on trade unions, working-class conditions and so on, but even these seem – at least given the hindsight of a hundred years and more – rather settled, rather unquestioning of basic nineteenth-century assumptions about self-help, and about co-operation between artisans (who must, however, keep their place) and employers (who also rarely speculate beyond the local conditions and events they know). Had Mrs Gaskell's political thinking been freer, I suspect that it would have been easier for her to make it relevant to the other, more personal and domestic, concerns in her novels.

Mary Barton for instance, though written during the 'hungry forties', and gloomier in tone than *North and South*, is if anything less radical in outlook than, say, James P. Kay's 1832 pamphlet on Manchester, or dozens of the reports that came in to Chadwick from his local doctors and poor-law officers:

> As they passed, women from their doors tossed household slops of *every* description into the gutter. . . . Our friends were not dainty, but even they picked their way, till they got to some steps leading down to a small area, where a person standing would have his head about one foot below the level of the street. . . . You went down one step even from the foul area into a cellar in which a family of human beings lived. It was very dark inside. The window-panes, many of them, were broken and stuffed with rags. . . . no-one can be surprised that on going into the cellar inhabited by Davenport, the smell was so foetid as almost to knock the two men down. . . . they began to penetrate the thick darkness of the place, and to see three or four little children rolling on the damp, nay wet brick floor, through which the stagnant, filthy moisture of the street oozed up; the fire-place was empty and black; the wife sat on her husband's lair [bed], and cried in the dark loneliness. (ch. VI)

The protest here against the injustice of working-class conditions in the industrial Midlands is obviously fair, and it is supported by literally hundreds of contemporary accounts, including of course those of Engels in his report on Manchester. But one's suspicions that, in context, Mrs Gaskell's protest may suffer not from any radicalism but from her un-thinking and basically sentimental conservatism, are born out by her handling of events generally in the novel. For example, after giving this and other perfectly clear instances of a system that condemns human beings to a sub-human existence, the novel neverthless concludes that master and servant may, *without any prior change in the system or in the living conditions of the men and their families*, be brought together in and by a kind of Christian humanism. In the end of the novel Barton, the by now broken and disillusioned trade-union delegate, meets Carson, the employer and the man whose son Barton has murdered. Under the stress of emotion class barriers break down; or rather, we are asked to believe that they might:

> The eyes of John Barton grew dim with tears. Rich and poor, masters and men, were then brothers in the deep suffering of the heart; for was not this the very anguish he had felt for little Tom, in years so long gone by . . .?

.   .   .   .   .   .

The mourner before him was no longer the employer; a being of another race, eternally placed in antagonistic attitude; going through the world glittering like gold, with a stony heart within, which knew no sorrow but through the accidents of Trade; no longer the enemy, the oppressor, but a very poor and desolate man. (ch. xxxv)

Writing in this softly sentimental prose, Mrs Gaskell almost makes it sound as if murder is the price we must pay for better class relations. And the moral tale that follows only makes matters worse: a little girl forgives a rough labouring lad for pushing her, with the words (italics Mrs Gaskell's or her editor's) '*He did not know what he was doing*, did you little boy?'

North and South is I think a better novel than *Mary Barton*, and in part it is better because Mrs Gaskell's enquiry into the phenomenon of industrial magnate *versus* working men, though still fairly conventional and limited, is by now slightly freer. The over-all pattern follows directly from her rather sentimental hopes at the end of *Mary Barton*, but here the writing is sturdier and more interesting. In *North and South* Mrs Gaskell is determined to bring the tough but likeably honest mill-owner, Thornton, to a better understanding of his men; and the men (notably the bluff, radically minded Higgins) to a better understanding of their free-enterprising master. The novel does this of course mainly through the heroine's influence, but also by forcing Thornton to ask himself tougher questions than he has done in his life to date. 'What do you want money for?' demands Mr Bell (Margaret's – the heroine's – godfather and fellow of an Oxford college). The question, though ironically put and only half serious from Mr Bell, is a faint precursor of Gudrun's famous question about Gerald in *Women in Love*: 'Where does his *go* go to?' Thornton's answer – unlike Gerald, he has the question put to him directly – is strongly enough shaped by Mrs Gaskell to give a clear, and in its unambitious way quite convincing, account of her hero's and to a large extent her own sympathies. (Thornton is by no means merely a mouthpiece for Mrs Gaskell's view, but such irony as is directed against him in this scene leaves his views about work and industry pretty much undisturbed.) These sympathies are neither so radically questioning nor so despairing of industrial society as Lawrence's, and they are, at least in this novel written in the more prosperous fifties, firmly in favour of a vigorous individualism in labourer and master alike. As such they seem both inoffensive and quite strongly put:

'But I belong to Teutonic blood ... we do not look upon life as a time for enjoyment, but as a time for action and exertion. Our glory and our beauty arise out of our inward strength, which makes us victorious over material resistance, and over greater difficulties still. We are Teutonic up here in Darkshire in another way. We hate to have laws made for us at a distance. We wish people would allow us to right ourselves, instead of continually meddling, with their imperfect legislation. We stand up for self-government, and oppose centralization.' (ch. XL)

The larger interest of Mrs Gaskell's political novels however is not so much in her own political position as, once again, in the enormous gap that identifying this reveals between the love-stories in her books on the one hand, and her attack on contemporary problems and abuses on the other. The love-stories, particularly that of Mary Barton's love for Jem Wilson, are in outline very like those of countless popular novels of the time.[1] Mrs Gaskell's, like those of the popular novel and indeed, if it comes to that, those of many of the greater nineteenth-century novelists, are generally affairs that flourish on ill-chance, separation, difficulties of degree and circumstances that force lovers apart before they can be united; and through it all the lovers lean yearningly on the very circumstances that part them or put difficulties in their way. In other words they, and Mrs Gaskell, thoroughly enjoy the pains of misunderstanding and separation. And if this sort of nostalgia is more marked in Mrs Gaskell than it is in Hardy, whose name obviously looms in any such discussion, it is so precisely because of the remarkable dichotomy between love and politics, at least in these two books of hers.

The most uncomfortable example of this tendency is Mary's totally unconvincing change of heart in favour of Jem in *Mary Barton*. Mary has for some time been dazzled by the local mill-owner's rakish son, but in the course of a few minutes' anguish, and after a pretty mawkish appeal from Jem, she drops Carson. 'What were these hollow vanities to her, now that she had discovered the passionate secret of her soul?' This is not just a technical slip or a moment of bad writing that one could happily forget, because in fact it governs the course of the succeeding tale in which Jem, who has rushed off without hearing Mary's declaration, and who despairs of her until she pleads for him in court at the end, leaves the district hurriedly and is wrongly but with some colour accused of Carson's murder. All the time it is Mary's father, driven to opium by hunger and despair at the failure of the trade-union petition to London, who, drawing the killer's lot in a working-men's ballot, has killed young Carson. Mary's character is improved – redeemed from flightiness, though she was always good at heart – by and in the *angst* of her apparently unrequited love for Jem; and the impetus of most of the second half of the novel, its own emotional charge as well as Mary's and Jem's, is diverted to this heroic stand of Mary's in the face of circumstance and of Jem's estrangement. The conditions that caused Carson's murder are left gradually behind – almost forgotten, indeed, except for the death-bed repentance–reconciliation scene between Mr Carson and John Barton.

North and South is emotionally tougher than this, and less of its energy

is diverted into the masochistic pleasures of an apparently tragic separation that ends happily for the lovers. In *North and South* the mutual suspicion of a pride and prejudice kind between Thornton and Margaret
(the proud daughter of an ex-Anglican minister who has given up his
ministry) is psychologically well done. Margaret's initial rejection of the
whole notion of trade and the cotton-spinning town of Milton is made a
real challenge to Thornton, in that it forces him to think as well as feel
differently about industry and its purpose in life. But again there is the
dependence on self-sacrifice and on unlikely chance separating the lovers.
Margaret's estrangement from Thornton is increased when he sees her
meeting a strange man (in fact it is her brother, whose life she is trying
to save); yet despite this she offers him all her new-found money (left
to her by the Oxford don) when he is financially endangered by his own
honesty and some bad years in trade. These circumstances produce again
that nostalgia and *angst*, so inseparable from one's remembrance of
nineteenth-century tales in verse and prose, that bedevils incipient
maturity. In Margaret, Mrs Gaskell has sketched a credibly strong-willed
and intelligent woman but one who, quite *in*credibly, has more fainting-
fits, illnesses, spells of weeping than any other heroine in reasonably
mature fiction. It is as if Mrs Gaskell will not allow genuine independence
and spirit without melting sentiment to make up for it. Whatever the
reason, sentimentality spoils any real development of the critique of
industrialism ('What do you want money for?') begun so interestingly
earlier in the book.

And always, side by side with love-affairs of this kind, but only very
insecurely related to them, Mrs Gaskell has what under the circumstances
becomes too often a potpourri of topical questions and issues – debates
and talks about all the problems, or a good many of them, of the 1840s
and 1850s. Into *North and South* alone she manages to cram the agricultural
poor in the South; the doctrine of self-help; drink and opium as the
refuge of the poor; atheism; ill-health and death caused by factory
conditions; the tyranny of the majority in trade-union affairs, and so on.
In *Mary Barton* she even has, in a speech of John Barton's, a version of
the labour theory of value: 'I say, our labour's our capital, and we ought
to draw interest on that.'[2] All these were, and many of them still are,
real issues, and at her best Mrs Gaskell dramatises them well. But even
at her best she can do no more than dramatise or illustrate a particular,
and usually fairly localised, issue (for example, Higgins giving up
drink for self-help – quite credibly, in fact). There is no possibility of
or room for expansion or questioning or exploration, because the scenes
so 'dramatised' have nowhere to go in terms of the governing stories,
the increasingly threatening love-affairs of Margaret and Thornton,
Jem and Mary. The love-stories are loosely conventional, and grow
apart from any urgent questioning of industrialism or politics; in turn,
questions of politics therefore remain under-developed, at points little

more than illustrations of well-known abuses that are documented equally well in journals and reports of the time.

If this split between an informed but truncated enquiry into sociological and political issues on the one hand, and thinly conventional love-stories on the other, were an isolated phenomenon, peculiar to Mrs Gaskell alone, it would not merit longer attention than simply the great regret one has for an intelligent novelist whose work is persistently flawed by what amounts to a fault of character in herself. But the more one looks at nineteenth-century novels, the more it becomes obvious that here is a case of an overriding convention hindering rather than helping literature. Indeed, the love-convention affects major novelists as well, and as Denis de Rougemont has suggested, love-stories of the kind Mrs Gaskell uses are much more than *simply* a literary convention or convenience.[3] Like most phenomena worthy of notice for good or ill in literature, this 'convention' is clearly rooted in human nature, rather than just in literary 'style' or form.

I want to consider some of the implications of Rougemont's thesis more fully in a moment. Before doing so it is essential to notice that all the other novels I have picked out, admittedly rather summarily, for discussion exhibit startlingly similar patterns of behaviour in their characters; and again these stories of frustrated love grow more or less irrelevantly apart from the political issues raised in the books. The result is that the personal love-stories tend to lose substance, to become *merely* personal anguish; the political and sociological enquiries tend to be, if not always impersonal, then at least undeveloped because they have no driving, compelling human action to work with or clash against.

Disraeli's *Sybil* is very much a case in point. Obviously knowledgeable about contemporary England, Disraeli gives accurate accounts of the disorganised nature of the Chartist groups in the 1830s and 1840s, and a slightly sentimentalised portrait of one of the 'moral force' leaders ('Gerard' in the novel), vainly opposing the 'physical force' tactics of some of his comrades. Disraeli sees very clearly the inevitability of the collapse of Chartism: it is doomed from the beginning by its own divided and confused aims and leadership, while at the same time, on the 'establishment' side, it faces a mixture of some sympathy (too weak to do more than encourage the men to present petitions that must fail), some apathy (the petition to Parliament is politely ignored by most), and superior force. In addition, he gives slightly stiffly written but credible pictures of working men's houses in the crowded lanes of 'Marney', each with its damp or flooded floors inside and its dunghill immediately outside; and he shows northern strike-parties of the late 1830s and 1840s, often starting out (as others have testified) with peaceful intentions, but as often inflamed to violence by a mixture of opposition from the soldiers and rabble-rousing speeches from demagogues ('Bishop Hatton' in the novel, a drunken, savage mobster with some brute energy and appeal).

Finally in this vein, Disraeli details the effects of the 'truck' system: workmen's wives and children have to take part of the husband's wages in 'tommy' (food and clothing bought at shops controlled or owned by the masters). Generally the best bacon, food, clothing goes to the 'butties' (who keep the shops), and nothing is left for the men but over-priced, under-weight goods.

All this is accurately described by Disraeli, though it tells one nothing that other accounts of Chartism and of conditions in Lancashire and Yorkshire at the time could not reveal equally well. The facts are not really in dispute. However, Disraeli's attempts to develop his account of the 'condition of England' beyond mere fact-finding are bedevilled by two things: first, his over-simple and nostalgic yearning for a past alliance and condition that never in fact existed, but that Disraeli wants to restore:

> In the selfish strife of factions, two great existences have been blotted out of the history of England – The Monarch and the Multitude; as the power of the Crown has diminished, the privileges of the People have disappeared; till at length the sceptre has become a pageant, and its subject has degenerated again into a serf. (Book VI, ch. 13)

Going along with this nostalgia for a past that must in fact have been much more brutal and much more inequitable than Disraeli is willing to allow, and indeed preventing him from breaking out of his own nostalgic dream of a perfect alliance between Church, monarchy and commons, is the story of the love of Egremont, younger brother of the mean and bullying Lord Marney, for Sybil, daughter of Gerard. Sybil wants to reinstate her father in his ancient rights to land – his family lost them with the dissolution of the monasteries under Henry VIII – and then rejoin a sisterhood with whom she is staying at the beginning of the novel. She is saved from a police attack on a secret Chartist meeting by Egremont (she has gone there to try and warn her father), and finally marries him instead of the sisterhood. In all this the threatened separation of Egremont and Sybil (they belong of course to opposite sides in 'the two nations' of modern England) produces an all-too-familiar note of anxious melodrama and sentimentality. Overstraining the notion of separation and threatening tragedy, Disraeli's prose – at its best factual though uninspired – at times adopts the weirdest contortions of false neo-feudalism. Sybil's rigorous purity, for instance, results in dialogue like this terrible *mélange* of colloquial and 'literary' English:

> 'Call it what you will, Walter,' replied Stephen; 'but if I ever gain the opportunity of fully carrying the principle of association into practice, I will sing *Nunc me dimittas.*'
> '*Nunc me dimittas,*' burst forth the Religious, in a voice of thrilling melody, and she pursued for some minutes the divine canticle. Her

companions gazed on her with an air of affectionate reverence as she sang; each instant the stars becoming brighter, the wide moor assuming a darker hue.

'Now, tell me, Stephen,' said the Religious, turning her head and looking round with a smile, 'think you not it would be a fairer lot to bide this night at some kind monastery, than to be hastening now to that least picturesque of all creations, a railway station . . .?'

'You must regain our lands for us, Stephen,' said the Religious; 'promise me, my father, that I shall raise a holy house for pious women, if that ever hap.' (Book II, ch. 8)

If there is a touch of intended humour in all this from England's future Prime Minister, it is only uncertainly and waveringly there. The fake old-English affected by Sybil is intended solemnly and seriously, and the humour, if it is there at all, only glances briefly and not at all slightingly at her. Disraeli's notion of this religious life is flimsy, and his notion of the love between Sybil and Egremont, which takes precedence later in the novel, is equally so. In such a setting, and with the novel's structure based largely on the unworldly lives and loves of Sybil and Egremont, it is not surprising that the 'political' element never develops beyond a hopelessly impractical neo-feudalism on the one hand – a vague aspiration towards 'community' instead of the mere gregariousness of modern cities – and on the other much more interesting but still limited notations of contemporary conditions.

George Eliot is quite obviously the most intelligent novelist in this group. The clear and sympathetic but unsentimental eye with which she gives us Mrs Transome's imprisonment and isolation in a masculine world is beyond the range of anything in Mrs Gaskell, Disraeli, or even Trollope. Indeed, even to call this society 'a masculine world' is misleading, though true in an over-all summarising sense. George Eliot's creation of the life and world of Matthew Jermyn, and of Jermyn fighting against his illegitimate son Harold Transome, is subtler than summarising terms can possibly suggest. As she says herself, Mrs Transome is a captive in a man's world, and the male dominance she cannot fight once Harold has returned to England (unaware of his birth but determined to get control of affairs and in addition to ruin his mother's man of business, Jermyn) is indeed a large factor, both in George Eliot's account of society and in her account of Mrs Transome's increasing loneliness. But though Jermyn is a scoundrel, he is far from the conventional villain of melodrama, merely seducing women and then using his power over property and money affairs to ruin them further; and he is also far from being unconvincingly 'masculine' in the way mere villains often are. ('How now, my pretty wench . . .' is a turn of phrase and personality that goes as far up the scale as Hardy's Alec d'Urberville, but which George Eliot is never even tempted to use.) Jermyn's relations with Mrs Transome include from the start both a dominance over her and a dependence on her finer nature. And a similar intelligence governs most of the characterisation of Harold Transome. Clearly George Eliot knew and shaped very well the sense in which a man like this can be – perhaps, in such a society and given a more determined clear-mindedness than other men, *has* to be – insensitively unaware of an intelligent woman's interest in life and in those affairs of business and property that Harold simply assumes she neither knows nor cares about. But George Eliot also knows the sense in which such a man may well behave decently and sensitively towards women, even though his quite genuine decency is at the same time serving his own ends (compare his courtship of Esther, in which Harold very often shows a genuine kindness to her and to Felix Holt which, as he well knows, will also heighten him in Esther's estimation).

All this, despite some minor flaws, could be documented easily from the clear, assured writing in that part of *Felix Holt* which concerns Mrs Transome, Harold and Jermyn. It means that there, as of course much more largely in her greater novels, George Eliot's interest in 'society' (including her interest in the politics of the period after the 1831 election) has been made subservient to ends that are less clearly summarisable, but far more interesting, than any imagined by Disraeli or Mrs Gaskell.

Nevertheless *Felix Holt* viewed as a whole is weak, structurally thin. This in itself might not be significant – a George Eliot is entitled to her failures, or comparative failures – but what is significant is that the weaknesses in *Felix Holt* are remarkably similar to ones that consistently limit or warp other political novels in the period. The story of Felix Holt and Esther bears distressing resemblances in tone and outlook to stories like that of Disraeli's Sybil and Egremont, or Mrs Gaskell's Mary Barton and the good artisan Jem Wilson. In all three cases the authors, in order to further the love affairs that lift the main characters clear of the dirt of politics and local conditions, give us the men, and to some extent the women, as both exceptional *and* idealised. Gerald, alone in the working-class milieu of *Sybil*, is against factionalism and violence; and he is alone because his nature is simply too pure to be relevant to the Chartist politics he is supposedly engaged in. Jem, alone of the artisans who influence the story in *Mary Barton*, has the purity of motive to save money and strike out on his own as a foreman/inventor, free alike from the squalor and the trade-union pressures that attack other men. More single-mindedly than either of these, Felix Holt, the son of a quack doctor, deliberately throws away his chance to rise in the world to stay in and with the working class as a clock and watch repairer. The trouble is that the way in which he does this is so idealised that neither his advice, nor his life as he lives it, can touch either working-class conditions or the men he has devoted his life to:

> He was considerably taller, his head and neck were more massive, and the expression of his mouth and eyes was something very different from the mere acuteness and rather hard-lipped antagonism of the trades-union man. Felix Holt's face had the look of habitual meditative abstraction from objects of mere personal vanity or desire, which is the peculiar stamp of culture, and makes a very roughly-cut face worthy to be called 'the human face divine.' Even lions and dogs know a distinction between men's glances; and doubtless those Duffield men, in the expectation with which they looked up at Felix, were unconsciously influenced by the grandeur of his full yet firm mouth, and the calm clearness of his grey eyes . . . (ch. xxx)

This is belittling and contemptuous of the men; it also underlines the noble shagginess and impetuous but other-worldly purity in Felix that 'redeem' his rough-cut features, lift him out of the working-class world he is allegedly part of and devoted to serve, and further the love between him and the reformed, no longer girlish Esther. The whole drive of the Felix/Esther stand in the novel is towards a love that thrives on obstacles and separation –

> And Felix wished Esther to know that her love was dear to him as the beloved dead are dear. He felt that they must not marry – that they would ruin each other's lives. But he had longed for her to know fully that his will to be always apart from her was renunciation, not an easy preference. (ch. xxxii)

These last two passages are practically a translation into novel terms of the Rougemont thesis about the inevitable course of love in Western society (a searching for obstacles rather than fulfilment, and union desired only in death or in some other transcendental state of being). And though this state of mind can be handled much more powerfully by some novelists, here the difference in tone between these passages and almost any on Mrs Transome, or on Jermyn and Harold, is obvious. The sugared isolation of Felix and Esther's stand has infected George Eliot's prose itself, and clearly has her backing. It leads, as similar tendencies do in *Mary Barton*, to a plea in open court by the heroine for her lover. George Eliot's prose at this point (the trial) shows glimpses of the conceptual intelligence that underpins her great work, and this is, even in its relatively weak form, beyond Mrs Gaskell's range; but otherwise the two women are not far apart when writing scenes of this nature:

> When a woman feels purely and nobly, that ardour of hers which breaks through formulas too rigorously urged on men by daily practical needs, makes one of her most precious influences. . . . Some

of that ardour which has flashed out and illuminated all poetry and history was burning to-day in the bosom of sweet Esther Lyon. In this, at least, her woman's lot was perfect: that the man she loved was her hero; that her woman's passion and her reverence for rarest goodness rushed together in an undivided current. And to-day they were making one danger, one terror, one irresistible impulse for her heart. (ch. XLVI)

Why should George Eliot's intelligence fail her, or be in abeyance, at precisely *this* point, and at others like it, in the novel? Even the more purely reflective prose of the novel is often, at such moments, irritatingly mannered, as if George Eliot were nervously aware that some stiffening was needed ('We have all felt the presence of . . .'; '. . . all of us – whether men or women – are liable to this weakness . . .'). The question is unanswerable in any full or complete terms, because one can only guess at factors of personality that must have been there, and that so disastrously combined with tendencies in the literature and society around her to produce such an absence of the rigour that determines the key scenes with Mrs Transome, and such a corresponding access of escapist sentimentality and buttonholing mannerism. Perhaps the closest one can get – and this is certainly not any full 'answer' to the question – is to point again to the gulf between the tendencies evident in the Felix/Esther conjunction on the one hand, and the political and sociological circumstances this conjunction allegedly arises from on the other. Whole sections of *Felix Holt* make dull reading because the circumstances of the 1831 election campaign and its aftermath – the details about a 'reformed' parliament, the parties that are voting and bolstering their candidates, the unfranchised workers' role in this – as well as the circumstances of nonconformist chapels (the book's rather rigidly minded 'religious' interest) – all these are cut off from the increasingly idealised love of Felix and Esther. As with Disraeli and Mrs Gaskell, these surrounding circumstances tend to remain either dully factual or, at best, interesting illustrations or dramatisations of essentially documentary material.

The sense in which this disjunction may provide a partial 'answer' to the question why George Eliot's intelligence failed her is that the gap between the transcendentalist love-story and the circumstances of Felix Holt's actual life points once again to a general failure rather than to a particular or local one (of 'characterisation', 'plot development', and so on). Tendencies in the age, and in George Eliot herself, to separate idealism – even simple emotion – from fact and reason were so strong that evidently even her intelligence was swamped in at least this novel. As Rougemont would put it in still more general terms: there is evidently a strong tendency, perhaps infecting Western society as a whole, for love ('passion') to cut loose from the practicalities of life, because it has become an emotion that only feeds on itself and must therefore end, at least in the most extreme cases, by feeding on death, the one absolute left that it can trust. George Eliot does not give Felix or Esther a tragic end (the Rougemont thesis fits Mrs Gaskell's *Ruth* much more completely),[4] but the overt idealisation combines with a long series of nostalgically treated separations, misunderstandings, failures between Felix and Esther to make his diagnosis relevant. Indeed the general cast of their story, in which absence and separation are longed for at least as much as successful consummation, would seem to expect an apocalyptic or tragic ending rather than the ending George Eliot in fact gives, with Felix freed, married to Esther, and living quietly in a village away from Treby Magna and its Reform politics. The drive of the story being what it is, such an ending is only possible by substituting for death and tragedy a sentimental transcendentalism that puts the lovers beyond the range both of their own passions and of the worldly interests and politics the novel started out to investigate.

'In the seventeenth century a dissociation of sensibility set in, from which we have never recovered . . .' T. S. Eliot's famous statement has of course been challenged in a number of ways, but personally I think it is substantially right, and certainly applicable to the sort of situations revealed by and in the nineteenth-century novels discussed and referred to in this chapter. Furthermore, Eliot's diagnosis can be linked both with Rougemont's thesis, and with D. H. Lawrence's comments on a Western civilisation in which, as he sees it, the impersonal intelligence has become divorced from the therefore too personal 'self'. One could add Blake, more gnomically but if anything still more trenchantly:

> Those who restrain Desire, do so because theirs is weak enough to be restrained; and the restrainer or Reason usurps its place and governs the unwilling.
>
> And being restrained, it by degrees becomes passive, till it is only the shadow of Desire. (*The Marriage of Heaven and Hell*)

The trouble is that Blake's own later writings in the rest of the Prophetic Books seem for the most part too cloudy to suggest any solution, or to adumbrate any true 'marriage' between the opposites he contemplates. And as the nineteenth century goes on, and develops into the twentieth century, even the best writing seems at times distorted by the dichotomy that makes for instance the intelligence of J. S. Mill rather dryly forbidding, the emotionalism of most of Victorian poetry and some parts of the Victorian and indeed twentieth-century novel rather gushingly unthinking. Dickens is one case in point here, and Lawrence is another; but even *Middlemarch*, solid and secure though it is in most respects, has the embarrassingly thin Dorothea/Will Ladislaw sections.

The 'Two Nations' split is indeed a threat, therefore, in nineteenth- and even early twentieth-century England; though to be fully meaningful the phrase has to be extended beyond Disraeli's original sense to include one or more of the senses sketched by Blake, Lawrence and Eliot. In this situation, what the novel at its best can and does do (though at the cost of virtually abandoning any specific commitment to politics or government as a major theme) is impart to wider spheres of enquiry the sort of resilience in dramatising personal affairs that George Eliot achieved in the Mrs Transome episodes of *Felix Holt*. *Middlemarch* itself is the clearest case of a novel in which this sort of writing ('political' in a sense, but also personal) is spread through a multiplicity of groups and situations within a middle-class society.

Before discussing *Middlemarch* in detail, however, I would like to look at some of Trollope's novels in which he too, though forced gradually to abandon parliamentary politics as a major interest, helps to forward a sense of purpose and enlargement in literature by concentrating on the sort of decisions that are made or at least attempted in ordinary daily living. Of course, Trollope never achieves anything remotely as impressive as either *Middlemarch* or the best of *Daniel Deronda*; and perhaps both writers suffer a little from having to limit the range of their strictly political interests (the politics of Reform and of parliamentary government might well have been a productive theme for novelists); but the Trollope novels from *Phineas Finn* to *The Duke's Children* are an impressive, and possibly underrated, achievement. Certainly they represent an interesting (and *very* readable) series in the history of the English novel.

6 Trollope's 'Political' Novels: *Phineas Finn* to *The Duke's Children*

In part, the Finn–Palliser series documents Trollope's growing realisation that, as he put it himself in *An Autobiography*, 'I could not make a tale pleasing chiefly, or perhaps in any part, by politics.'[1] Indeed, by the time he was writing the last two of his 'political' novels, he had virtually abandoned any hope of making such things as the details of parliamentary alignments, his own interest in election procedures and open ballot, or the arguments for and against 'Mr Monk's' proposals for Ireland the primary materials for writing a novel.

In many ways, this indeed is a matter for regret. If anyone could have closed the gap – quite obvious in earlier political novels – between literature and the day-to-day political life of the nation, it would have been Trollope. On the other hand, what he did develop in the course of writing this series, and out of his initial absorption in the raw materials of political in-fighting, was a slightly more generalised but very impressive drama focused on the two main characters in the series, Lady Glencora and her husband, Plantagenet Palliser. These two, together with the socio-political characters and situations around them, bear comparison with a good deal in the acknowledgedly great English novels from Jane Austen to Dickens, George Eliot, James, Conrad and Lawrence. One striking thing about the more famous novels is that, in skirting around the more specifically political situations and themes that naturally arise from time to time, they often dramatise situations that are 'political' in a much wider sense than any merely parliamentary one; and more and more Trollope himself is drawn to doing this too. His best novels, therefore, are only political in a sense of the word that is, necessarily, rather hard to define.

One way of approaching a critique of Trollope's own sense for a wider political arena than simply that of parliament and the civil service is to note his very clear class-affiliations. Whatever may have been the case with earlier social and political novelists, and with the society they worked in, Trollope is avowedly and unhesitatingly middle-class in outlook, sympathies and tone. Apart from a few cases like Quintus Slide, editor of *The People's Banner* – 'You'll find, Mr Finn, that in public life there's nothing like having a horgan to back you' – lower-class people in Trollope are usually transients, party and electioneering agents, small landlords and the like; never main characters like Felix Holt or Mary Barton and her father. Even Trollope's aristocrats behave (much more markedly than, for instance, the gentry in Jane Austen) in middle-class ways. In the political novels they tend to group themselves around the middle-class figure of Phineas Finn, the country doctor's son from Ireland, or around Palliser and his wife Glencora. And it is these groupings, rather than any specifically parliamentary ones, that really interest Trollope.

Plantagenet Palliser (the comic name is actually misleading) spends the happiest years of his life working very hard indeed in the House of Commons and at the Treasury. Later he becomes Duke of Omnium, the richest and most important peer in the realm, and as such he can and does behave very much like an aristocrat – often, indeed, objectionably so. But he still longs for the middle-class virtues of hard work at some useful, specific task (actually, the details of decimal coinage proposals), and his theory of English nobility includes the thoroughly standard notion that the nobility must recruit strength, stamina and money by intermarriage with commoners. This is, one would guess, Trollope's theory too, though he is perfectly aware of the snags in it: while the Duke is explaining the notion to Isabel Boncassen, the American heiress, he is shown as naïvely unaware that his son Silverbridge has proposed to her; he also appears temporarily to have forgotten his own anger and disgust at his daughter Mary's proposing to marry Tregear, a penniless gentleman-commoner.

Despite this irony, it is arguable that Trollope's commitment to middle-class virtues comes out even more strongly in this last pair of his political novels (*The Prime Minister* and *The Duke's Children*) than in the earlier ones which centre on the plainly middle-class figure of Phineas Finn. Like most of Trollope, the two later political novels include commoners (like Tregear) and a Tory squirearchy (the Fletchers), as well as a varied selection of Liberal and Tory peers. All of these, however, centre on the Duke and Lady Glencora: it is these two who hold the interest and who colour the novels most strongly. And certainly Lady Glencora (as she is known even after she becomes Duchess of Omnium) is the most obviously and wholeheartedly middle-class of all Trollope's aristocrats. She has more money in her own right than the Duke has in his, so that their two fortunes combined are practically inexhaustible. As far as money goes, Lord Silverbridge's racing debts of £70,000 are negligible; and even Glencora's expenses as the Prime Minister's wife, entertaining half London practically every week, do not endanger the two estates. But where the Duke prefers to accumulate money rather than spend it – he is more like someone born into 'the rise of capitalism' than a landholder of ancient properties – Glencora spends both lavishly and, as the Duke almost says to her on one occasion, vulgarly. These two are both aristo- crats who take as much from middle-class virtues and vices as they do from the nobility; though Glencora takes different things, and takes them more determinedly, wholeheartedly, and unthinkingly.

Two episodes in particular (both from *The Prime Minister*) show the growing differences between Glencora and the Duke, and at the same time show Trollope's own (I think very finely balanced) interest in their lives and their position. First, there is Glencora's transformation of the white elephant Gatherum Castle (built by the Duke's uncle, and vulgarly opulent) for her big summer house-party; and second, there is her indiscreet lobbying (actually no more than stopping her carriage and dropping a hint to a Liberal agent) on behalf of Ferdinand Lopez in the Duke's own borough of Silverbridge. Both episodes take place while the Duke is Prime Minister in a coalition government.

Trollope's dramatising of these events is indeed more complex – though that is too modern a word for Trollope – than I have suggested so far. With the Gatherum business, once again it is not the enormous expenditure itself that angers the Duke. He has indeed an un-aristocratic prudence in money affairs; but since there is more than enough to spend, he can also be enough of a nobleman not to care about the losing of it, particularly if the spending has pleased Glencora. The expenditure on Gatherum offends him in other ways than the purely financial.

On the occasion in question the Duke comes to Gatherum earlier than Glencora wants or expects, so that there is already a quarrel between them. She quarrels a bit unfairly in this instance, as in others, because she knows he will not like the changes and so has wanted him to stay in London until they are complete, irrevocable, and anyway masked by a flood of guests. But he arrives early, wanders out into his own grounds, and, though he has never liked the place, is immediately offended by what looks to him like wanton expenditure for the sake of mere enter- tainment; or worse, like using his money to help maintain the Coalition. Tents have been set up, a new conservatory built, a road built and new lawns planted, an archery-ground enclosed:

'What are you doing this for?' he said to one of the labourers. The man stared at him and at first seemed hardly inclined to make him an answer. 'It be for the quality to shoot their bows and harrows,' he said at last, as he continued the easy task of patting with his spade the completed work. He evidently regarded this stranger as an intruder who was not entitled to ask questions, even if he were permitted to wander about the grounds. (Vol. I, ch. XIX)

The Duke likes grandeur that is his proper due: '. . . he walked up and saw the flag waving over the Castle, indicating that he, the Lord Lieutenant of the County, was present there on his own soil. That was right. That was as it should be . . .'

> But here was an assumed and preposterous grandeur that was as much within the reach of some rich swindler or of some prosperous haberdasher as of himself, – having, too, a look of raw newness about it which was very distasteful to him. And then, too, he knew that nothing of all this would have been done unless he had become Prime Minister. Why, on earth, should a man's grounds be knocked about because he becomes Prime Minister? (Vol. I, ch. XIX)

Of course this annoyance the Duke feels is the product of other things too – mainly, his unease at having to bear the pin-pricks of office. It culminates in a scene with his wife in which he accuses her of, in effect, middle-class vulgarity. He does not actually use the word 'middle-class', but he does come close to calling Glencora's preparations vulgar. It is this accusation that angers her, and our sympathies are nicely divided between the two. She has indeed been vulgar in her attempts to influence society and members of parliament; though she has done it all generously, and very much for his sake. She is right to resent the word used against her, and right also in accusing her husband of being thin-skinned and over-sensitive; but even her very strength of resentment, both at the moment when the Duke brings out the word 'vulgar' to her and later on her own, shows her as half-conscious that he is at least partly right. This is not *just* a middle-class world, and she should have known it. There is a real danger that the Duke's opponents will make political capital out of the house-party – indeed Quintus Slide, having asked for an invitation and been refused, does precisely that – but more, they may now do so by injuring him personally in ways they could not injure either 'prosperous haberdashers' or more hardened politicians:

> 'Vulgarity!' She uttered the word aloud to herself, as she sat herself down in the little room upstairs which she had assigned to herself for her own use. . . . Perhaps it was vulgar. But why shouldn't she be vulgar, if she could most surely get what she wanted by vulgarity? . . . Of course she was prepared to do things, – was daily doing things, – which would have been odious to her had not her husband been a public man. . . . She lavished her smiles, – so she now said to herself, – on butchers and tinkers. . . . When a man wants to be Prime Minister he has to submit to vulgarity, and must give up his ambition if the task be too disagreeable to him. The Duchess thought that had been

understood, at any rate ever since the days of Coriolanus. (Vol. I, ch. XIX)

The Duchess is right, both about politics (the Coriolanus comparison is perfectly apt) and about the Duke's personal character, his hyper-sensitivity as a man. The dilemma is that in the nature of the case she can only be right by being partial, by taking the part of the world against her husband. Indeed, as the Silverbridge affair draws to a head, events take charge of her own impetuous nature and force her to the logical, extreme position against the Duke. She says to Mrs Finn:

> 'I hate people to be sensitive. It makes them cowards. A man when he is afraid of being blamed, dares not at last even show himself, and has to be wrapped up in lamb's wool.'
> 'Of course men are differently organised.'
> 'Yes; – but the worst of it is, that when they suffer from this weakness, which you call sensitiveness, they think that they are made of finer material than other people. Men shouldn't be made of Sèvres china, but of good stone earthenware.' (Vol. II, ch. LI)

Once again, this is all true; or at least it is true to the very real necessities of political and social behaviour in a world largely dominated by tougher and far less scrupulous characters than the Duke's own. He is vulnerable because, pedestrian and 'middle-class' though many of his interests are, he will not learn lessons that the haberdasher and Glencora might both have taught him. What is left understood, but I think quite clear, in dialogue such as this is Glencora's own feeling or intuition that the Duke's intransigence is worth something, despite the realities of political life. Trollope's is not highly 'complex' prose, but he can register at once the need for dependence on attitudes like Glencora's worldly toughness of mind, and at the same time a feeling (his own, and indeed also Glencora's) that this toughness can be inflexible and insensitive. Glencora's personality is very taking indeed, and her programme of action is certainly more in tune with the world than the Duke's; but by the same token she cannot really accommodate his quite unworldly pride in himself, his family, and indeed his office. The only sustained discussion of these events that the Duke's reserve of manner ever allows between them registers the significance of their two personalities very well. Glencora advocates ignoring the malice of Quintus Slide, and ignoring imputations that the Prime Minister bribed agents in a local election (Silverbridge):

> 'What is it that you fear? What can the man do to you? What matter is it to you if such a one as that pours out his malice on you? Let it run off like the rain from the house-tops. You are too big even to be stung by such a reptile as that.' He looked into her face, admiring the energy with which she spoke to him. 'As for answering him,' she continued to say, 'that may or may not be proper. If it should be done,

there are people to do it. But I am speaking of your own inner self. You have a shield against your equals, and a sword to attack them with if necessary. Have you no armour of proof against such a creature as that? Have you nothing inside you to make you feel that he is too contemptible to be regarded?'

'Nothing,' he said ... (Vol. ii, ch. li)

That seems to me a fine passage – a piece of characteristically nineteenth-century English prose from a novel indubitably of its period. For all its limitations, it seems almost by a different man from the man who wrote, for instance, *The Three Clerks*: 'Ah! Mrs Woodward, my friend, my friend, was it well that thou should leave that sweet unguarded rosebud of thine to such perils as these?'

That, too, is obviously and unfortunately characteristic of its period. But Trollope had no real subject in *The Three Clerks*; at least he had none that was as big an issue as the position of the Duke in the political and social world of *The Prime Minister*. Glencora's personality alone would be almost enough to sustain that novel, but in fact it is backed by the Duke's, and by the very real dilemma produced for both of them by the combination of her public indiscretions and his sensitivity (perfectly genuine, but quite unable to adapt to, or compromise with, the world as it goes). Just after the above exchange, she tries her last card, namely telling the truth publicly:

'You must throw me to the whale. Let somebody say in so many words that the Duchess did so and so. It was very wicked no doubt; but they can't kill me, – nor yet dismiss me. And I won't resign. In point of fact I shan't be a penny the worse for it.'

'But I should resign.'

'I couldn't do it, Cora. Though the stain were but a little spot, the thing to be avoided political destruction, I could not ride out of the punishment by fixing that stain on my wife. I will not have your name mentioned. A man's wife should be talked about by no one.'

'That's high-foluting, Plantagenet.'

'Glencora, in these matters you must allow me to judge for myself, and I will judge. I will never say that I didn't do it; – but that it was my wife who did.'

'Adam said so, – because he chose to tell the truth.'

'And Adam has been despised ever since, – not because he ate the apple, but because he imputed the eating of it to a woman. I will not do it.' (Vol. ii, ch. li)

I said that Trollope was wholeheartedly middle-class in outlook. He is I think clearly that, but at his best – and the Finn–Palliser series, together with *The Way We Live Now* and *Orley Farm*, is I think his best – he can

make that label 'middle-class' convincingly individual, and indeed something quite other than a label. He is not a brilliant writer: he has not the
massiveness of a George Eliot, and even his palpable faults in these novels
(of occasional sentimentality, careless indirection coming out in plots
loosely strung together or thinly motivated) are not gross in the way
that, say, Dickens's can be. And he has hardly a touch of Dickens's
brilliantly inventive imagination. But he has a surer, more developed
and more sophisticated sense of purpose and form in novels than probably
any earlier 'middle-class' English writer except Jane Austen; and he
combines this with enough feeling for the possibilities of drama and
dramatic interplay of personalities to make him a novelist, rather than
simply a recorder of events and society external to himself. As far as
social and political outlook goes, one can therefore use the term 'middle-
class' of Trollope in order to point to a certain stability, and to an assured,
if unimaginative, *sense* in his handling of the world of House of Commons
politics and London society of the fifties and sixties (and this includes, of
course, his handling of people whose position in society is well above his
own position and habitual outlook). But one must also grant him a
greater individuality than these qualities alone would imply, and a
deeper seriousness of purpose.

By itself, the phrase 'seriousness of purpose' is perhaps off-key for most
of Trollope, including most of the 'political' novels. The seriousness I
mean is really something that grows out of his earlier political interest
and comes to dominate the two last novels of the series in the form of a
quite un-political deepening of interest in the Duke and Glencora. *The
Prime Minister* was first published complete in 1876; *The Duke's Children*
in 1880 (two years before Trollope's death). Before this we have had
Can You Forgive Her? (1864–5), *Phineas Finn* (1869), *The Eustace Diamonds*
(1872), and *Phineas Redux* (1873), all of them a good deal lighter in tone,
and all dependent for their popularity (now revived after a lapse during
the 1890s and the early part of this century) largely on qualities of simple
narrative interest and sheer readability. Trollope shares with the Hardy
of, say, *Far From the Madding Crowd* (published the year after *Phineas
Redux*) an ability to write novels which keep one reading, amongst
other reasons, simply in order to find out 'what happens next?' And
though this can obviously be a merely flimsy interest – it is, for instance,
in *The Belton Estate*, where an ostensibly hopeless love affair goes far too
readily towards the happy ending we know all the time will come – it
could also, in the nineteenth century, be the basis, or at least the framework, for sturdier writing. Certainly it is pretty safe to say that a
twentieth-century Trollope would be highly unlikely, a contradiction in
terms almost. Even Hardy, at the age of thirty-three or thirty-four when
he wrote *Far From the Madding Crowd*, shows both metaphysical and
sexual interests of a kind not paralleled in Trollope, and of course these

grow in later Hardy and push him much more firmly towards the twentieth century than Trollope ever ventured. After the turn of the century, literary interests have become irreversibly still more 'difficult', if not indeed overly intellectual, and for good or ill some of Trollope's best qualities have disappeared from the scene altogether. Even C. P. Snow (often likened, I think for the most part wrongly, to Trollope) does not write with the necessary lightness of touch that might equate his 'political' interests with Trollope's.

The limitations and dangers of Trollope's vein of sophisticated popular writing are obvious. The outline of a typical Trollope story, even of the 'political' series, would look dismayingly like one of the merely conventional love-stories of the same period or earlier. Typically, there is an impoverished but good-hearted and spirited hero or heroine who is in love with somebody who is much richer or whose parents are firmly opposed to the match. Generally there are also real or suspected love-affairs, like those of the impetuous Irishman Phineas Finn, that stand in true love's way. In the course of one novel Phineas proposes to Lady Laura Standish, Violet Effingham, and Mary Flood; and in the same novel he rejects a proposal from the interesting Madame Max Goesler (unfortunately Mary has by then accepted him). Similarly in *The Belton Estate*, the engagingly impetuous hero meets his poor cousin, re-orders her father's estate for her, buys her a cow for company, and all this only to discover that she is, she thinks, in love with someone else. And in *The Duke's Children* Mary's engagement with Tregear is put off hopelessly by her father's opposition; Silverbridge's with Isabel is put off by the same opposition and by his affair with Mabel Grex. In each of these cases, and in dozens of others, parental opposition finally melts, old love-affairs are put aside, and where necessary money is suddenly forthcoming. (There are a few, but very few, people in these novels who marry without a comfortable income.)

Writing within this sort of framework (and it is one that he uses in the political novels very successfully indeed), there are times when Trollope's easy-going nature yields so far, or so easily, to the needs of conventional writing that he affronts the basic realism that is also essential to his best work. *Framley Parsonage* and *The Three Clerks* are among the weakest of his novels in this regard. In *The Three Clerks*, for instance, Trollope is helplessly torn between two conventions: one would have the charmingly pure Katie die tragically of a fever induced by a hopeless passion; the other would have her recover and marry a reformed and financially better-off Charlie. In *Framley Parsonage*, it is hardly credible that the Mark Roberts we are shown early in the book – a respectable clergyman, with a good wife and family and prospects of further advancement – should put his name to a bill for £400 simply to oblige his rakish friend Sowerby; quite incredible that he should later sign a separate bill for £500, thinking that it is merely a slightly increased renewal of the original. Trollope uses this formula (of an innocent man caught by scoundrels) tellingly enough elsewhere: for instance, it is perfectly likely that Phineas Finn would indeed sign a bill for Laurence Fitzgibbon, thinking it merely a temporary loan. With the Robarts story, however, he has done so merely in order to wring more *angst* from the tale than it could properly yield.

There is one other local sign of a careless reliance on conventions that afflicts even the otherwise much more solid political novels. That is, the appearance in some passages of a Thackeray-like 'irony' and padding that, in an otherwise serious novel, simply puts one's teeth on edge. *The Duke's Children* is I think the most tightly knit of all the political novels, but even it has paragraphs where, for instance, a serious consideration of a woman's influence on a man will turn to trifling of the 'fair sex' kind:

> There are men, who do not seem at first sight very susceptible to feminine attractions, who nevertheless are dominated by the grace of flounces, who succumb to petticoats unconsciously, and who are half in love with every woman merely for her womanhood. (ch. LXXIV)

The notion of the Duke as a man who might give way to women is true (though he hardly ever does to Glencora when there is something really at stake between them); the Duke talked down to in this tone of voice diminishes the novel.

Trollope never breaks quite free from the modes, conventions and tricks of the trade that lead him so badly astray at times. What he can do in the better of his novels even before *The Prime Minister*, is turn these into something which, though still conventional in outline and substance, is both more developed, neater, and more substantial than comparable stories in earlier popular novels, or in the political fiction of Mrs Gaskell and Disraeli. Of the novels in Trollope's middle period that concern politics, the two Phineas stories (*Phineas Finn*, 1869, and *Phineas Redux*, 1873) are I think clearly the best. Substantially, they are episodes in Phineas's political, social and matrimonial career, less closely knit than the main stories in the later novels, but more so than the strands of, for instance, a typical Dickens novel. It is in these novels that Trollope's unpretentious, tolerant worldly wisdom is most to the fore, enabling him quite effortlessly to keep us reading for the pleasure and interest of finding out what the impetuous and generous-minded Phineas will do when faced with a political dilemma (for instance, having to vote against the Irish Bill he thoroughly believes in, or lose the government place he both likes and needs); and how, if at all, he can sort out his love, or rather loves, for Lady Laura, Violet Effingham, Madame Goesler and the girl he forgets when in London but loves when at home in Ireland (the genuinely nice, but thoroughly innocuous, Mary Flood). All this is easy going for Trollope, and the writing has precisely that quality, a quality impossible to recapture without risking complete vacuity after

Trollope had thoroughly done it, or after the course of the English novel had been changed by circumstances and by writers like Hardy, Conrad, James.

The checks and breaks in the telling of this tale – even the practised Trollope cannot avoid some – are minor. He is trapped here and there by the necessary habit in such tales of every now and then breaking off one strand of a story at the end of a chapter and switching in the next to another, often with a related but different set of characters involved.[2] But Trollope's ease of manner can make a virtue of necessity, and one's momentary irritation on turning the page and finding, for instance, that Phineas's first attempt to speak openly to Violet Effingham (*Phineas Finn*, Vol. i, ch. xxxiv) is to be left in the air for 'Mr Monk upon Reform' (Vol. i, ch. xxxv), is quelled by the narrative impulse, promising more, and by Trollope's own undisguised, relatively uncomplicated interest in the fates of his characters. Even if Trollope hadn't said so himself,[3] one would be able to sense, I think, that often he didn't know what these might be until the story developed later on; but the end of Chapter xxxiv (Vol. i), for instance, just before Mr Monk upon Reform, shows Trollope's ability to write about men and women easily, but with enough electricity in the air to make the promise of further developments, and of links with the political interest, a real one instead of simply a trick of the trade:

> 'Mr Finn,' she said, 'I wonder whether I may ask a question?'
> 'Any question,' he replied.
> 'Is there any quarrel between you and Lady Laura?'
> 'None.'
> 'Or between you and him?' [Laura's violent brother Chiltern, also in love with Violet.]
> 'No; – none. We are greater allies than ever.'
> 'Then why are you not going to be at Loughlinter? She has written to me expressly saying you would not be there.'
> He paused a moment before he replied. 'It did not suit,' he said at last.

The reason for Phineas's staying away from Laura is her husband's jealousy, but he cannot say this because it would be breaking a confidence. A little later he continues:

> 'The cause, whatever it be, has been full of sorrow to me. I would have given my left hand to have been at Loughlinter this autumn.'
> 'Are you so fond of it?'
> 'I should have been staying there with you,' he said. He paused, and for a moment there was no word spoken by either of them; but he could perceive that the hand in which she held her whip was playing with her horse's mane with a nervous movement. 'When I found

how it must be, and that I must miss you, I rushed down here that I might see you for a moment. And now I am here I do not dare to speak to you of myself.' They were now beyond the rocks, and Violet, without speaking a word, again put her horse into a trot. He was by her side in a moment, but he could not see her face. 'Have you not a word to say to me?' he asked.

'No; – no; – no;' she replied, 'not a word when you speak to me like that. There is the carriage. Come; – we will join them.' Then she cantered on, and he followed her till they reached the Earl and Lady Baldock and Miss Boreham.

In context, this is not the mere coyness on Violet's part that perhaps it might seem here, because it is part of a shrewd and much more extended judgement of Phineas and of his whole career. Phineas's political career is dogged by women (as his enemies tend, very publicly, to put it), helped by their sympathy and interest (as Phineas himself, on the whole much more fairly, puts it). Violet Effingham's own shrewd diagnosis of Phineas as a man is put by Trollope as a question that must extend, as Laura Kennedy's fervent and sometimes ill-judged championship of him also extends, to touch his career as a politician. Violet is womanly, apparently flippant though in fact very intelligent. She acknowledges herself attracted, as almost all women are, to Phineas's handsome figure and generous, impulsive nature, but she chooses finally to marry the fierce 'red man', Lord Chiltern. Chiltern drinks, has lost all his own money (though fortunately not his father's) on the turf, has been sent down from Oxford – 'He had taken by the throat a proctor's bull-dog when he had been drunk at Oxford, had nearly strangled the man, and had been expelled' – and he has killed a man who attacked him at Newmarket. Violet chooses him because she loves him (and that marriage, despite Chiltern's violent nature, proves successful); and also because she guesses that marriage to Phineas would be interesting and pleasant but, though he would be true to her despite his present flirtations, it might well be no more than this. She doesn't intend to put up with the mad bull side of Chiltern, but if he calms down a bit, his will be the deeper nature of the two.

Chiltern does not enter politics, so the comparison between the two men does not overtly extend to include Phineas's political career. But, as Violet senses (though Laura never does, or if she does, won't admit it), Phineas, for all his freshness and the genuineness of his interest on entering the House of Commons, will never come within reach of being a Gladstone or Disraeli, or even a Mr Monk (Phineas's immediate political hero; an independently minded Liberal whose convictions and thinking about politics carry him to some eminence even when he leaves the Cabinet). Phineas's place and career in parliament is, one might fairly guess, something like what Trollope imagined might have been his own had he won the seat he stood for in 1867. Whether this is so or not, Phineas is a man whose nature, though nowhere near as sensitive to insult as Plantagenet Palliser's, is sensitive and eager enough to put him well above the common ruck of party hacks, but not ruthless enough to rival a Daubeny, or full enough to think and act with the originality of a Monk or a Gresham. With all this, his career in politics is a test, not only of his own character, but also of party politics. Disraeli himself wrote at length about the corruption of the Whig and Tory party system, but I am not sure that he saw it as shrewdly or as truly as Trollope did in his quiet realisation of the hopelessness of a man like Phineas attempting to move the inertia of Liberal–Tory alliances and oppositions.

The issue that Phineas faces from quite early on in his career is the quite simple and familiar one: how to reconcile the demands of his party with the demands of principle and his own convictions. This issue is raised by each of the three main parliamentary debates in the series; on Reform and the Ballot; on the Irish question; and (in *Phineas Redux*) on Church disestablishment. On each occasion there are the party hacks who vote Liberal or Tory at command, but there are also better men than these. Some, like Daubeny, are better only in the sense that they are ruthlessly opportunist. Daubeny (who, despite differences, does seem to be Trollope's portrait of Disraeli) cares little for Tory principles, but has devoted his life to dishing the Whigs, stealing liberal measures from under their very noses. The interest Trollope has in him – apart from the negative one of disliking the man and his trickery – is that Daubeny's nature is clearly that of a very strong and effective leader, and this in matters where a man like the Duke is obviously over-scrupulous. In addition to Daubeny, the field includes the old-world Mr Mildmay (a premier who can play politics in the old way, but whom Trollope sees as lacking the fire needed to lead now that parliament faces the bigger questions of the post-1832 era); Mr Gresham (a man whom Europe listens to when he speaks in parliament); and Mr Monk, a man well aware of the need for compromise and expediency but who also lives by principle and ideal.

Phineas and Mr Monk both resign over the Irish question, and it is an essential part of Trollope's fairness and thoroughness that he puts the dilemma squarely to Phineas: if Phineas resigns, his conscience over Irish tenant-right will be at peace; but as Mr Monk himself and others point out, a man cannot do this without in some sense endangering his party, the only effective organ for most men to get anything done at all in parliament. (At this stage, towards the end of *Phineas Finn*, Mr Monk sees himself as an exception to this general rule, a popular critic of government who can do his best work when in opposition or at least when not in government office.) Even if the motives of some party men in urging Phineas to stick with the government and party are contemptibly selfish, their arguments cannot be ignored.

Phineas's resignation over Irish tenant-right is the result of a very credible, and creditable, mixture of self-doubt (he knows he needs the money that his under-secretaryship carries, and can't clear himself of the suspicion that he is over-compensating in consequence); bafflement at the dilemma that being a party man presents; and a genuine concern for Mr Monk's ideals and for his arguments on the Irish question. This is much more than simply a matter of character-portrayal and character consistency: similar issues confront Phineas, and later on the Duke, when other debates come up, and though he becomes much more assured during his later years – indeed, weary of politics, finally – Phineas's career, like the Duke's, focuses Trollope's own concern for the future of parliamentary democracy and Liberalism.

I think we may take Trollope's final position to be close to, but not *quite* the same as, the Duke's cautious optimism when, in Chapter LXVIII (Vol. II) of *The Prime Minister*, he explains to Phineas Finn his vision of a very gradual equalising of classes in England under the influence of careful Liberal leadership. We may also fairly imagine, knowing the Duke, that this version of Liberal leadership would include absolute freedom of conscience for any party member acting wholly sincerely. Trollope himself, though clearly liking the Duke's rather starry-eyed scheme for the future (and though he doesn't himself show any greater awareness of the nature of the working classes who are demanding reform and the ballot), is sharper than this. He contrasts the Duke's pleas for a gradual democratisation very sharply with the Duke's intense dislike of his daughter's marrying a penniless commoner and his son an American heiress; and he also shares, and blends into the fabric of the novels, a good deal of Phineas's later bitterness and scepticism about the ethics of party management.

The blending of these elements is finely done in the Phineas series, and the moral issues involved are carried over into *The Prime Minister* and *The Duke's Children*. The early and middle stages of Trollope's political novels are therefore good, and good in ways that make them very much a part of the sort of considerations that George Eliot capitalises on in *Middlemarch*, clearly the epitome of English middle-class fiction. Yet in these novels Trollope, like George Eliot earlier in *Felix Holt*, fails finally to close the gap between fiction and reality in politics. In particular, there is a telling split in the novels' characterisation. With the exception of Mr Palliser and Mr Monk, the House of Commons leaders (Mildmay, Daubeny, Gresham, Turnbull) do not appear as actors in the novels' main stories. They remain parliamentary figures, and whether or not they can be equated, wholly or partly, with men of the time like Lord John Russell, Disraeli, Gladstone, Bright, they act in the novel as if they could be. A. O. J. Cockshut refers to Trollope himself, and Frederic Harrison backing him up, saying that no such parallels were intended; and indeed, as Cockshut points out, none of the possible parallels, in character or in situation, can be complete.[4] Nevertheless it seems likely that some of these figures are partial portraits (Daubeny/Disraeli certainly, and perhaps Gresham as a version of Gladstone); others are put together, consciously or unconsciously, from various figures of the mid-century, and then modified as the action of the novel demands.

None of this would matter one way or the other if it were not that all these men, whether they represent historical figures or not, remain almost entirely actors in the House of Commons, hardly ever meeting other characters or other situations. Phineas himself (a comparatively minor figure in the House) does, and I can think of no 'political' scene in the English novel that is psychologically as telling, or as sensitively done, as Trollope's rendering of Phineas's paralysing nervousness when, as a young member, he is asked to reply to Mr Turnbull's speech about the ballot and his attack on Mr Monk. In the end, Phineas cannot get to his feet and has to let another man, Bonteen, do the job on this occasion; and he is not in much better shape when he does finally force himself to his feet in the House and speak for the freedom of the people to ask for the ballot without fear of persecution from the authorities. Again, the state of mind is well rendered, and its relevance to Phineas's probable place in parliament and office clearly suggested. (Phineas learns to speak well and fluently, but this ability coincides with his growing concern over the necessary insensitivity of and in party politics.)

But Phineas, and to a lesser degree Monk, are very much exceptions. Some other men from the main story, like Palliser, do speak and act frequently in the House, but in these cases we do not see much of their speech or action, only hear of it as something virtually completed and of the past. This is not a fatal or crippling gap in the novel's span of attention, but it is a significant pointer to Trollope's future course as a novelist and to the way in which his interests are developing. Gradually during the Phineas series, and much more markedly during the last years of his writing life, Trollope allows other issues than specific parliamentary debate on Reform to dominate his writing. Partly this is no doubt because many political debates are of their nature too local and particular for a novelist to digest readily; but partly too, I think, it is because even Trollope, for all his interest in parliament, and for all the importance of this in the Phineas novels, is not at bottom a political novelist. Certainly he is not in the last novels. In *The Prime Minister* the real issues, though they incorporate the Duke's political worries easily and fluently, are not – despite the book's title – political ones. And in *The Duke's Children*, the chapter on Sir Timothy Beeswax as a consummate but empty-minded manager of the House is like a reminder of events that are now important only in so far as they impinge on the Duke's personal dilemma. In the course of the novel these events do impinge strongly on the Duke's life; but in this context the actual discourse on Sir Timothy (ch. xxi) looks, and is, mere padding. Trollope's interests have moved away from the details of party management considered as a fact of political life generally; they have moved, in fact, much more fully into the natural sphere of novelists like the later George Eliot and Conrad, to whom politics is real, but only real as one part of the warp and woof of life itself. As such it comes and goes in their novels naturally and unobtrusively, but is never the main course of a man's life.

I began this chapter with the claim that what underpins the best Trollope novels (including the last two of the political series, *The Prime Minister* and *The Duke's Children*) is a commitment to certain specifically middle-class ways of life, and to the sort of broad common sense that he can distil from these, even – or perhaps especially – when his characters are at odds with each other and acting from anything but common-sense motives. The scenes involving the Duke and Glencora in *The Prime Minister*, or the Duke and his children in the later novel, are among the best cases in point.

However (and without bringing into consideration the case of a novel like *He Knew He Was Right*, 1869), there is something else in the late Trollope that must be added to this picture of a sane and balanced English novelist. Trollope was that; but it is also significant that the more personal his fiction becomes – that is, the more it concentrates on personal confrontations such as those between the Duke and Glencora – the bleaker is his vision of life and of the future (politics included). In these last two of the political novels there are familiar elements, including some, such as his portrait of Arthur Fletcher as the ideal Englishman, that are merely a corruption of the qualities that led George Eliot to admire him as 'so thoroughly wholesome-minded' and Hawthorne as so 'solid and substantial'. One could live with the notion of Arthur bursting into tears, if only it didn't go together with Trollope's concluding picture of him welcoming Emily Wharton to Longbarns: '. . . fair-haired, open-eyed, with bronzed brow and cheek, and surely the honestest face that a loving woman ever loved to gaze on.'

But these lapses are more than balanced, in the late novels, by a relatively new toughness of mind that extends Trollope's range beyond the sentimental, beyond even the soundly conventional (for example, his portrait of Lord Silverbridge) that we have grown used to from early on. Certainly, there are examples of this tougher and bleaker outlook among the earlier novels. In particular there is *Orley Farm* (1862), where Trollope sticks firmly and steadily to Lady Mason's guilt (for her son's sake, she has forged a codicil to her husband's will) in the face of what must have been strong temptations to reveal her finally as innocent after all, or at least as having suffered enough to expurgate her sin. What distinguishes both *The Prime Minister* and *The Duke's Children*, however, is the contemplation of a greyness in the nineteenth-century, middle-class living that is the more impressive because it spans not merely the strains evident in the Duke's marriage to Glencora and his future after she dies, but the lives of certain of the minor characters as well. One very clear and good example is Lady Mabel Grex in *The Duke's Children*.

Lady Mabel is impoverished (her own modest portion has gone towards paying her father's gambling debts), but she is also young, beautiful and clever. By all the canons of the popular novel she should have had a loving and good husband by the end of the book, whatever the difficulties and disappointments on the way. But Mabel's two lovers, Tregear and Silverbridge, do in fact both marry other women, and I think it is an important part of reading late Trollope to see that, in giving a woman like Mabel that sort of bleak future, he is quite clearly departing from a convention which would have given a quite different ending to her life. Indeed, there is even a slight strain in the writing at the end of the book that reinforces the feeling that Trollope is, probably consciously, departing from a given mode: Mabel's accusations against Frank Tregear that, though they agreed to part, he deserted her for Mary Palliser very easily and quickly are true – to the point indeed where they endanger the balance of the novel slightly (Tregear must be supposed to be thoroughly worthy of Mary).

But Lady Mabel's accusations are far from melodramatic in substance, and they reach back into the novel's whole development. Mabel has known all along that she cannot marry Tregear – their natures are both such that poverty would be unendurable – but she also knows that Tregear's calm and complete acceptance of this situation, though it lowers him in some respects compared to the impulsive Silverbridge, also heightens the sophisticated and adult quality in him that she admires and loves. Silverbridge is by far the more engaging of the two men and would have stuck to her, had he really loved her, whatever the barriers between them might have been; but compared with Tregear he is a 'boy' (her own word, though Silverbridge feels this himself). Silverbridge indeed recognises that in some ways Mabel is his superior: 'Lady Mabel as his wife', he reflects, 'would be his superior, and in some degree his master. Though not older she was wiser than he, – and not only wiser but more powerful also.' This is from Chapter XIX and it parallels Mabel's feelings early on that not only is Silverbridge too unsophisticated for her, she herself is rapidly becoming too sophisticated for her own good. 'What would she be in ten years, she who already seemed to know the town and all its belongings so well?' She sees through things too easily and too quickly for her present life to have much substance in it; yet she also knows that women in her position lack the freedom and the opportunities that men have.

In all this Trollope is clearly hinting that in Lady Mabel we have something of the exhausted, or at least over-used quality of even the best of the London and county society he himself admires. The contrast with Miss Boncassen, of course, makes the point clearly – perhaps a shade too clearly – later on; but all through the treatment of Mabel, and even when

Miss Boncassen is not present, there is the implication that she is tainted, and this not from any convention of novel-writing, but simply from belonging so thoroughly to the society Trollope is writing about. Silverbridge and his brother and sister are not 'tainted'; but, reflecting on the later novels, it becomes clear that many people in them are. The weariness evident in the London and county living described is unmistakable; though Trollope's quite considerable tact in writing makes this far less an accusation than a condition that his intelligent women, and some of his men (the Duke, and even Phineas in later life), have to face.

A bleak future indeed; but also one that is very *strongly* realised in the novels. Lady Glencora and Plantagenet Palliser – now of course Duke of Omnium and for a time Prime Minister – are the centres of interest in this world of late Trollope. Except for the improbable Emily Wharton/ Ferdinand Lopez marriage, with its brief overtones of a very unpleasant anti-Jew strain in Trollope, the course of events in the two novels focuses on the Duke's career and conscience, and on his struggles with his wife and children, whom he senses as in different ways allying themselves with a world that he feels to be hostile to him and impertinently vulgar in its pretensions.

There are some lapses of taste and insight in Trollope's developing account of the Duke and his family, but these are brief and not of a kind to threaten the main achievement. Occasional gushes of bathos and sentiment from the otherwise witty and intelligent Miss Boncassen are unpalatable, but mercifully short:

> 'Love you! Oh, my darling! – No, no, no,' she said as she retreated from him round the corner of the billiard-table, and stood guarding herself from him with her little hands. . . . 'From the sole of your foot to the crown of your head I love you as I think a man would wish to be loved by the girl he loves. You have come across my life, and have swallowed me up, and made me all your own. But I will not marry you to be rejected by your people.' (*The Duke's Children*, ch. LII)

For the most part Miss Boncassen is spiritedly, and charmingly, independent; and her entrance into English society extends the novel's range by forcing a new and unfamiliar but very tangible presence on to Silverbridge, the Duke and Mabel Grex. Flanked by a father whose American seriousness appeals to the Duke (though it is credibly different from his own), and a mother who simply wants to get home as quickly as she can, Miss Boncassen responds to England with an American tough-mindedness that is witty and alert, but very far from parody or merely surface charm. Certainly her response to poor Dolly Longstaff's repeated proposal is anything but superficial. Dolly begins:

> 'I will never deceive you. Only say that you will love me, and I will be as true to you as the North Pole.'

> 'Is that true to me?'
> 'You know what I mean.'
> 'But if I don't love you?'
> 'Yes, you do!'
> 'Do I?'
> 'I beg your pardon,' said Dolly. 'I didn't mean to say that. Of course a man shouldn't make sure of a thing.'
> 'Not in this case, Mr Longstaff; because really I entertain no such feeling.'

Dolly blunders on – 'But I want you to know that I can afford it. You might perhaps have thought that I wanted your money . . .' – until the point where Isabel draws a deliberately far-fetched analogy to indicate that she would not marry even an English prince merely for his position:

> 'That's quite out of the question,' said Dolly, 'They can't do it, – by Act of Parliament, – except in a hugger-mugger left-handed way, that wouldn't suit you at all.'
> 'Mr Longstaff, – you must forgive me – if I say – that of all the gentlemen – I have ever met in this country or in any other – you are the – most obtuse.' (*The Duke's Children*, ch. xxxii)

Isabel is one of the facts of life that make Mabel Grex feel old in comparison, and that fling her back, when Silverbridge has finally left her, on to a by now hopeless love for Tregear. Still, Mabel's bleak future is not quite the novel's. Even apart from Silverbridge, who will always be young, and English, the two novels together throw up other, less tangible possibilities to answer the brief American challenge in the last. Like the bleak strains in Trollope's vision, these 'possibilities' stem mainly from the Duke and Glencora. But they also reverberate throughout the books, so that the sum total of both novels is an impressive openness to the familiar but still daunting question: what will or can happen to ideals when once they are immersed in action? The question itself is familiar indeed within Trollope's own earlier novels; but the note he sounds in these last two of the political series is deeper than perhaps one might have expected from reading any of his earlier novels except the Lady Mason story in *Orley Farm*. Indeed, except for George Eliot in *Middlemarch*, James in *The Awkward Age* and *The Ambassadors*, and Conrad in *Nostromo*, *Victory* and others, it is not easy to think of any novelist who has treated the theme more impressively than Trollope.

Lady Mason's taut composure, the Duke's sensitive retirement from the world together with his longing to act in it, Glencora's vivacity facing the Duke's rigidity of manner, Miss Boncassen's challenge to Mabel Grex and others – all these things are a long way from specifically political writing, though mostly they stem from Trollope's interest in parliament and involve political issues. Certainly they belong to a middle-class world and a middle-class outlook that, different though the range of society pictured by the two novelists is, it is not surprising to hear George Eliot recognising as 'thoroughly wholesome-minded'. And indeed I do not think it is too improbable a jump of the mind to move from thinking of Trollope's characters and the way they act – particularly the Duke – to thinking of Strether, Mr Longdon, Nanda. James is in another class altogether as a novelist from Trollope, and any comparisons are, for this reason alone, shaky. But so is George Eliot, and if it is not absurd to mention her name, neither is it to mention James's in connection with Trollope. All three differ obviously and importantly, but all three create characters who live impressively, if also foolishly or weakly at times, in a recognisably late nineteenth-century society that they see and feel, for somewhat the same reasons, as inimical. So do the authors, though they also welcome it as in some sense their natural element and environment. All three authors – particularly Trollope and George Eliot, but also I think James – would be unhappy if the *only* way were retirement or with-drawal or isolation, however strong, or even valid, may be the need that their characters feel in particular circumstances for some such retirement. James's bulwarks against the world (Strether, for instance, or Mr Long-don) are not peevish, as the Duke sometimes is, or even compromisers, as Lydgate finally is; and it may well be that James himself was sturdier, at least in *The Awkward Age* and *The Ambassadors*, than even George Eliot. For all the complexity of his writing, he was certainly sturdier than the more sensibly unadventurous Trollope; but nevertheless, in the Duke in his world, and in Lydgate and Strether in theirs, one can see a lot of late nineteenth-century living that Trollope, George Eliot and James must have felt, and liked, in common.

7 *Middlemarch* and Modern Society

To go back for a moment to Jane Austen: after her conservative certainty about social issues – and her achievement marks the last point in literary history at which intelligent satire could at once criticise and bolster an exclusive society – the majority of nineteenth-century novelists dealt only precariously with social problems which, by the time George Eliot began to write, had assumed threatening proportions. The monstrous growth of bureaucracies, suburbias, governmental controls and industry which began soon after Jane Austen too often forced later novelists into a disastrously oversimplifying position. Trollope is indeed an exception here, and his best novels (especially the later ones in the political series) are firmly unterrified and unevasive in the face of problems that clearly dismayed a good many other mid-century writers, including some who were by nature more imaginative than Trollope himself. As the century went on, however, and as the initial Romantic impulse both weakened and spread more widely through the literate community, the temptation grew to sidestep social problems by adopting one version or other of the too-neat formula: the individual *versus* society.

In particular, the sentimentality that dogs almost every chapter of Dickens – potentially the most imaginative writer of the age – springs directly from this pervasive tendency to split personalities, individuals, away from the society in which, after all, they must live and act. In Jane Austen's world, close-knit societies, for all the acid comment she directs towards them and towards individuals in them, are still present possibilities. Clearly the Darcys, Emmas, Knightleys exist in and for their narrowly exclusive societies, rather than in opposition to them. In Dickens, however, Donwell Abbey has turned into Sir Leicester Dedlock's nightmare estate in Lincolnshire, and London has engulfed Highbury. The consequence is, very often, the cloying sentimentality of an individualism which has no support from anything outside itself ('He wos wery good to me, he wos ...'); or, alternatively, the unhealthy attraction Dickens feels towards nihilistic fantasies of the Krook, Grandfather Smallweed kind. All the great Dickens novels raise sociological matters crucial to the nineteenth century, but constantly his prose (when it is not cloyingly sentimental in the Jo the crossing-sweeper vein) turns all to horrified animation. That grotesque comedy, of the kind evident in the Barnard's Inn passages of *Great Expectations*, for instance ('dry rot and wet rot and all the silent rots that rot in neglected roof and cellar . . .'), whatever its life and animation, is shying away from the problem of commercial London, rather than facing and coping with it. There is a sense in which Wemmick's drawbridge is a necessary expedient for Dickens as well as for Wemmick. And the way in which that brilliantly imaginative beginning of *Bleak House* turns, after three or four pages, into the laboured irony and symbolism of the Lord Chancellor sitting in *his* fog is a further manifestation of the same inability to cope.

My comment on Dickens is obviously highly selective – for this reason many would consider it unfair – but I will stick to it without modification because I think it is sufficiently representative of central weaknesses in Dickens to make the contrast with George Eliot interesting – indeed a *sine qua non* of reading nineteenth-century novels at all. My case in the following analysis of *Middlemarch* will be that, though George Eliot in this novel is less lively, and certainly less animated, than Dickens is on social matters, her prose and her thinking are more honest and more direct. In the terms of *Middlemarch* there appears to be a straight fight between individualism of, say, the Dorothea–Lydgate kind, and the conservative, nearly corporate unity of Middlemarch citizens and traders and 'county' families. On the surface it looks as if George Eliot is taking the position she adopts in novels like *Felix Holt* and *Daniel Deronda*, with the heroes and heroines in isolated opposition to a hostile society. In actual fact *Middlemarch* demonstrates an acceptance, rather than a rejection, of modern society. Some sections of the novel are tedious (is there a long novel in English which is not dull at points?), but even this tedium springs from George Eliot's steady refusal to evade the central fact of nineteenth-century sociology: the age of individualism and Reform was also the age that had to confront the most startlingly rapid growth in history of bureaucracies, business associations, corporate government of all kinds. In addition, there is of course the perennial, implacable hostility to new ideas evident in the Mr Crabbes and the Mrs Dollops of Middlemarch itself:

> 'I say, I've seen drops myself as made no difference whether they was in the glass or out, and yet have griped you the next day. So I'll leave your own sense to judge. Don't tell me! All I say, is, it's a mercy they didn't take this Doctor Lydgate on to our club. There's many a mother's child might ha' rued it.' (ch. LXXI)

.   .   .   .   .   .

It is for this reason that the first consideration in a study of the unusual quality of *Middlemarch* should be the firmness with which George Eliot presents the failure of the idealists in the novel, the men and women who are indeed merely annoyed by the petty restrictions which surround them and by the rock-like stupidity of the Mrs Dollops contemplating medical reforms. George Eliot is of course not always successful in this direction. Dr Leavis has very clearly shown that there is a strong emotional tie which makes her – particularly as the novel goes on – virtually incapable of seeing Will and Dorothea in true relation to the society around them:

> ... but she drew her head back and held his away gently that she might go on speaking, her large tear-filled eyes looking at his very simply, while she said in a sobbing childlike way, 'We could live quite well on my own fortune – it is too much – seven hundred-a-year – I want so little – no new clothes – and I will learn what everything costs.' (ch. LXXXIII)

This is the 'St Theresa' complex taken to embarrassing lengths, thinned out and sentimentalised to the point where Dorothea's personality is presented as ignoring everything outside Will and herself. It is a different case altogether from the sentimentality in Dorothea's view of the poor, and her scheme to build them cottages, for on the whole George Eliot sees Dorothea's cottages for the evasion they are. In the scenes with Will, however, the sentimentality in the prose itself is unmistakably endorsing a nineteenth-century individualism of the very weakest kind.

However, if this is sometimes a worry with Dorothea and Will, it is never so, as Dr Leavis notes, with the treatment of Lydgate, the strongest of the novel's idealists. He fails unequivocally – in marriage, as a doctor, as a reformer – and there is no attempt to gloss the failure or smooth it over in any way. Moreover, this failure is clearly presented as brought on by an idealism very similar to that which George Eliot attempted to endorse in the case of Dorothea. Both are impulsive, generous, impatient of petty restrictions; but Lydgate, we know, gets precisely what he deserves. Personally, he is likeable, sincere, intelligent; it is impossible not to sympathise with such a man in such an all-too-familiar situation. But his failure is the very crux of the novel in that it springs from a habit of mind which attempts to mould Middlemarch to fit an abstract idealism. This attempt is presented as not merely impossible, or unlikely to succeed, but actually undesirable. Reformers who cannot, or will not, see that the society they reform is also the medium in which they must, almost by definition, exist and act, are self-doomed to failure. The idealism even of a man as vigorous and intelligent as Lydgate withers when it sets itself *above* the society which should be its natural source of strength:

> For the first time Lydgate was feeling the hampering threadlike pressure of small social conditions, and their frustrating complexity. . . .

It would have seemed beforehand like a ridiculous piece of bad logic
that he, with his unmixed resolutions of independence and his select
purpose, would find himself at the very outset in the grasp of petty
alternatives, each of which was repugnant to him. In his student's
chambers, he had prearranged his social action quite differently.
(ch. xviii)

If the irony of this is directed against the 'small social conditions', it is
also clearly directed against Lydgate.

Lydgate will not see that Middlemarch itself, rather than the isolation
wards of the hospital (where the 'isolation' refers to fever but to other
matters as well), is the sphere in which he must live. On the plane of
personal contact, he is better equipped to fight, and he does not shy away
from the problems of marriage with Rosamond: 'Lydgate's anger rose;
he was prepared to be indulgent towards feminine weakness, but not
towards feminine dictation. The shallowness of a waternixie's soul may
have a charm until she becomes didactic. But he controlled himself . . .'
(ch. lxiv)

If Lydgate's life could ever have been conceived as a struggle on the
personal plane alone, he would have triumphed. But George Eliot's
insight is crystal clear on this issue – for her, as again Dr Leavis has shown,
a particularly tricky one. Lydgate's life could never, she sees, have been a
matter of personal conflict divorced from social issues, and so she makes
Rosamond, with her maddeningly beautiful curve of the neck, precisely
typical of the kind of mindless stubbornness that Middlemarch at its
worst can display. The key scenes are in Chapter lxiv, and the picture
we are given of Lydgate is, for all the sympathy it evokes, unequivocally
one of failure:

He was feeling bitter disappointment, as if he had opened a door
out of a suffocating place and had found it walled up; but he also felt
sure that Rosamond was pleased with the cause of his disappointment.
He preferred not looking at her and not speaking, until he had got over
the first spasm of vexation. After all, he said in his bitterness, what
can a woman care about so much as house and furniture? a husband
without them is an absurdity. When he looked up and pushed his hair
aside, his dark eyes had a miserable blank non-expectance of sympathy
in them, but he only said, coolly –
   'Perhaps some one else may turn up. I told Trumbull to be on the
look-out if he failed with Plymdale . . .' (ch. lxiv)

Middlemarch, quite rightly, failed to respond to the arid idealism of
Casaubon's 'The Key to all Mythologies'. It is now clear that it will not
respond either to the idealism that projected Lydgate's 'Homogeneous
Origin of all the Tissues'. Lydgate's personal problems are different from
Casaubon's, and he deals with them far more impressively; but on the

other hand his personal life is, through Rosamond, linked to his public life. And in the wider sphere of public relations both these men have failed because they could not, or would not, see life as anything more than subject to their own idealism.

I want to return shortly to the matter of Lydgate's dealings with Bulstrode, and to the light they throw on the nature of moral choice and action in a modern society; in the meantime, the question arises of what the novel sees in Middlemarch society that Lydgate fails to see, or fails to respond adequately to. Middlemarch itself, in contrast to Lydgate's idealism, has a sustaining solidity and actuality. Stupidity, blindness, self-interest are rampant, and George Eliot sees these things with dismaying clarity; but the point of her essentially comic vision of Middlemarch is the perception of ways in which society gains from this very blindness a rock-like immovability of substance which, to people like Celia, Chettam, the Vincys and even Mr Brooke, is a source of strength.

The beginning of the novel is brilliant in this regard. Celia and Dorothea, when together in these early scenes, bring out the strength and resilience of George Eliot's comedy; essentially this is seen and described as a 'Middlemarch' strength:

> 'It is so painful in you, Celia, that you will look at human beings as if they were merely animals with a toilette, and never see the great soul in a man's face.'
>
> 'Has Mr Casaubon a great soul?' Celia was not without a touch of naive malice. (ch. 11)

There is clearly a good deal that is worth while in Dorothea's searching for the 'great soul in a man's face', but Celia's shrewdness is indispensable if we are to catch – as we do at this early stage – exactly what is true and what is dangerously false in Dorothea's attitude. Reflecting on Sir James Chettam's wooing of Dorothea (which Dorothea has mistaken for the natural politeness of a country gentleman) Celia sees the matter very clearly indeed, even managing to include a half-conscious reflection on her own views of Chettam:

> She had never been deceived as to the object of the baronet's interest. Sometimes, indeed, she had reflected that Dodo would perhaps not make a husband happy who had not her way of looking at things; and stifled in the depths of her heart was the feeling that her sister was too religious for family comfort . . . (ch. 11)

In some respects, or viewed in some lights, Celia is a brainless featherweight compared with her sister Dorothea (here seen truly for what she is and not sentimentalised). But it is obvious from this passage that Celia has a core of common sense that Dorothea most notably lacks. She also has a resourceful wit and humour. More important, she has these qualities *because* she is in many ways representative. Middlemarch is not peopled with Celias; but Celia is *of* Middlemarch in a sense that her sister is not. She vividly typifies, and draws on, certain solid Middlemarch, middle-class virtues.

The sense that Celia's insights, and her limitations, are common property, or at any rate that they interlock with other people and other things in Middlemarch, spreads throughout most of the scenes and events in these early chapters. Thus Mrs Cadwallader, the clergyman's wife, in violently unclerical phrase, strengthens Celia's view of Casaubon's idealism: '[Dorothea] says he is a great soul. – A great bladder for dried peas to rattle in!' Even Sir James Chettam is given his moments of insight, notably into Dorothea's nature, and they clearly relate to Celia's and to the common Middlemarch view of 'dreamers' and idealists:

> 'Your sister is given to self-mortification, is she not?' he continued, turning to Celia, who sat at his right hand.
> 'I think she is,' said Celia, feeling afraid lest she should say something that would not please her sister, and blushing as prettily as possible above her necklace. 'She likes giving up.' (ch. 11)

Of course Chettam doesn't consciously realise the importance and essential truth of what he has said, any more than Celia does (less so, in fact). The point is that his remark *is* true, and it is his limited county assurance and intolerance that has led him to it; just as, in fact, the same qualities lead him inevitably away from Dorothea herself.

Later Featherstone and Brooke, in different ways, further extend the novel's grasp. Both these men are in many ways pitiably weak and foolish, but they are not entirely so. More important, the note of comedy with which their weaknesses are presented is a note of acceptance, not dismissal. What distinguishes *Middlemarch* from George Eliot's other novels is her clear realisation that the valuable and the good gain strength and solidity from the confusion and error of actual (Middlemarch) life. For instance, the tenacity of the dying Featherstone is remarkable. He is a miserable hoarder, and clearly seen as such by George Eliot; but the comedy of that scene where the still more rapacious relations are held off (barely) by Mary Garth is broadly tolerant – to the point, in fact, where it can see strength in the almost wholly commercial society of which Featherstone himself is a grotesque representative:

> He was propped up on a bed-rest, and always had his gold-headed stick lying by him. He seized it now and swept it backwards and forwards in as large an area as he could, apparently to ban these ugly spectres, crying in a hoarse sort of screech –
> 'Back, back, Mrs Waule! Back, Solomon!'

The comedy of this, and of the lines that follow, so far from being a bitter repudiation of Featherstone's wealth, accepts it as something to be reckoned with. Jane Austen could not have permitted herself the note of tolerant farce which characterises these scenes –

> 'Brother Peter' [Solomon] said, in a wheedling yet gravely official tone, 'it's nothing but right I should speak to you about the Three Crofts and the Manganese. The Almighty knows what I've got on my mind . . .'
> 'Then He knows more than I want to know,' said Peter, laying down his stick with a show of truce which had a threat in it too, for he reversed the stick so as to make the gold handle a club in case of closer fighting, and looked hard at Solomon's bald head. (ch. xxxii)

In all this it is important to see how, in George Eliot's clearly rational prose, the question of Featherstone's tenacious hold on his money links with the hold that Casaubon, Bulstrode, Lydgate, Dorothea and other purposeful characters (the novel is crammed with them!) have on their own particular spheres of interest and influence. The above scenes are not simply an investigation of Featherstone's character, or an illustration of an eccentric of provincial society. Taken in the context of surrounding scenes they severely question, for instance, Dorothea's sentimental repudiation of wealth and Lydgate's impatience over petty matters like the money he owes to tradesmen. Featherstone quite obviously lacks any sense for Lydgate's idealism; on the other hand Lydgate's idealism is crippled by his irresponsibility about money. In the end, the new Fever Hospital sinks, as no purpose of Featherstone's would have done, under the sheer weight of furniture bills. Reduced to essentials, it is money – or rather the lack of power over money – that forces on Lydgate the moral compromise which ends in Raffles's death and his own disgrace. In the closing scenes not even Dorothea's wealth, offered with a sentimentally conceived generosity far beyond the imagination of Featherstone, can save Lydgate. In Chapter lxxvi, which is in the final book 'Sunset and Sunrise', she goes to Lydgate and proposes that he stay in Middle-march after all and, with her financial help, keep on his work at the hospital. But Lydgate has – too late – learned his lesson: he has not the ability to use the power that is potentially there in Middlemarch money. The tone of the writing in 'Sunset and Sunrise' wobbles in places to the very edge of sentimentality, but generally speaking it is clear and uncompromising:

> 'God bless you, Mrs Casaubon!' said Lydgate. . . . 'It is good that you should have such feelings. But I am not the man who ought to allow himself to benefit by them. I have not given guarantees enough. I must not at least sink into the degradation of being pensioned for work that I never achieved. It is very clear to me that I must not count on anything else than getting away from Middlemarch as soon as I can manage it . . .' (ch. lxxvi)

Constantly Lydgate and Dorothea extend the range of the novel beyond the imagination of solid Middlemarch citizens. On the other hand the novel constantly returns to the events and life of ordinary Middlemarch as to a source of nourishment – for solid food, in fact. In the early stages of the novel, for instance, the Vincy household, for all Fred's flightiness, is established as having a solidly real, workable domesticity of a kind hopelessly beyond the grasp of Casaubon, Dorothea and Will. The comedy is steadily unemphatic:

'Have you got nothing else for my breakfast, Pritchard?' said Fred, to the servant who brought in coffee and buttered toast; while he walked round the table surveying the ham, potted beef, and other cold remnants, with an air of silent rejection, and polite forbearance from signs of disgust.
'Should you like eggs, sir?'
'Eggs, no! Bring me a grilled bone.'

Nobody could imagine Dorothea sitting down to a grilled bone for breakfast. In the Vincy household, and in other comparable scenes, it is the density and force of deliberately ordinary detail – both of things and personalities – that impresses us as being utterly, unimaginatively, reliable: '"Mamma," said Rosamond, "when Fred comes down I wish you would not let him have red herrings. I cannot bear the smell of them all over the house at this hour of the morning . . ."' (ch. XI)

It is in connection with the comedy of these scenes that Mr Brooke, despite his own foolishness, looms large. Mr Brooke's household, and his conversation, notably lack the 'potted beef' solidity of the Vincys; but Mr Brooke's foolishness is related to the Vincy household in that it *belongs* to Middlemarch. The importance of what he says (or doesn't say!) is in the very close relationship it bears to surrounding scenes and dialogue. Thus in Chapter II Dorothea is talking of the value of spending money on land-improvement instead of on hunting and dogs. A few minutes later, contemplating Mr Casaubon, whom she has just met, she transfers these thoughts to the (for her) still higher plane of Mr Casaubon's nobility of purpose and scholarship. In the meantime, however, and before Dorothea turns from land-improvement to Casaubon, Mr Brooke is allowed *his* comment:

'Young ladies don't understand political economy, you know' said Mr Brooke, smiling towards Mr Casaubon. 'I remember when we were all reading Adam Smith. *There* is a book, now. I took in all the new ideas at one time – human perfectibility, now. But some say, history moves in circles; and that may be very well argued; I have argued it myself. The fact is, human reason may carry you a little too far – over the hedge, in fact. It carried me a good way at one time; but I saw it would not do. I pulled up: I pulled up in time. But not too hard.

I have always been in favour of a little theory: we must have Thought
. . .' (ch. 11)

Lord David Cecil once accused George Eliot of being unhumorously
puritanical. I think the evidence suggests that George Eliot could have
seen Lord David himself with tolerant irony. For here, in terms of an
unbelievably fragmented mind, are the novel's true concerns; as indeed,
they were also present in Dorothea's ardent praise of land-improvement
and of Casaubon's scholarship. What Mr Brooke's conversation (sand-
wiched between Dorothea's reflections on her cottages and Casaubon)
gives us is fragmentation of purpose and ideal. The further, and more
important, implication is that the true quality of purpose and nobility is
such that it can only be glimpsed, not through, but *as it resides in* the
quality of fragmentation itself. What *Middlemarch* is saying in the strong
comedy of these scenes could be summarised as the perception of ways
in which idealism gains an essential strength and solidity *from* that compromise with life which Lydgate and Dorothea refuse to make.

In the later sections of the novel, it is the developing relation between
Lydgate and Bulstrode which gathers these threads together and pushes
the novel towards a consideration of a new, but related, problem: the
nature of moral choice and action in modern society. The problem is
forecast early on with the voting for the chaplaincy of the Infirmary
(Tyke or Farebrother), and from then on, through the business of Lydgate's gradual commitment to Bulstrode, it becomes a dominating concern in the novel: what kind of decisions are being taken? what relation
do they bear to the motives that prompt them? and how far can they be
thought of at all as 'decisions taken' in a place like Middlemarch which
tends, as Lydgate knows, to hamper all freedom of decision? From all this
nothing emerges as a summarisable conclusion in ethics or philosophy –
indeed conclusions of this kind would not be within the proper sphere of
a novelist – but certain possibilities emerge. For instance in the Infirmary
business Lydgate, naturally, is irritated by the need to make a choice at all.
For him at this stage, higher work on scientific and medical discoveries is
all-important, and he feels it can only be hampered by parish-pump
politics. For the first time Lydgate was feeling the hampering threadlike
pressure of small social conditions, and their frustrating complexity . . .'
In action, these issues are clarified by the actual presentation of Lydgate's
moment of choice (the first of several which lead finally to his accepting
the fatal loan from Bulstrode). Purposeful and decisive though he is,
he puts off the moment of choice until 'the energy which is begotten by
circumstances – some feeling rushing warmly and making resolve easy'
shall decide for him. That 'energy begotten by circumstances' is doubly
ironic in context. For though Lydgate cannot see it, the whole weight
of the novel has made it clear that it is precisely the 'circumstances' he
despises which should provide the real energy, or a necessary part of it,

for all moral choice and action. But as it is, of course, he is totally blind to this; his idealistic concern for the hospital is divorced from the necessary practical details of who will run the place and how it will be financed. Therefore the 'circumstances' he despises use him, rather than responding to his control. Angered by Wrench's taunt – '"The thing is settled now ... We all know how Mr Lydgate will vote."' – Lydgate, pencil poised and still, at this last moment, undecided, votes defiantly for Tyke.

In doing so he votes also, of course, for Bulstrode. Bulstrode himself presents almost the opposite case from Lydgate. His grasp on financial detail (for example, on the trading interests of the Vincys and the Brookes) and on the ways in which pressure-groups in Middlemarch work, is firm to the point of becoming a stranglehold. On the other hand his idealism – and he is, or persuades himself that he is, an idealist – is selfishly concentrated where Lydgate's was, however impractical, generous and broadminded. In the course of the novel these men, who dislike and distrust each other, are faced with common, or at least related, sets of frustrations and decisions. There is a sense of nearly physical entanglement which gradually surrounds them, as indeed it surrounds almost everybody else in the novel:

> Mentally surrounded with that past again, Bulstrode had the same pleas – indeed, the years had been perpetually spinning them into intricate thickness, like masses of spider-web, padding the moral sensibility; nay, as age made egoism more eager but less enjoying, his soul had become more saturated with the belief that he did everything for God's sake, being indifferent to it for his own ... (ch. LXI)

It is in the context of imagistically strong writing of this kind, presenting the thread-like entanglements of Middlemarch as almost a solid presence to be dealt with and faced, that Bulstrode makes the crucial decision to allow his housekeeper to give Raffles the port-wine and brandy Lydgate had pronounced against as fatal.

The ways in which Bulstrode is brought to his choice in this scene are strikingly similar to the ways in which Lydgate was brought to vote for Tyke and Bulstrode earlier. The action presents both men as being acted upon by circumstances and their own selfish concerns. On the other hand, the way in which the writing presents these scenes leaves open the possibility of more genuine, and more valuable, moral choice. The run of the prose encompasses the directing power of circumstance, hampering freedom of choice; but on the other hand it has not that rigidly deterministic quality which comparable scenes in, say, Ibsen have. In Ibsen the past determines action to the point where not merely the individuals concerned, but the very possibilities of individualism and choice are presented, often, as simply a hollow mockery. George Eliot is more open than this, for she presents at once the power of circumstances and the past, and the force of present personalities coping, however wrongly, with circumstance. It is in this regard that Bulstrode's killing of Raffles is very similar to that pencil-poised 'decision' of Lydgate's earlier on. It is also similar to Lydgate's decision, taken during Raffles's illness, to accept a loan from the conscience-ridden Bulstrode. The whole chain of inter-locking circumstances and personalities leads finally to Lydgate's identify-ing himself publicly with Bulstrode after the council meeting which ends Book VII ('Two Temptations'):

> Bulstrode, after a moment's hesitation, took his hat from the floor and slowly rose, but he grasped the corner of the chair so totteringly that Lydgate felt sure there was not strength enough in him to walk away without support. What could he do? He could not see a man sink close to him for want of help. He rose and gave his arm to Bulstrode, and in that way led him out of the room; yet this act, which might have been one of gentle duty and pure compassion, was at this moment unspeakably bitter to him. It seemed as if he were putting his sign-manual to that association of himself with Bulstrode, of which he now saw the full meaning as it must have presented itself to other minds. (ch. LXXI)

Both Lydgate and Bulstrode are presented during this later part of the novel as under the influence of a half-conscious rationalising process in which guilt, their own immediate desires, and a chain of circumstances beyond their control all have a tremendous influence on their actions. But mixed with these influences is a strong feeling of being *in fact* respon-sible for events, and also a strong feeling of responsibility for others – notably for Rosamond and Mrs Bulstrode – besides themselves. It is in these scenes that George Eliot's sense for a largeness of purpose in life, and her knowledge of the circumstances that restrict this, are brought closest together. Her prose falters just occasionally towards sentimentality and an oversimplification of issues, but predominantly it is vigorous and assured:

> There was a benumbing cruelty in his position. Even if he renounced every other consideration than that of justifying himself – if he met shrugs, cold glances, and avoidance as an accusation, and made a public statement of all the facts as he knew them, who would be convinced? It would be playing the part of a fool to offer his own testimony on behalf of himself, and say, 'I did not take the money as a bribe.' The circumstances would always be stronger than his asser-tion. . . .
> But then came the question whether he should have acted in precisely the same way if he had not taken the money? . . . if he had not received any money – if Bulstrode had never revoked his cold recommendation of bankruptcy – would he, Lydgate, have abstained from all inquiry even on finding the man dead? (ch. LXXIII)

If the novel ends with the defeat of these two men, it also ends with a clear-minded sympathy for them. The last book of *Middlemarch* is at its weakest when dealing with Will and Dorothea precisely because it tends again to endorse Will's and Dorothea's own contempt for money and the petty details of Middlemarch living. It is at its strongest in the picture it gives of Lydgate's retirement from Middlemarch and the final, silent scene between Bulstrode and his wife. In the case of these two men George Eliot has tested and explored the nature of moral action *in* the field which is the natural arena for action and choice – the 'circumstances' of Middlemarch life.

The early seventies, and the publication then of *Middlemarch*, mark clearly and decisively one of the great achievements of Victorian fiction. After this, there will be some changes of emphasis. In particular, later novels will be rather more explicitly concerned with some of the impulses that are clearly present earlier on, but that are, at least in part, outside the range of terms like 'middle-class', 'urban', 'political', or even (to use the more general term commonly applied to literature) 'cultural'. There is certainly no distinct break in the history of the novel at this point, but from now on Hardy, Conrad, James, Lawrence will each bring various matters more specifically to conscious recognition: fears of man's being permanently and ineradicably alienated from society; some fear that the universe itself may provide for such a condition of aloneness; and a sense of dislocation from the ordinary, day-to-day experience that has been up to now, and with certain very interesting exceptions, simply assumed as the staple of man's existence.

What sustains the best of the later novelists in these and related enterprises, however, is a knowledge and experience of life that is still very close to the solid middle-class base so firmly established by George Eliot in *Middlemarch*.

8 'Fits of Spiritual Dread': George Eliot and Later Novelists

Middlemarch concentrates the strengths and weaknesses of the English middle class more steadily than probably any other novel before or since. And it does this in a way that gathers together some of the stablest forces evident even in later, more 'modern' and complex novels by people as different as Conrad, James and Lawrence. But before discussing some of these later writers, it is important I think to look a bit more closely at some of the *unstable*, even threatening, components evident in George Eliot's own writing and in the life around her. By this, I don't mean so much the notorious sentimentalities that weaken parts both of *Middlemarch* and lesser George Eliot novels; but, rather, a sense in her work that both the mistakes she makes, and, more interestingly, some of her strongest writing, are of a kind that cannot be entirely comprehended or explained in terms of her more widely acknowledged virtues, such as her engagement with society and the challenge and choices it presents to the individual.

There is a passage early on in *Daniel Deronda* that lingers constantly in the mind in this connection: 'What she [Gwendolen] unwillingly recognised, and would have been glad for others to be unaware of, was that liability of hers to fits of spiritual dread ...' This is from the scene in Chapter VI in which one of Klesmer's 'thunderous chords' from the piano opens the movable panel to disclose – for the second time, but now very unexpectedly – the picture of 'an upturned dead face, from which an obscure figure seemed to be fleeing with outstretched arms'. If the phrasing here is a shade melodramatic, the effect of the scene as a whole is not. Everybody is surprised; but Gwendolen actually collapses, and this in a way that none of the offered explanations – even, perhaps, George Eliot's own at the end of the chapter – quite comprehends.

Klesmer's comment ('A magnificent piece of plastik that!') comes first, and is obviously intended kindly, though not as offering any complete understanding of what has happened. Gwendolen's mother and friends conclude simply that these 'fits of terror' to which Gwendolen is subject are the result of her sensitive and excitable nature. But this is close to tautology, and one is struck by the fact that Gwendolen's own private admissions, which she would do anything rather than make public, or confess even to her mother, cut closer to the bone. To herself, though only half consciously, Gwendolen admits a quite general 'susceptibility to terror'. She then immediately tries to bury this fact about herself in a piece of wishful thinking that lays the blame for her timidity on her circumstances and upbringing: '... this shortcoming seemed to be due to the pettiness of circumstances, the narrow theatre which life offers to a girl of twenty, who cannot conceive herself as anything else than a lady, or as in any position which would lack the tribute of respect.'

This brings into play, comically but very pertinently indeed, the difficulties, not just of provincial life in general, but of women in particular. However spirited and independent by nature the heroines of many nineteenth-century novels may be, their position in life forces them into a kind of idleness and subjection that even Lydgate, for instance, is not subjected to. Whatever its frustrations and restrictions, Lydgate's life has, as he himself acknowledges, wider boundaries than the house and home that Rosamond – or if it comes to that Dorothea herself – is bound to. However, what is interesting about Gwendolen's reflections here is that, though they bring considerations of this kind once again very sharply to mind, they also include an element that operates almost independently of any sociological considerations. Thus, the fact that Gwendolen's statements about the 'pettiness of circumstances', and the 'narrow theatre which life offers to a girl of twenty', are for all their truth essentially rationalisations, is underscored by her more private thoughts turning, at precisely *this* point, to the still more compelling reflections about 'that liability of hers to fits of spiritual dread'.

George Eliot's own explanation or comment follows immediately; and, though it reads perhaps a shade literal-mindedly, it clearly builds on – is in fact really part of – Gwendolen's own innermost, half-recognised admissions. It also offers these as of much more general significance than any that could be attributed simply to a girlish sensitivity constricted by the circumstances of county society. Clearly, this side of Gwendolen's character would have been much the same, no matter what class or circumstances she had been born into:

> Solitude in any wide scene impressed her with an undefined feeling of immeasurable existence aloof from her, in the midst of which she was helplessly incapable of asserting herself. The little astronomy taught her at school used sometimes to set her imagination at work in a way that made her tremble: but always when some one joined her she recovered her indifference to the vastness in which she seemed an exile; she found again her usual world in which her will was of

some avail, and the religious nomenclature belonging to this world was no more identified with those uneasy impressions of awe than her uncle's surplices seen out of use at the rectory. With human ears and eyes about her, she had always hitherto recovered her confidence, and felt the possibility of winning empire.

The mention here, and earlier in Chapter VI, of the fact that religion has had no meaning at all for Gwendolen other than the externals of an Anglican service is an uneasy reminder of ways in which not merely Gwendolen, but unfortunately George Eliot herself later on, takes refuge in Daniel; or worse still, in George Eliot's own case, in Mordecai's empty phrase-making ('Seest thou, Mirah . . .'). By the time we get to Mordecai's interminable sermons, George Eliot's critical intelligence has weakened to fits of defensive irony only, coming the more faintly because channelled through the sentimentalised Mirah:

> 'In this moment, my sister, I hold the joy of another's future within me. . . . I recognise it now, and love it so, that I can lay down this poor life upon its altar and say: "Burn, burn indiscernibly into that which shall be, which is my love and not me". Dost thou understand, Mirah?'
> 'A little,' said Mirah faintly . . . (ch. LXI)

Yet the failure of virtually the whole of the Daniel/Mordecai/Mirah sections of the book has at least the negative interest of pointing exactly what it is that both Gwendolen and George Eliot are running away *from*. And that is best recollected in terms of the accuracy with which, in the more public scenes earlier on, Gwendolen's boredom at the prospect of domestic life meshes with her strongly physical repulsion to any form of love or tenderness – the scene giving us Rex's proposal is brilliantly done – and also with the 'sick motivelessness' that attacks her from time to time, and that is so tellingly close to certain states of mind that Grandcourt, both before and after he marries Gwendolen, shows. Grandcourt and Gwendolen are the centre of this novel; and they are so in wholly positive ways that make a silly nonsense of both Mordecai's and Daniel's ostensibly more constructive behaviour and ideals. At first sight most of Gwendolen's behaviour, and Grandcourt's, looks passive, indeed 'motiveless'. It looks as if what George Eliot is saying is that these two people exemplify, in different ways, the boredom and pointlessness of contemporary life; a life, that is, in which even the riches of a yacht on a Mediterranean cruise can do nothing to alleviate, and may indeed exacerbate, the feeling of helplessness that can assail people who lack the positive assurances of a religious, or quasi-religious, belief of the kind that Mordecai, Daniel, Mirah differently exemplify. And so, indeed, part of her wants to say. But the fact is that the scenes in the novel that render Grandcourt's and Gwendolen's boredom are so telling, and so memorable, that any accurate and fair reading must surely remember these scenes as in some way positively charged. Gwendolen, for all her disadvantages, and quite certainly Grandcourt, are forces to be reckoned with. Both of them far exceed any merely diagnostic reading of what can happen to people who, given certain circumstances, have either too little money, and/or too little to do with the money they acquire or inherit.

In her early life, Gwendolen has of course always been in command of the small world around her. Indeed, her fits of loneliness apart, she cannot merely command other people – servants at a hotel, her mother's household, her own family – but, for all that her life lacks any sense of direction or purpose, she can effortlessly instil alacrity and life into others, whether family or servants or friends. It is simply part of her nature to feel herself perfectly confident, 'well equipped for the mastery of life'. And the fact that she fails, unequivocally, in the end does not, somehow, make her power over people and things illusory. Because almost all the way through the book, the very unusual thing one notices about Gwendolen is that her very weaknesses – as for instance the physical repulsion she feels to Lush, or to Rex's very different intimacy, or, finally, her utter failure to master Grandcourt – carry also a wholly positive charge. There is, for instance, the extraordinary scene in Chapter XI when the 'physical antipathy' she feels to Lush's prominent eyes, fat person and grey-sprinkled, frizzy hair prompts her instantly effective repulsion when he offers the burnous she had asked for: '. . . holding up the garment close to Gwendolen, he said, "Pray, permit me?" But she, wheeling away from him as if he had been a muddy hound, glided on to the ottoman, saying, "No, thank you."'

It is much the same with the more serious scene, cutting still closer to the bone, of her reaction to Rex's proposal earlier. In both cases, Gwendolen is clearly in the grip of an irrational, physical repulsion that she cannot control, and that is I think strongly linked with her more general feelings of loneliness and dread. But one never feels that scenes of this kind, at least up to and including the yachting 'accident', make her the slightly sad spectacle that Lydgate for instance is in some of his moments of defeat, or Bulstrode at the end of *Middlemarch*. The scene with Rex, and with her mother after Rex has left (Chapter VII), is one of the most powerful in this connection, because here the physical antipathy is quite explicitly linked with those feelings of 'spiritual dread' – of a contact, however devastating, with powerful, inimical forces in the very universe around her – that overcome Gwendolen occasionally. These are frightening moments, certainly, but Gwendolen's, and George Eliot's, response to a certain blankness in the universe has an electricity in it that makes their sensitivity quite different from that focused on Lydgate's failure of nerve and will:

'Should you mind about my going away, Gwendolen?'
'Of course. Everyone is of consequence in this dreary country,'

said Gwendolen, curtly. The perception that poor Rex wanted to be tender made her curl up and harden like a sea-anemone at the touch of a finger.

The 'certain fierceness of maidenhood' in Gwendolen then makes her come out explicitly and more curtly still with her 'Pray don't make love to me! I hate it'; and then finally, after Rex has left, there is the sudden and devastating collapse – quite out of proportion to her careless feeling for Rex himself – and the confession to her mother that she feels there is 'nothing worth living for', and that 'I shall never love anybody. I can't love people. I hate them.'

The whole scene is psychologically very acute; but more important still than this, it has a probing, investigatory quality in it that is directly and positively in touch, through Gwendolen's sensitive but highly charged nature, with a certain threat that the universe (rather than *just* the intractable nature of middle-class county society) poses. And it is instinctive feelings and perceptions of this kind, rather than simply the need for money, security and power, that make Grandcourt first of all so attractive to Gwendolen, and then, when she has discovered that he is virtually a human embodiment of all that she has feared as powerfully alien in the world around her, make her hate him, and finally kill him, or at least let him drown without throwing the rope that might well have saved him.

Grandcourt is an extraordinarily powerful figure. At first sight, of course, he is simply the embodiment of a cultured, quite undemonstrative boredom that must appeal to Gwendolen after Rex's youthful eagerness and naïvety. But we hardly need the very excellent scene at the beginning of Chapter XII, where Grandcourt and Lush are at breakfast, to sense the threat and power in his quiet, effortlessly contemptuous mastery over men and animals alike. He is like Gwendolen in that he has both a sure and quick intelligence, and an instinctive response to the powerful and quite unmalleable forces that must, in the end, govern even his strong will. But he is much more advanced in his experience of these, and of course of the world in general, than she is, and he uses this experience to govern her almost as easily as he has used it earlier on with Lydia Glasher and Lush. What is remarkable about him – what makes him, for instance, both more menacing and more interesting than James's Gilbert Osmond in *The Portrait of a Lady* – is the quality at once of an extremity of boredom, and at the very same time of a latent quick activity, that invests all the images George Eliot uses to describe his states of mind and behaviour. His is a very powerful boredom, and the 'lotus-eater's stupor' that invades him in Chapter XIII during the ride at Diplow very quickly and actively invades ('benumbs') Gwendolen and others too. The same is true of his appearance – 'as natural as an alligator' – after Gwendolen has been frightened away by Lydia; of his state of mind when lazily following her back to England, and when Lush notices that the likelihood of poverty making Gwendolen accept him after all has induced a familiar state of mind where 'the certainty of acceptance was just "the sort of thing" to make him lapse hither and thither with no more apparent will than a moth'; and, finally, of his still more powerfully effective inactivity in the close confines of the yacht, when Gwendolen finds that quarrelling with Grandcourt is not merely ineffective, but actually impossible: '. . . and even if she had not shrunk from quarrelling on other grounds, quarrelling with Grandcourt was impossible: she might as well have made angry remarks to a dangerous serpent ornamentally coiled in her cabin without invitation . . .'

Even more positively than Gwendolen's states of 'sick motivelessness', Grandcourt's behaviour – apparently negative, but actually strongly and powerfully active – testifies to impulses beyond the bounds of his own personality and situation. There are forces at work here that neither character can wholly control, but that demand, even in their most destructive vein, some kind of assent, both from the writer and I think from the reader:

> Gwendolen's will had seemed imperious in its small girlish sway; but it was the will of a creature with a large discourse of imaginative fears: a shadow would have been enough to relax its hold. And she had found a will like that of a crab or a boa-constrictor which goes on pinching or crushing without alarm at thunder.

Daniel Deronda was completed in 1876, and was of course the last of George Eliot's novels. Given the wisdom of hindsight, one can see why she was tempted, towards the end of her life, to try for the broadness and sublimity of vision that the Mordecai sections – as it turned out, most unfortunately – outline. In *Middlemarch*, a few years earlier, she had written a novel that is at once much livelier and more readable than popular estimate usually allows, and also a normative, *directing* experience as to both the difficulties, and the sheerly solid possibilities in ordinary day-to-day living. But of course both *Middlemarch* and earlier novels had also contained, however imperfectly, sections that pointed to some quite different kind of awareness: a sense of 'otherness' (the more modern word, 'alienation', would be too definitive) that some of the characters experience. Mrs Transome's musings are a case in point, as also are some of the scenes concerning Casaubon, quite cut off from any of the life around him, or Bulstrode towards the end of the novel, or even Fare-brother, man-of-the-world in some ways though he is. Presumably, the element of threat – again, it is quite independent of class circumstances or of social pressures – in each of these scenes pressed on George Eliot so much that she tried to conceive a life that would either transcend these threats, or offer some answer to them that might gather all 'lesser' lives into an encompassing whole.

That the 'Mordecai' sections (excepting some scenes where Daniel is talking, not to Mordecai or Mirah, but, interestingly enough, to the much more worldly Gwendolen) – that these scenes fail so badly is a tragedy for George Eliot, but also, one cannot help feeling, for the nineteenth-century English novel as a whole. Or, since 'tragedy' is far too melodramatic a word for what is happening to the English novel at this time (1876), it represents a severe limitation as to what the distinctively English novel can do. Neither Dostoevsky nor Tolstoy would have been troubled to write very interesting scenes that could arise from the worries that assail Daniel early on in his life, or the events that happen to Mirah and Mordecai early on in theirs. George Eliot fails abysmally.

What, then, might she have done? Short of suggesting that she attempt another novel, one cannot answer this question, since it encompasses far more than merely the metaphysical doubts and speculations that both Mordecai and Daniel indulge. What one can do is keep in mind what she has indeed done, and done well; and perhaps link this with some of the prevailing impulses in other quite distinctively English novelists – writers, that is, who are for the most part temperamentally sceptical of the worth of any abstract or conceptual thinking.

Of the writers before George Eliot, Jane Austen must clearly be the most interesting in this connection. With the possible exception of *Mansfield Park*, she does not attempt anything at all like the sort of 'answer' to doubts and queries that George Eliot attempts in the Mordecai sections of *Daniel Deronda*. But throughout her career, as D. W. Harding has shown, she is most sharply aware of the possibilities in human nature for inconsistent, even vicious behaviour of a kind that is not unconnected with impulses that dominate some of the best of the Gwendolen/ Grandcourt scenes. The two writers are separated by a very telling half-century that makes George Eliot closely and intimately aware of the impact on English culture of the German Idealist philosophers who, in Jane Austen's day, were unregarded by, and indeed probably quite unknown to, most important English writers except Coleridge. It is only later on that a John Stuart Mill can see and write about the significance that this un-English activity might have for everybody in England, including even the most unaware of natively Anglo-Saxon writers and readers of literature, politics, and philosophy. It is largely this difference – a difference of horizon, influence, awareness – that deepens the tone at least of the more 'serious' passages in George Eliot's writing. And yet, though Jane Austen would never have been tempted to say of one of her own characters that 'Solitude in any wide scene impressed her with an undefined feeling of immeasurable existence aloof from her, in the midst of which she was helplessly incapable of asserting herself ...' – though such a sentence would be inconceivable in a Jane Austen novel, the hard core of doubt, much more Anglo-Saxon in origin than it is Germanicmetaphysical, is common to both novelists, and furthermore inspires some of the very best writing of each.

Jane Austen's 'hatred' for certain traits that she clearly regards as permanently embedded in human nature, and that tend therefore to isolate people even within the close communities she describes; and George Eliot's sense of a threatening loneliness that is equally engrained, though by this time it is seen to be so within the wider frame of the universe generally – at first glance these tendencies in both, and differently again in some later writers like Hardy, Conrad, James, could well represent some sort of Achilles' heel in the developing middle-class confidence and solidity on which, I have been claiming, the quality of all the great nineteenth-century novels largely rests.

What is remarkable about the novelists, however – and indeed about some other prose writers in English – is the way in which they can turn such threats, and the resulting doubts and fears, to wholly productive ends. When Dr Johnson kicked the stone and simply said, of Berkeley's theory of perception, 'I refute it *thus*', he may have been wrong about Berkeley, or misinterpreting him, but he was surely very right – and characteristically English – in placing so much of his faith in the solid ordinariness of simple, obvious, everyday existence. The English middle-class novel is very like Johnson in this regard; and it is like him too in that its trust in simple fact and common sense is an active, enquiring – even, at points, aggressive – quality, not a passive or purely defensive one. What is interesting in the Johnsonian response as it lives on through the next century is not that it dispels all shades of doubt and speculation (it doesn't), but that it is prepared actively to participate in these. Thus even the middle-class (and in many respects rather un-Johnsonian) confidence so clearly there in the densely populated area of *Middlemarch* is rendered, not in terms of a bulwark of stoicism against an encroaching blankness and alienation, but as a way of life much more actively interested in the forces threatening it than any such metaphor would imply, and prepared in consequence to gain from these, rather than simply retreat, defensively, before them. And many later novels, even ones which, like *Daniel Deronda*, fail badly in segments, continue just such an active participation.

To test this claim and make it more specific, I want now to look briefly at three very different novels, none of which seems to me quite as good as the novels I will be discussing in later chapters, but each of which is responding very clearly to specific forms of modern life – or better still, life itself – as, at least in part, a threat. In Hardy's *Jude the Obscure* (1895), James's *The Awkward Age* (1899) and Conrad's *Victory* (1915), we have middle-class figures (together with Jude, who is of course a working-class man trying to master middle-class attainments) all either killed or driven into some form of retreat in the face of problems of modern living and modern unbelief, doubt, alienation. Quite clearly the problems these people face are not new. The social inequalities and religious doubts that Jude faces, the brittle rootlessness of the small (and dwindling) group in *The Awkward Age*, and Heyst's inability finally to trust even Lena – all these have been either prefigured, or at least given some impetus, in both the breakdown of social conventions (of the kind Mr Longdon, for instance, had known) and the ramifications of a by now well-established mechanistic science and philosophy that, however genuinely impressive, has tended to emphasise man's relative helplessness – even unimportance – in the face of a universe seemingly dominated by principles enunciated by Lyell, Darwin, Huxley and others. On the other hand, each of these novels shows such a strong and continuing base in Victorian middle-class certainties that they can afford to be almost as exploratory in the realm of Victorian *un*certainties as later, more technically experimental, novels are in the problems they tackle.

What singles out Hardy, first of all, in such a context, is his naïvety. What I mean here is the kind of 'naïvety' in *Jude* that results in some melodrama, certainly, and some over-specific writing that is close to mere propaganda against 'the iron contract' of marriage, but that results also in a story and scenes with quite unusually strong lineaments. The best and the worst scenes, as in Hardy generally, are separated by a hair's breadth, and what they share is a strong simplicity that makes the melodrama of Father Time's hanging of himself and Sue's children ('Done because we are too menny') quite as memorable, and in its way as close to the heart of the novel, as the splendid scenes in which Sue is shown as driven to torment both Jude and Phillotson (and in these we remember also, of course, the story of the undergraduate earlier on in Sue's life). Admittedly, the details of Sue's relationships with her young (and not so young) men have a complexity about them that reminds one of later, rather than earlier, novels. Nevertheless, what lingers in the mind from Hardy's rendering of these scenes is just such a clarity of outline as characterises the presentation of Father Time in the train, his walk to Jude's house, and later on his suicide.

And this remains true, I think, even in those scenes in which Hardy himself is probably only partly conscious of what is going on. One of the most remarkable things that he renders about Sue (and I think this is indeed unconscious, rather than fully conscious, on his part) is her tendency to give one excuse after another, and each of them different, for not marrying Jude and for thinking marriage in general disastrous. These 'excuses' include her claim that marriage is a 'dreadful contract to feel in a particular way', enforced by an inflexible modern civilisation (the rather crude but telling analogy with the rabbit caught in a steel trap follows this outburst of Sue's in Chapter ii of Part iv); that she and Jude are ahead of the times, and an 'irrevocable path' is doubly risky for them (v, iv); that a bride can be nothing but a heifer led to sacrifice, the flowers wilting in her hand (same chapter); that popular disapproval of her will ruin Jude's career (v, vi); that in conscience she must return to Phillotson (VI, iii); and so on.

As Freud remarked some years later (and as his colleague Ernest Jones detailed in the case of Hamlet), when somebody gives a number of different excuses for not doing something, it is more than likely that they are hiding, even from themselves, whatever the real reason is. Sue does glance at the real reason (her tendency to destroy men by some kind of sado-masochistic 'flirting'), but only to reject it immediately. Even Hardy himself, perhaps, is unwilling to keep this fact about Sue in the forefront of his *conscious* mind for long. But in his telling of her tale he does place it – whether consciously or not doesn't matter – at the centre. In fact, the best scenes between Jude and Sue are a very telling mixture on Hardy's part of certain quite real difficulties in the way of the marriage – most of them put to us by Sue, but real none the less – and Hardy's own recurrence, again and again, to the fact of Sue's fastidious, 'Shelleyan' nature being at the same time rapacious, driven all the time, no matter what the social circumstances or obligations acting upon it, towards actions that turn her ethereal qualities into the pretty vicious cruelty of scenes like the mock-wedding she forces on Jude just before her actual marriage to Phillotson. What Hardy is doing in these scenes, then, is recognising the relevance, to people like Jude and Sue, of the social, conventional pressures symbolised in the marriage bond; and at the same time insisting on the primacy of certain instinctual forces of the kind here concentrated in Sue's very nature, 'quite unfitted by temperament and instinct to fulfil the conditions of the matrimonial relation with Phillotson, possibly with any man . . .' (IV, iii) The social bonds and pressures that Hardy renders are quite real (more so, I think, than Lawrence, in his 'Study of Thomas Hardy', is prepared to admit); at the same time, it is clear that Sue herself would be much the same no matter what society she was born into, and the clear, single-minded (or single-spirited) strength with which Hardy renders this fact is the most telling thing about the book.

In all this, Hardy is indeed rather unusual in the nineteenth-century landscape, fictional or otherwise. And within Hardy's own works, *Jude* stands out – warts and all – as exceptional. Certainly no other nineteenth-century writer one can readily think of renders sex as a single, driving impulse in men and women as strongly or as openly as he does. Yet there are certain aspects of this quality in Hardy that do make one turn back and reflect, however tentatively, on the most un-Hardy-like nineteenth-century novels. Because in the first place, even Hardy's open and frank rendering of sexual drives and impulses is still done very much, and at its best, very impressively, in nineteenth-century terms. Even in *Jude*, his is a *pre*-Freudian, rather than a Freudian, analysis – much simpler and more telling, in fact, than that of many more complex novels since. And he is not merely perfectly happy with, but actually very good at, the 'old stable *ego* of the character' that binds even the most exceptional people strongly to the society around them, dismayingly and massively immovable though this may be. In the second place, and given Hardy's quite distinctively nineteenth-century characteristics, one is bound I think to reflect that both the most apparently conformist of novels, like most of Jane Austen's some eighty years before *Jude*, and the most discreetly 'un-Freudian', like those of Henry James's that were written about the same time as Hardy's, all render, and indeed depend in part upon, certain aspects of human behaviour that cannot be *entirely* explained by, or even referred to, the social circumstances that were nevertheless so clearly important to all these writers.

Henry James's *The Awkward Age* came out just after *Jude*; Conrad's *Victory* some sixteen years later still (1915). One thing I would like to stress about the James, because it is reflected also in the other two (clearly very different) novels, is that, whatever the importance to Nanda of local circumstances – and the vicious in-breeding of much of her mother's circle clearly is important, both to her and to James – it is not these that *cause* her self-condemnation to perpetual spinsterhood. It is all too easy to read this novel (as it is to read Conrad's *Victory* or Hardy's *Jude*) as if the author were saying, 'Had circumstances been different . . .' Yet in fact, like both the other novelists, James is saying, I think very clearly, that local circumstances, though they are indeed definitive in certain ways as far as his characters are concerned (Nanda, but also Mitchy, Mrs Brookenham, Van and the rest) are nevertheless not a first cause of the self-imposed isolation that most of these people – especially Nanda – in the end exemplify. The same is true of the Conrad: Heyst's father, and all that he exemplifies in the way of nineteenth-century rationalist/determinist thinking, moulds his son's character and beliefs into inescapable patterns; and though Conrad's recurring to the father is a trifle forced or even unnecessary, his presentation of the shaping element of rationalism in modern life is crucial to the novel's success. Even in this case, however, there is a residual, instinctual element that is finally self-sufficient as a cause of Heyst's inability to admit his love for Lena, or to make it real. Heyst might very well have agreed with Sue Bridehead's virtual confession that it is her very nature not to be able to love any of the men she tempts; just as he might also have agreed with Nanda's proclamation to Mr Longdon, 'I shall be one of the people who don't' (that is, marry). And in each of these three cases, Gwendolen's sudden confession to her mother springs again to mind: 'I can't love people, I hate them.'

But *The Awkward Age* is in some ways *the* crucial example here, because it is one of the most closely involved of all English novels with the very texture and substance of the society into which the characters are born or (in Mitchy's case at least) precipitated. Even on first reading, and with a comparatively dim understanding therefore of exactly what is going on, one is aware from the start of the close-knit texture of the life these people are living. Mr Longdon's first late-evening talk to Van, bringing together as it does Mr Longdon's half-idealised memories of the past, and Van's oblique, crowded references to the Brookenhams' house in Buckingham Crescent, the mystery of what they live on, the four puzzling children, his own impulse (which he calls a necessary part of London 'friendship') to betray Mrs Brookenham's real age as a bit older than what she has claimed – all this testifies to what we are to see, even in the larger gatherings later on, of the hot-house atmosphere which the group has fostered, and on which it depends for its continued, if rather precarious, existence. Actually, the whole thing is much better done by James than any phrase like 'hot-house atmosphere', relevant though it is in a way, can possibly render; because all through the novel one is struck by the fact that what might so easily have turned into a bitter but rather facile denunciation of 'modern' London life, yields instead the most striking combinations of, for instance, the sheer enmity between Mrs Brookenham and her son Harold, and a kind of honesty in both of them – like most of the rest of Mrs Brook's circle, they are devious but far too intelligent to be less than honest – that is too striking to be condemned as simply degenerate. If Harold's stealing of his mother's five pounds, and his open admission of having done so, are unpleasant, the resulting dialogue between the two, in the first chapter of Book 11 ('Little Aggie'), so far from betraying any note of tired resignation or complaint on James's part, registers very clearly an open enquiry into just what will be revealed if, in a closed society, people's intelligence and intuition are such that literally nothing at all either can be, or need be, concealed. The deviousness of it all is an essential part of the game being played, but the intelligent people concerned – and they certainly include the apparently listless Mrs Brook – know all the moves, and all the intimate details of others' making the moves; and furthermore face, at least as far as they can, the consequences of such a 'knowing'.

This is a novel, then, in which the dense atmosphere of *Middlemarch* (particularly its second, more concentratedly urban, half) is narrowed to a fraction of the area George Eliot explores, but in which the resulting intensity of vision – bringing people as close together as they could possibly be brought without the social group simply exploding into fragments – is still essentially that of the social novel. *The Awkward Age* could not have been written if it had not been for James's close involvement with both the possibilities and the impossibilities of and in certain kinds of communal life.

Yet what is most interesting about this novel (and in a different way about *Victory* later on) is James's also bringing into play certain states of mind that *look* as if they are wholly the result of, say, the kind of upbringing that Nanda has had, and that the Duchess so much and so spitefully objects to, but that on inspection turn out to be also, and independently, the product of James's own feelings about certain indelible qualities in life itself. Like others of its kind, this 'middle-class' novel clearly knows that human nature – or, in wider terms, nature itself – produces behaviour that can, in certain cases, run parallel to socially induced actions, motives, feelings, but that is in fact alarmingly autonomous. Some examples from *The Awkward Age* include, for instance, Mitchy's exchange with Mrs Brookenham about himself and Nanda:

> 'I like her as much as I dare to – as much as a man can like a girl when, from the very first of his seeing her and judging her, he has also seen, and seen with all the reasons, that there's no chance for him whatever ...'
>
> 'I think you exaggerate,' his hostess replied, 'the difficulties in your way. What do you mean by "all the reasons"?'
>
> 'Why, one of them I've already mentioned. I make her flesh creep.' (ch. 111)

There could be an echo here of the comic phrase from Dickens's Fat Boy ('I wants to make your flesh creep'), but I doubt it. Mitchy's comic guise (mainly his clothes) cuts much closer to the bone than the horror-fun in *Pickwick*; and though part of the reason for it is indeed his origin as a wealthy shoe-maker's son who must feel something of a raw newcomer in the West End, both his very acute intelligence, and his honesty, reflect also the range of James's own intelligence: Nanda's antipathy to Mitchy is an antipathy that could perfectly easily be overcome if social origins were all that was in question – indeed, she likes Mitchy very much; what she can't overcome is firstly her own love for Vanderbank, and secondly a physical reaction that Mitchy's slightly comic but surely very acute phrase catches immediately: 'I make her flesh creep'.

This reaction of Nanda's is very close to Gwendolen's reaction (also quite removed from any social considerations) to Rex's too timid overtures. The parallel is not complete, because Gwendolen is never shown by George Eliot to be in love with anyone in the way Nanda clearly is with Van; and in addition, Nanda's very intelligent, but much quieter, personality means that her motives are not so much on public display as Gwendolen's, for all their tangled and partly hidden nature, sometimes are. Of the two however Nanda's motives are at least *as* telling as Gwendolen's (in the sense that they have a general, rather than just a local and psychological, interest); and in some ways the quieter presentation perhaps allows a slightly more flexible and suggestive exploration of the ways in which even the most closely knit social groups are subject to tensions, impulses, emotions that have a quite non-social origin, and so are finally beyond the control of the group itself or of anyone in it.

In this sense, perhaps the most commanding, and puzzling, fact about Nanda is her clear choice of spinsterhood, most obviously at the end of the novel, but also in fact much earlier ('I shall be one of the people who don't'). Certainly the brittleness of modern life that Mr Longdon detects and so distrusts, even as early as his first talk to Van ('You don't care, you don't care!' he says when Van airily dismisses 'friendship' to Beccles and the countryside) – this, clearly, is a determining factor. Nanda's nature is too serious to fit at all into this world. But there are other worlds, and over the run of the story as a whole the clear impression is not that Nanda is being driven into exile by London life, but that it is her own *nature* driving her to it, and so to the very sad future at the end.

It is an impulse in Nanda very close to the self-destructive, and its significance is widened by the rest of the novel giving us different, but clearly related, impulses in others of the group. Most of these are people who fit much more easily and willingly into the London life James is giving us than Nanda ever could, and so they are the more fully moulded by it. But even so, there is often a marked suggestion that their actions are more precipitate, or more extreme, than the situation necessarily demands. Thus Harold's sheer delight in a career of sponging might have been changed a bit had his upbringing been healthier, but it surely would not have been wiped out of his nature; while his father's choice of a completely separate life, ironically distanced from all the goings-on around him, is indeed *his* choice, not merely something dictated by circumstances and Mrs Brook.

But at the end of the novel, and despite her apparent control of many of the events in it, it is Mrs Brook herself who is left as the book's most isolated figure. And, paradoxically, the reasons that have driven her to this isolation have an odd kinship with the impulses in Nanda that have left her (one takes it) a perpetual spinster. Paradoxically, because the moments when Mrs Brook's self-isolating impulses are most clearly apparent tend also to be those when she is most actively concerned to close off her daughter's future.

One of the most striking scenes in this regard – one where, quite suddenly and unexpectedly, Mrs Brook seems almost as intent on bringing the whole house of cards tumbling about her own head as on keeping it up, or drawing her friends more closely round her – is the one in Book 11 ('Mrs Brook'), Chapter 11, where she 'blurts out' to Mitchy, in Van's presence, the fact that Mr Longdon has offered Van money if he will marry Nanda. Mr Longdon, of course, has been quite uncorrupt – idealistic, even – in making this offer, which is in any case one in which Mitchy not merely concurs, but wishes to share. They both wish to see any impediment there may be to Nanda's happiness removed.

Mrs Brook's interest in the matter is, however, very different from theirs. Clearly her main purpose, or one of her main purposes, is indeed to bind Van closer to her by 'exposing' him publicly, or at least in Mitchy's presence, as a man who has been made an offer of money which he has then kept to himself. She wants Van to stay with her, the star in her *own* orbit, rather than marry her daughter. If therefore she brings out the fact of Mr Longdon's offer before Van himself has told Mitchy about it (supposing he ever would), it must make Van feel so exposed, so much like a man who has been bribed to marry Nanda, that he will never do so. And, in her boldly devious way, Mrs Brook capitalises further on this by stating aloud what must indeed be Van's own near certainty: 'He thinks I want him myself.' This forces the normally safely reticent Van into an impossible situation: he must now either deny the accusation (which he cannot, because everyone present knows it is true – he does think Mrs Brook wants him herself); or he can admit it, thus increasing even further the for him quite unusual state of embarrassment into which Mrs Brook has forced him. Either way the marriage, always unlikely, is now definitely off because, as Mrs Brook again explains (tightening the noose still further), Van's pride will make it impossible for him to propose under these circumstances. Her parting dig at Van (actually just after he has left) is almost contemptuous: in his presence, she and Mitchy have agreed that the likelihood is that Mr Longdon will leave even more to Nanda if Van does not propose; and Mrs Brook keeps Mitchy behind for a moment simply to add, 'Now – by that suggestion [that is, that Nanda will benefit financially by Van's *not* proposing to her] – he has something to show. He won't go in.'

So much would seem to leave Van virtually a prisoner in Mrs Brook's circle. But the oddest twist to the whole scene is that it is Mrs Brook herself who really knows, more clearly and certainly than any of them, that this badgering of Van is quite unnecessary. In the previous chapter she has told Van, quite directly, that she is scheming for Mitchy's help as well as Mr Longdon's for Nanda's 'desolate old age'; and when he asks why, she comments:

'What can relieve me of the primary duty of taking precautions ... when I know as well as that I stand here and look at you –'
'Yes, what?' he asked as she just paused.
'Why that so far as they count on you they count, my dear Van, on a blank. .... You won't do it.'

Very true. But the more we see this, the more we must see Mrs Brook's tormenting of Van as something supererogatory. The only end it really achieves is that of making life in her drawing-room impossible for him, and so breaking up the small circle which has been her main – indeed, her only – interest in life outside the gossip provided by the carryings-on of Petherton, Mrs Donner, and others.

Nanda only cuts her*self* off from life – no doubt depriving Mitchy and others of her company, but not doing this perversely. In her mother, the same impulse is stronger still, and includes the uncontrollable and contradictory urge to twist all her moves to draw Van closer, into ones that will in fact drive him away. Mitchy's proffered explanation, that the modern girl (specifically, Aggie) 'knows too much', is part of the truth, and it is clearly meant to touch all of them, not just the women and, as Mitchy comically admits, himself. The life these people lead is so intellectual, and so very much on the defensive about emotions like the 'friendship' and love Mr Longdon wants for Nanda, that it must be unstable. But what even these facts cannot explain quite by themselves is the eagerness with which they all – particularly their leader, Mrs Brook – embrace the final isolation that comes to seem for all of them (to use that favourite, and telling, Jamesian phrase) 'a doom'.

The degree of sophistication and self-consciousness in all this – the characters' self-consciousness, but also James's own – is clearly a long way on from that given us in any of Jane Austen's novels, even the more persistently reflective ones like *Persuasion*. But this progression (in any case far from unambiguously in favour of the much more modern world rendered by James) should not be allowed to conceal the presence in the work of both writers of certain rather similar, because permanently *un*social, and unselfconscious, feelings. And I think the comparison is strengthened if we add to it some of those apparently wayward impulses in people and in nature itself that also command part of Conrad's *Victory*. Indeed reading a book like this, as also reading some of the Tales like 'The End of the Tether' or 'The Secret Sharer', brings out some key facts about Conrad rather more obviously than does a book like *Nostromo*, though this is certainly a more massive, and also I think far greater, work. Like the rest of Conrad, the *Tales* and *Victory* realise very strongly the stabilising force of a conventional, 'middle-class' society and even economy; but they also put a bit more into prominence both the strains inherent in the very notion of such societies (Heyst's upbringing is a case in point), and the strongly *un*balancing but potentially productive forces of some impulses in human – and indeed non-human – nature itself. In terms of *Victory*, what I mean here is not so much the paragraphs of rather over-declamatory prose about every age being 'fed on illusions, lest men should renounce life early and the human race come to an end ...', and 'Man on this earth' being 'an unforeseen accident which does not stand close investigation ...' – these, like roughly comparable passages in Hardy, spoil the author's best insights by turning them into stiffish, rather literal-minded pronouncements that are not nearly adaptable enough to fit the changing facts that the tale itself produces. What strikes one much more forcibly is Conrad's ability to call to mind certain totally ordinary, day-to-day things in such a way as to put the solid realities of life cheek-by-jowl with its totally unpredictable qualities. For instance, Chapter IX of Part IV gives us Heyst's rage at the absurdity of his having nothing better than blunt kitchen knives to defend Lena against the three bandits: 'Absolute rubbish – neither edge, point, nor substance. I believe one of these forks would make a better weapon at a pinch. But can I go about with a fork in my pocket?'

This is the very best of Conradian comedy, and it is continued in Heyst's reflections that there might perhaps be a crowbar or so in one of the sheds, but he has given up the keys anyway. 'And then, do you see me walking about with a crowbar in my hand? Ha, ha! . . .' One might call it pre-absurdist comedy, and indeed it is a kind of comedy that has all the unstressed but perfectly real element of pain that Beckett, for instance, renders in his plays thirty or forty years later. But what differentiates Conrad from later writers in roughly the same vein is that, in *Victory*, the notion of the 'absurd' is only one element (though admittedly crucial) in an otherwise stable universe. To a Beckett, the spectacle of gentleman Jones in his dressing-gown 'executing a dance of rage in the middle of the floor' would be the centre of the whole tale: 'Heyst looked on, fascinated by this skeleton in a gay dressing-gown, jerkily agitated like a grotesque toy on the end of an invisible string. It became quiet suddenly.' (IV, xi)

To Conrad – as the sanity of his prose, in particular, demonstrates – Jones is only one element in the story. He is crucial certainly, but crucial in the sense that he is, like Pedro, Ricardo, Schomberg, one of those things that just will not fit into what is nevertheless a solid, logically predictable world. Conrad sees the world (as Hardy, though in very different terms, also sees it) as a place where most things fit together and make sense, but where a few do not and never will. And it is not that we haven't yet learnt or seen why they do not. Neither of these writers is tempted to look to some 'beyond' where, when all is known, all will be made clear. Indeed, very few English novelists are. To all these writers it is the collocation of the stability of things, and a certain oddness – even instability – in them, which is permanent, challenging and far beyond the reach either of any social change, or of any metaphysical or religious insight.

9 Hardy's Universe: *Tess of the d'Urbervilles*

Hardy said once that all he really wanted to be was 'A good hand at a serial'. And of *Tess of the d'Urbervilles* itself he adds in the Preface to the fifth edition, July 1892, '. . . the novel was intended to be neither didactic nor aggressive, but in the scenic parts to be representative simply, and in the contemplative to be oftener charged with impressions than with convictions . . .' Well, if these statements are meant as some sort of contrast to the muddle that goes on in late Meredith novels, for instance, they are certainly true. They are also true if we think of the genuine complexity of, say, *The Portrait of a Lady*, first published ten years before *Tess* (1891). On the other hand, phrases of Hardy's like 'representative simply' cannot possibly cover prose like this:

> At half-past six the sun settled down upon the levels, with the aspect of a great forge in the heavens, and presently a monstrous pumpkin-like moon arose on the other hand. The pollard willows, tortured out of their natural shape by incessant choppings, became spiny-haired monsters as they stood up against it. She went in, and upstairs without a light. (ch. XXVIII)

That might almost as easily have come from, say, the early Patrick White writing in the 1950s, as from Hardy or anybody of his generation. The fact of the matter is that Hardy is a more extraordinary writer than his own disclaimers would allow or even hint. He is clearly right about the very telling simplicity in the best of his tales: 'A good hand at a serial' indeed. But all his own statements miss the still more extraordinary combination of this simplicity with an adventurousness of thought, and so of writing, that makes him in my opinion unique.

I have picked *Tess* to concentrate on here because I think it is the best of Hardy's novels, and also because I think it shows, more clearly than anything else he wrote, an effortless combination of simplicity and sheer inventiveness. At first glance, this looks a ridiculous claim to make.

If *Tess* hasn't got anything like the hanging of the children in *Jude* ('Done because we are too menny'), it does have the sentimental coincidence of Tess's honeymoon happening at what had been a d'Urberville mansion; of Angel's brother happening to probe the hedge with his umbrella at just the spot where Tess had left her boots when she changed, after the long walk to Emminster, into the pretty shoes Angel had given her; the fact that Alec's blood soaks through Mrs Brooks's ceiling in the shape of a 'gigantic ace of hearts', and so on. In adition, there are whole passages of writing in parts of the novel that are notoriously and obviously loaded. It is of course a disaster for the Durbeyfields that their horse Prince is killed by the mail-cart, and in a way the fact that it is a chance occurrence like this that drives Tess into Alec's arms is tellingly true to Hardy's sense of the world we live in. But none of this justifies the over-specific and literal-minded interpretation put on the incident by Tess and young Abraham, both of them pretty obviously philosophising in Hardy's name:

> 'Did you say the stars were worlds, Tess?'
> 'Yes.'
> 'All like ours?'
> 'I don't know; but I think so. They sometimes seem to be like the apples on our stubbard-tree. Most of them splendid and sound – a few blighted.'
> 'Which do we live on – a splendid one or a blighted one?'
> 'A blighted one.'
> ''Tis very unlucky that we didn't pitch on a sound one, when there were so many more of 'em!' (ch. iv)

Then a couple of pages later and after the accident we get Abraham's famous, or infamous, summing-up: ''Tis because we be on a blighted star, and not a sound one, isn't it, Tess?'

It is not really to the point to say, as so many reviews at the time and later have said, that this is the author speaking through the characters. (Why shouldn't he, if he has something interesting to say?) The trouble here is that Hardy has slipped, momentarily, into a stiffly synoptic, summarising view of things that simply is not true to the facts his own novel renders. Because, in the first place, Hardy appears not to have noticed the discrepancy between Tess's claim that she thinks all the stars are 'like ours', and her following statement that most of them are 'splendid'; and in the second place, as Hardy perfectly well knows and as he shows elsewhere in the book, any notions of translating Tess and the rest of us to a 'splendid star' would be oversimplifying day-dreaming. The terms and tone of all his best work, verse and prose alike, declare with perfect confidence that there are none such.

On the other hand, and far more characteristically, even this scene from Chapter iv about the killing of Prince has much stronger and truer writing in it, including some that is on the same topic – the world and universe we live in. For instance, the description of the actual accident, though it has one or two rather stiffly literary phrases in it, comes across as completely unpretentious and tellingly direct:

The pointed shaft of the cart had entered the breast of the unhappy Prince like a sword, and from the wound his life's blood was spouting in a stream, and falling with a hiss into the road.

In her despair Tess sprang forward and put her hand upon the hole, with the only result that she became splashed from face to skirt with the crimson drops. Then she stood helplessly looking on. Prince also stood firm and motionless as long as he could; till he suddenly sank down in a heap.

By this time the mail-cart man had joined her, and began dragging and unharnessing the hot form of Prince .

'You was on the wrong side', he said. 'I am bound to go on with the mailbags, so that the best thing for you to do is to bide here with your load. I'll send somebody to help you as soon as I can. It is getting daylight, and you have nothing to fear.'

Certainly there is no hint of sentimentality or melodrama in the mail-cart man's brief, unpretentious speech. It presents quite simply the factual truth; something that Hardy does not attempt either to gloss over or to magnify beyond its natural significance.

The paragraph that follows is obviously wider in import. The Hardy 'universe' or world-view is indeed taking a more direct hand here:

He mounted and sped on his way; while Tess stood and waited. The atmosphere turned pale, the birds shook themselves in the hedges, arose, and twittered; the lane showed all its white features, and Tess showed hers, still whiter. The huge pool of blood in front of her was already assuming the iridescence of coagulation; and when the sun rose a hundred prismatic hues were reflected from it. Prince lay along-side still and stark; his eyes half open, the hole in his chest looking scarcely large enough to have let out all that had animated him.

But unlike young Abraham's sentence ("'Tis because we be on a blighted star . . .'), this paragraph, though quite unblinking in its depiction of the blood on the road, the hole in Prince's chest, the indifference of the natural life around to Tess and her plight, does not close its options there. What further 'options', if that is the word for it, Hardy can see or sense he does not attempt to summarise, at least at this early stage. But nor does he, so far as I can detect, resort to any sentimental bitterness in this contrast between the wretchedness of the girl and the calmly understated beauty of the morning around her. Even the coagulating blood, despite the periphrasis that so many people have objected to ('the iridescence of coagulation'), is beautiful, and the irony that contrasts this unpretentious beauty in the whole scene with Tess's is not of a kind that makes the natural scene (including the blood) a hollow mockery. It is as if Hardy were saying – and indeed I think that something like this is what his whole novel *is* saying, though it's tactfully unspelt out here – that the ugly hole in Prince's chest, and the simple naturalness of the morning, are and always will be at once incompatible (in the sense that no holistic notions of the universe can possibly reconcile them) and truly facts.

Writing like this seems to me distinguished, and distinguished in the sense that it manages to be at once perfectly individual (including the slight tendency to periphrasis), and also representative of some of the strongest and best insights of its period. Nobody but Hardy could possibly have written this; yet the passage is at the same time intensely representative. There is a strain of what one might call *positive* agnosticism in a whole cluster of very different writers from essayists like Mill and Arnold, through novelists like George Eliot, Conrad, James, even perhaps early Lawrence (though obviously Lawrence, at least, would have shuddered at the mere use of the term). It is a philosophy of doubt, certainly, but one that also hints or adumbrates possibilities rather than simply a succession of negations. Hardy's own particular world is one where, if one may deny his own rather bitter joke from *The Woodlanders*, the 'Unfulfilled Intention' is crucially *not* that, because clearly there was no such intention in the first place. In Hardy at his best (including the best parts of *The Woodlanders* itself), and in different ways in other nineteenth- and early twentieth-century writers, the universe we live in is a universe *part* of which continues to make clear and good sense, part does not and never will. Hardy's real challenge is to say to us, why assume that nothing is good and valuable unless it is or might be part of an unseen whole? There is another possibility, namely that the existence of certain obvious and permanent injustices – facts of experience that are unjustifiable in any terms, human or divine – does not negate or even weaken the rightness and trueness of other pieces, large and small, of life.

Two other, still more characteristic, pieces of Hardy may help to justify this reading of him. Like other Hardy novels, *Tess* includes a lot of descriptions of landscapes in which people and objects move like automatons. The first paragraph, for instance, reads:

On an evening in the latter part of May a middle-aged man was walking homeward from Shaston to the village of Marlott, in the adjoining Vale of Blakemore or Blackmoor. The pair of legs that carried him were rickety, and there was a bias in his gait which inclined him somewhat to the left of a straight line. He occasionally gave a smart nod, as if in confirmation of some opinion, though he was not thinking of anything in particular. An empty egg-basket was slung upon his arm, the nap of his hat was ruffled, a patch being quite worn away at its brim where his thumb came in taking it off. Presently he was met by an elderly parson astride on a gray mare, who, as he rode, hummed a wandering tune.

Durbeyfield's half-sober ruminations are characteristic of him personally, of course; but more than this, the jerky gait and bearing of that figure – and at this stage he is no more than that, an impersonal figure in the land-scape – is characteristic Hardy, a small but very telling instance of his view of man's role in a universe that can be at once full of promise (though not particularly here), and also completely indifferent to any notion of individual volition or will. This I think is the point of and in the good-humoured portrayal of Durbeyfield in those passive impersonal terms: 'The pair of legs that carried him ...'; 'a bias in his gait ... inclined him somewhat to the left of a straight line ...' 'An empty egg-basket was slung upon his arm, the nap of his hat was ruffled ...' In different but related terms later on we get Tess not so much dwarfed, as effortlessly ignored, by the rich valley of the Froom which she has just entered; and later still the two girls at Flintcomb-Ash, seen from a distance and looking like flies crawling over the face of a huge expanse.

The second of the two passages I want to quote makes this point, of an individualism that is all the time mixed in with inflexible laws of conduct and behaviour, in absolutely typical Hardy prose. This is the scene where Tess takes her baby to the wheat-reaping and binding, and despite what must have been, for Hardy, a strong temptation to abuse society and the Fates for crushing Tess further, the irony here is open-minded, intelligent and interested in its object:

But of all ruddy things that morning the brightest were two broad arms of painted wood, which rose from the margin of a yellow corn-field hard by Marlott village. They, with two others below, formed the revolving Maltese cross of the reaping-machine, which had been brought to the field on the previous evening ... The paint with which they were smeared, intensified in hue by the sunlight, imparted to them a look of having been dipped in liquid fire ...

Two groups, one of men and lads, the other of women, had come down the lane just at the hour when the shadows of the eastern hedge-top struck the west hedge midway, so that the heads of the groups were enjoying sunrise while their feet were still in the dawn. They disappeared from the lane between the two stone posts which flanked the nearest field-gate.

Presently there arose from within a ticking like the love-making of the grasshopper. The machine had begun, and a moving concatena-tion of three horses and the aforesaid long rickety machine was visible over the gate ... Along one side of the field the whole wain went, the arms of the mechanical reaper revolving slowly, till it passed down the hill quite out of sight. In a minute it came up on the other side of the field at the same equable pace; the glistening brass star in the forehead of the fore horse first catching the eye as it rose into view over the stubble, then the bright arms, and then the whole machine. (ch. xiv)

If it weren't that the passage is so good, I would be tempted to call this a Hardy manifesto, and one that makes him a leader in nineteenth-century thought. But the passage resists labels of the manifesto kind, and so I will simply claim that this *is* Hardy: the quality of movement, for one thing, concentrates the very essence of his beliefs and feelings. And I take it, from reading this scene and others like it in Hardy, that these beliefs and feelings are such as have no truck either with synoptic, holistic views of life and the universe, or with any that see life as only meaningless chaos.

For instance, I believe that Hardy's point here includes a perfectly good-humoured comment on the sheer irrelevance, to any hopes or despairs Tess might have at this moment, of the attractiveness of the brightly painted arms of the machine rising above the yellow cornfield and just now touched by the rising sun ('... dipped in liquid fire'). On the other hand, what he shows in addition to the tragedy threatening Tess is that the scene's attraction is perfectly genuine, as also, of course, is Tess's own. There is no purely destructive or negative irony at work here. Hardy is quite confident in his beliefs: in part the scene he renders is indeed true, fruitful and meaningful; in part it is not and never will be.

What of Tess herself, though, and the other human beings — even the ineffectual Angel – who are in fact caught up in all this? The above account is still too limited to include their part fully, and if left alone would be an incomplete account of the novel.

One difficulty in deciding what part Hardy intends people to play in the world as he sees it is, notoriously, the characters of the two men in Tess's life. From the early reviews onwards, a majority of readers has seen Tess as splendidly done by Hardy, but one or both of Alec and Angel as feebly drawn. Clearly there is a good deal more than a grain of truth in this accusation, but I would myself want to distinguish Hardy's presentation of Alec very sharply from his indeed feeble presentation of Angel Clare. On the whole, Alec seems to me well done. Admittedly, some of the early scenes where he appears are dismayingly melodramatic. The short review in *Punch* of 27 February 1892 said, "'Tis a great pity that such a penny-plain-and two-pence-coloured scoundrel should have been allowed so strong a part among Mr Hardy's excellent and un-conventional *dramatis personae*', and indeed one can see why *Punch*, along with a good many other reviews, should have said this: 'D'Urberville looked round upon her, nipped his cigar with the tips of his large white centre-teeth, and allowed his lips to smile slowly of themselves.' But in fact most of Hardy's description of that ride to Trantridge is good. The *Punch* parody of it ('Aha! a day will come! ... She must and shall be mine!') is wide of the mark because it exaggerates the melodrama, and at the same time ignores both a sensuous openness in Alec's behaviour and the consequence of this, namely a very real personal relationship already springing up between him and Tess. More true to the real spirit of the scene than the quotation about Alec's large white centre-teeth is this account of the first ride downhill:

> Down, down, they sped, the wheels humming like a top, the dog-cart rocking right and left . . . the figure of the horse rising and falling in undulations before them. Sometimes a wheel was off the ground, it seemed, for many yards; sometimes a stone was sent spinning over the hedge, and flinty sparks from the horse's hoofs outshone the daylight. The aspect of the straight road enlarged with their advance, the two banks dividing like a splitting stick; one rushing past at each shoulder.
>
> The wind blew through Tess's white muslin to her very skin, and her washed hair flew out behind. She was determined to show no open fear, but she clutched d'Urberville's rein-arm . . . (ch. VIII)

At this point Alec persuades her to clutch his waist instead, as safer; and then finally, threatening her with another downhill ride, to let him kiss her:

> He was inexorable, and she sat still, and d'Urberville gave her the kiss of mastery. No sooner had he done so than she flushed with shame, took out her handkerchief, and wiped the spot on her cheek that had been touched by his lips. His ardour was nettled at the sight, for the act on her part had been unconsciously done.

The scene ends with Tess's stratagem (later on both Alec and Angel are to accuse her of many more) of making her hat blow off so that she can get out of the dog-cart, and Alec is left stranded.

The whole Trantridge sequence, including this ride and also Tess with her 'community of fowls' in the thatched cottage, presages others in the novel that show her as sharing, however unwittingly, some at least of Alec's physicality and sensuousness. Despite some of Hardy's emptier protestations ('Why it was that upon this beautiful feminine tissue, sensitive as gossamer, and practically blank as snow as yet, there should have been traced such a coarse pattern as it was doomed to receive . . .'), Alec is important in the novel, and the relationship between the two of them essentially convincing. Tess herself puts one side of this explicitly to Angel at the end, when he discovers her in Sandbourne (Chapter LV): 'He has won me back to him.' Before this, and more actively on Tess's part (though less consciously) we have seen her in the wheatfield 'holding the corn in an embrace like that of a lover' (Chapter XIV); appearing to Angel at Talbothays with 'the suspended attitude of a friendly leopard at pause' (Chapter XXX); and being accused at various times by both Alec and Angel of 'tantalising' and tempting appearance and behaviour. Indeed Alec, in his period of conversion, makes her swear on what he thinks is a holy cross that she will never tempt him again 'by your charms or ways'. (The impact of this is not entirely lost, I think, by the heavy irony of Hardy's then introducing a labourer who explains to Tess that this is no cross at all, but simply 'a thing of ill-omen' marking the burial-place of someone who was tortured and hanged because he sold his soul to the devil.) Of course, Tess is not *consciously* a temptress, let alone, as Angel claims at Talbothays, 'almost a coquette' or a flirt. It is simply a very real and convincing part of her nature and physique that, unlike Angel, she is actively sexual.

All these hints, and more besides in the novel, make the bond between Tess and Alec much more convincing than her union with Angel. Hardy's hesitations about Angel's role in Tess's life are explicit in these few sentences from Chapter xxxvi (italics mine): 'It was the third day of the estrangement. Some might risk the odd paradox that with more animalism he would have been the nobler man. *We do not say it.* Yet Clare's love was doubtless ethereal to a fault, imaginative to impracticability.'

Why on earth not say it, especially when everything in the honeymoon scenes in particular has shown it to be true? Of course, Hardy does have his criticisms of Clare ('ethereal to a fault'); but he seems reluctant to press these, or admit the particular significance for Tess of the man's nature and behaviour. The question at issue is not exactly one of Hardy's 'characterization' of Angel. Indeed, in itself this seems reasonably well done, at least to the point where it is quite possible to believe in those four girls (especially Tess in reaction against her seduction by Alec) falling in love with the 'Mr Clare' who comes to Talbothays and plays the harp. What I cannot see is that Hardy has put enough in Angel to make one believe that two of the four could have their whole lives ruined as a result, and that Tess's tragedy is bound up with her losing something worth while in him. There was never all that much to lose (or for Liza-Lu, at the end, to gain!), and so the story of Tess's life and death misses a bit of the sharpness it has elsewhere in the book. Certainly this relative blankness in Angel Clare seems much more of an issue than Alec's seduction of Tess earlier. Hardy is perhaps a bit too polite or hesitant about this latter point ('The Maiden'/'Maiden No More'); though I think there is no doubt that it was seduction, not rape. But he is far less ambiguous about the whole incident than he is about how worth while he intends Angel really to be.

Fortunately, there is so much that is solid and worth while in the novel as a whole that in the end Hardy's hesitations over Angel do not weigh all that heavily in the scale. *Tess of the d'Urbervilles* seems to me one of the really great novels in English and at the same time, particularly in the person of Tess herself, one of the most unusual. When nineteenth-century writers attempt to link intelligent and attractive women to markedly artistic or scholarly men, even the greatest falter a bit. And they falter not so much about the men, as in developing and placing the idealist impulses that must be a real part of such a woman's make-up. I don't think Hardy does with Tess. She seems to me clearly the most impressive of his women, and this impressiveness includes a radical innocence of a kind that would have been dangerous ground for Dickens, and very probably also for George Eliot, Conrad, or Henry James.

One of the most impressive things about Tess is something I have already mentioned – the physicality, even seductiveness, that Hardy gives her. In the best scenes, this is clearly and confidently linked to answering qualities in the natural world around her:

... Angel entered, and went through the silent passages of the house to the back quarters, where he listened for a moment. Sustained snores came from the cart-house, where some of the men were lying down; the grunt and squeal of sweltering pigs arose from the still further distance. The large-leaved rhubarb and cabbage plants slept too, their broad limp surfaces hanging in the sun like half-closed umbrellas ...
She had not heard him enter, and hardly realized his presence there. She was yawning, and he saw the red interior of her mouth as if it had been a snake's. She had stretched one arm so high above her coiled-up cable of hair that he could see its satin delicacy above the sunburn; her face was flushed with sleep, and her eyelids hung heavy over their pupils. The brim-fulness of her nature breathed from her. It was a moment when a woman's soul is more incarnate than at any other time; when the most spiritual beauty bespeaks itself flesh; and sex takes the outside place in the presentation. (ch. XXVII)

There are some over-literary phrases here ('the most spiritual beauty bespeaks itself flesh') that are clearly at odds with the sweltering pigs and the snoring men. More seriously, later on in the Talbothays scenes, Hardy is tempted into a disastrous literal-mindedness in his attempts to link the human and the natural: 'In this way Clare persistently wooed her in undertones like that of the purling milk – at the cow's side, at skimmings, at butter-makings, at cheese-makings, among broody poultry, and among farrowing pigs ...' (ch. XXIX)

He would; 'purling milk' is about right for Angel, though Hardy will not admit this openly. But whenever the scenes focus on Tess herself, as for instance in the quotation above from Chapter XXVII, the openness and frankness with which Hardy presents her attractions as a woman quite easily prevent the sort of idealising of womankind that bedevils most nineteenth-century novels, including some major ones like *Middlemarch*.

The way Hardy deploys this quality in Tess, and links it with his other themes and interest, can perhaps best be described in terms of Tess's journeying – it comes to have some of the qualities of fable, but with all the actuality of life pressing in on her too – her journeying from her home district, through the rich valley of the Froom to Talbothays, and then to Flintcomb-Ash and beyond. In outline these contrasts (for instance between Talbothays and Flintcomb-Ash) look merely notional – an over-obvious fable indeed, in which an innocent girl is removed from the safety of her home and Talbothays to suffer the rigours of the sterile uplands and, finally, death for ancestral faults or crimes. In fact, the three key places in this journeying – Tess's home, Talbothays and Flintcomb-Ash – are each so real that no dangers of this kind, or very few, threaten the commandingly simple outline of the book or detract from the poignancy of her death.

Her life at home is certainly real, and it is also worth while – more so, I think, than is generally recognised. Most of those early scenes in the novel, including Durbeyfield himself, but especially Joan, cradle-rocking on the flagstone floor of the untidy cottage, water and washing suds dribbling from her elbows, and singing away at 'The Spotted Cow' (or whatever other ballad she has caught) are excellent. Together they represent one of those rare sequences in English literature (Lawrence has others) that capture a quality of and in working-class life that offers to the Tesses and the Annas and even the Paul Morels a point of vantage. As with the Morel household in Lawrence, all the Durbeyfield untidiness, irresponsibility and drunkenness somehow includes moments of comic surety denied to more sophisticated, self-conscious generations. Hardy doesn't blink at the nastiness of this life, any more than Lawrence does. There is no doubt whatsoever that Durbeyfield drunk, or even sober, is a mindless daydreamer who will do his family no good whatsoever, and possibly a deal of harm. Nevertheless, scenes like the return home from Rolliver's in Chapter IV show a kind of instinctive sanity in this life that even its degenerate qualities cannot entirely negate. Hardy's simple, unpretentious realism renders the ugliness of the scene far better than, say, Dickens's more excited prose could do: 'They went home together, Tess holding one arm of her father, and Mrs Durbeyfield the other.' At the same time the comedy of it all, with the two women trying to steer 'Sir John' home in a reasonably straight line, is equally telling: 'On reaching the fresh air he was sufficiently unsteady to incline the row of three at one moment as if they were marching to London, and at another, as if they were marching to Bath . . .'

Tess's first move out of this village life is to Trantridge, Alec and the first phase of that very telling relationship. Her next move, to Talbothays, is in all sorts of ways more singular still. In outline, Talbothays may seem to resemble a pastoral idyll, a haven of retreat from the hurry and bustle of modern life. In actual fact, Hardy renders it as both quite remarkable, and demandingly real. A perfectly ordinary milking scene, from the end of Chapter XVI, makes the point:

They were the less restful cows that were stalled. Those that would stand still of their own will were milked in the middle of the yard, where many of such better behaved ones stood waiting now – all prime milchers, such as were seldom seen out of this valley, and not always within it . . . Their large-veined udders hung ponderous as sandbags, the teats sticking out like the legs of a gipsy's crock; and as each animal lingered for her turn to arrive the milk oozed forth and fell in drops to the ground.

By any standards this is remarkable prose, most particularly, of course, the last sentence. Virtually nobody one can think of in English literature after Shakespeare can show that sort of confidence in the physicality of nature and in its details: 'Their large-veined udders hung ponderous as sandbags, the teats sticking out like the legs of a gipsy's crock . . . the milk oozed forth and fell in drops to the ground.'

That is one of the more original pieces from the Talbothays sequence. Some other of Hardy's best renderings of the impact of such a place on Tess, in fact the majority of them, are less obviously noticeable. For instance, his 'Phase the Third: the Rally' begins, far less ostentatiously than the title would lead you to expect,

On a thyme-scented, bird-hatching morning in May, between two and three years after the return from Trantridge – silent reconstructive years for Tess Durbeyfield – she left her home for the second time.

Having packed up her luggage so that it could be sent to her later, she started in a hired trap for the little town of Stourcastle . . . (ch. xvi)

The opening phrases of this have the slight oddness so characteristic of Hardy (a 'bird-hatching morning'), and so are tinged, very aptly, with Hardy's own sense for the incongruity of things. But the oddness is not in the least insisted on here. On the contrary, the writing stays on the whole perfectly neutral-toned and unremarkable. Even the parenthetical phrase – 'silent reconstructive years for Tess Durbeyfield' – which, except for the country name, might have come from some more sophisticated or intellectually minded novelist, is here played down. Hardy simply shows Tess doing what must be done, and doing it with no fuss and very little of the self-conscious concern that naturally has to affect more educated and sophisticated characters in the modern novel: '. . . she left her home for the second time.'

The rest of the Talbothays sequence follows much the same note and gives us a quite remarkable girl, Tess, in surroundings that are, as Tess herself also is, unstrainedly natural. In a sense, this is comparatively easy for Hardy to do, because Tess has not the burden of self-consciousness that other nineteenth- and twentieth-century heroines, even at the age of twenty, often have. She is a country girl, and the country is not relevant in any obvious way to modern life, nor modern life to it. But the chapters are the reverse of escapist or incidental, and one reason for this is the demanding, day-to-day reality of Tess's life at the farm and of her response to this life. The place is extraordinary, even in Hardy's own agricultural world; at the same time there is more here that one can recognise as familiar than in most literature in English about the country-side:

> Dairyman Crick kept his shirt-sleeves permanently rolled up from Monday to Saturday; open windows had no effect in ventilation without open doors, and in the dairy-garden the blackbirds and thrushes crept about under the currant-bushes ... The flies in the kitchen were lazy, teasing, and familiar, crawling about in unwonted places, on the floors, into drawers, and over the backs of the milkmaids' hands ... (ch. xxiv)

These stubborn practicalities are so interwoven with the daily life at Talbothays, and so much part of Tess's own person and personality, that even the generally rather flimsy Angel takes on enough substance to make him a real issue, at least for Tess herself. He has his moments, such as perhaps, in his coy way, during the rainy drive with the milk to the station, or when he carries all four girls through the flooded part of the road on the way to church (fortunately the early version, in which Hardy gave Angel a wheelbarrow to carry them in, has sunk into oblivion). The strongest forces in him are not revealed until the sleep-walking scene during the honeymoon, and then only momentarily; but at Tal-bothays there is enough of him, just, for us to allow full credibility to the extraordinary, absolutely single-minded devotion that springs up in Tess:

> 'Do you care for me? I wish you would prove it in some way.'
> 'How can I prove it more than I have done?' she cried, in a distrac-tion of tenderness. 'Will this prove it more?'
> She clasped his neck, and for the first time Clare learnt what an impassioned woman's kisses were like upon the lips of one whom she loved with all her heart and soul, as Tess loved him. (ch. xxx)

But the general significance of Talbothays for Tess, and also for Hardy, is caught perhaps best of all in the brilliant scene at the end of Chapter xx, when Tess and Angel are seen wandering about alone at dawn, just before milking. These are the 'non-human hours', as Hardy calls them, that bring out most strongly the compelling and unusual mixture of the ordinary and the extraordinary that pervades the whole of the Talbothays sequence:

> They could then see the faint summer fogs in layers, woolly, level, and apparently no thicker than counterpanes, spread about the meadows in detached remnants of small extent. On the gray moisture of the grass were marks where the cows had lain through the night – dark-green islands of dry herbage the size of their carcasses, in the general

sea of dew. From each island proceeded a serpentine trail, by which the cow had rambled away to feed after getting up, at the end of which trail they found her; the snoring puff from her nostrils, when she recognized them, making an intenser little fog of her own amid the prevailing one . . .

Minute diamonds of moisture from the mist hung, too, upon Tess's eyelashes, and drops upon her hair, like seed pearls. When the day grew quite strong and commonplace these dried off her; moreover, Tess then lost her strange and ethereal beauty; her teeth, lips, and eyes scintillated in the sunbeams, and she was again the dazzlingly fair dairymaid only, who had to hold her own against the other women of the world . . .

The milking progressed, till towards the end Tess and Clare, in common with the rest, could hear the heavy breakfast table dragged out from the wall in the kitchen by Mrs Crick, this being the invariable preliminary to each meal; the same horrible scrape accompanying its return journey when the table had been cleared.

It is as if Hardy were saying, here is a place brimful of natural energies and life, but one where the details, when you really look at them, are just slightly askew. It is not so much that the 'horrible scrape' of the table jars against what would otherwise be a serene pastoralism, but rather that the scrape of the table is as natural as nature itself, though distinctly not part of it. Even the cows, which obviously are part of nature, are tinged very aptly by Hardy's querying mind: those serpentine trails, purposefully yet in a way irrationally wandering to feeding places, and each in the very pleasing oddness of 'the snoring puff from her nostrils . . . making an intenser fog of her own amid the prevailing one'.

Tess's journey to Flintcomb-Ash clinches certain disjunctions in the Hardy universe that were imminent, and I would be pretty sure intended, in the presentation of an almost threateningly fruitful Talbothays. At first glance, Flintcomb-Ash is perhaps a little close to an over-simple, merely illustrative contrast to Talbothays. Moreover, these chapters have one or two passages in which Hardy's over-insistence on the alienness of the world now facing Tess produces some notoriously literal-minded, even silly writing. The birds 'from behind the North Pole' are perhaps the worst example of Hardy straining his beliefs to breaking point:

> . . . gaunt spectral creatures with tragical eyes – eyes which had witnessed scenes of cataclysmal horror in inaccessible polar regions of a magnitude such as no human being had ever conceived, in curdling temperatures that no man could endure . . . been half blinded by the whirl of colossal storms and terraqueous distortions; and retained the expression of feature that such scenes had engendered. (ch. XLIII)

The prose is uncomfortably inflated (to put it mildly) and quite uncharacteristic of the best of the Flintcomb scenes. Hardy's attempts to bring the polysyllables back into contact with ordinary life merely underline how badly he has gone astray: 'These nameless birds came quite near to Tess and Marian, but of all they had seen which humanity would never see, they brought no account.'

Fortunately, one might add. Because the straining after meaning ends with that paragraph, and for the rest one is mainly conscious of detail and description that is far less pretentious than this, and that renders a threat much more real than any the birds themselves ever dreamt of. Tess is now high up on the table-land that divides her own childhood valley from Talbothays. 'Here the air was dry and cold, and the long cartroads were blown white and dusty within a few hours after rain.' Again, as at Talbothays, it is simple detail like this and the work in the field that renders Hardy's real meaning: this is no simple contrast to the sometimes oppressive fruitfulness of Talbothays, but a scene that asks the question, how far, if at all, can the two districts be thought of as part of the same country? The most threatening possibility is not that they cannot, but that parts of them can, while others remain forever disjunct:

> The upper half of each turnip had been eaten off by the live-stock, and it was the business of the two women to grub up the lower or earthy half of the root with a hooked fork called a hacker, that it might be eaten also. Every leaf of the vegetable having already been consumed, the whole field was in colour a desolate drab; it was a complexion without features, as if a face, from chin to brow, should be only an expanse of skin. The sky wore, in another colour, the same likeness ... So these two upper and nether visages confronted each other all day long, the white face looking down on the brown face, and the brown face looking up at the white face, without anything standing between them but the two girls crawling over the surface of the former like flies. (ch. XLIII)

Quite obviously this is a farm and a part of England that is not merely physically more demanding than anything could be at Talbothays, but also grimly sterile where that was fruitful, a piece of country *asking* to be farmed and enjoyed. What is still more disturbing about Flintcomb-Ash, however, is that there is a kind of beauty here too, an absoluteness that also asks to be admired. One might have expected, given the run of the story and of Tess's career to date, *simple* sterility and ugliness, all set in opposition to the farm where Tess had met and married Angel. In fact, there is a bare finality here, a sense of completeness and rightness that rivals, and in certain ways exceeds, the scenes we have by now grown used to in the valley. What jars in the Flintcomb scenes – quite deliberately and rightly on Hardy's part – is the fact that the ugly reality of hacking swedes is somehow part of a geometrical simplicity that Talbothays must, by its very nature, lack:

The wide acreage of blank agricultural brownness, apparent where the swedes had been pulled, was beginning to be striped in wales of darker brown, gradually broadening to ribands. Along the edge of each of these something crept upon ten legs, moving without haste and without rest up and down the whole length of the field; it was two horses and a man, the plough going between them, turning up the cleared ground for a spring sowing. (ch. XLVI)

The last sections of the novel, when Tess has left Flintcombe-Ash, continue the same outlook of Hardy's, but he does add one new and very significant element. Tess leaves Flintcomb-Ash just after one of the novel's most impressive scenes, the building of the straw-rick. This scene dominates the whole ending of the book more significantly than any of the ones, such as the operatic Stonehenge scene, that actually end it. In the straw-rick scene, Alec is waiting to press his claims on her. He is dressed now as a sporting character ('a little ratting was always done'), while Tess, very much on the contrary, is a field-woman, untying the sheaves of wheat that have to be fed ceaselessly to the threshing machine.

Hardy's brief introduction of machinery from the North, and his engineman – 'He served fire and smoke; these denizens of the field served vegetation, weather, frost and sun' – seems to me very impressive indeed, and impressive because, whatever his conscious intentions, he is very far from condemning this invasion. At this late stage in the novel he adds a new element, and it is one which, though obviously doubtful about it, he also admires. The whole thing is very similar to Dickens earlier on with railways. Ideologically, to both Dickens and Hardy, machinery is bad simply because it is mechanical, not natural. In fact, both recognise rather more power and justness in this relatively new phenomenon than most later writers can bring themselves to do:

A panting ache ran through the rick. The man who fed was weary, and Tess could see that the red nape of his neck was encrusted with dirt and husks. She still stood at her post, her flushed and perspiring face coated with the corn-dust, and her white bonnet embrowned by it. ... The incessant quivering, in which every fibre of her frame participated, had thrown her into a stupefied reverie in which her arms worked on independently of her consciousness. ...

By degrees the freshest among them began to grow cadaverous and saucer-eyed. Whenever Tess lifted her head she beheld always the great upgrown straw-stack, with the men in shirt-sleeves upon it, against the gray north sky; in front of it the long red elevator ... on which a perpetual stream of threshed straw ascended, a yellow river running up-hill, and spouting out on the top of the rick. (ch. XLVIII)

For all the very real exhaustion and pain this process causes Tess, 'shaken bodily by its spinning . . . cadaverous and saucer-eyed', it is pretty clearly felt by Hardy as an almost illimitable energy, suddenly introduced into a world whose energies had up to now been simply natural ('weather, frost and sun'). In a way, it is easier for Hardy to recognise this than for writers like Lawrence, oppressed by a whole society dominated by money and machinery. Even by the standards of the 1880s and 1890s, Hardy was talking in terms of isolated communities, relatively unaffected by what had begun to dominate the Midlands and the North at least fifty years earlier, or, if we think more particularly of the cotton-spinning districts, seventy or eighty years earlier. For all this, his look at this new phenomenon that life has thrown up, and that all his instincts must surely have led him to distrust, is not in the least hysterical or frightened: 'The man who fed was weary, and Tess could see that the red nape of his neck was encrusted with dirt and husks.' On the contrary indeed, there seems to me something very close to a note of confidence in Hardy's description of the new power that can drive 'a yellow river running up-hill, and spouting out on the top of the rick'.

After this, Tess returns briefly to more purely agricultural pursuits back home at Marlott. But Hardy's resourcefulness in the straw-rick scene lingers in the mind, partly because that scene, too, was essentially agricultural and so very much a part of the dominant impulse and shape of Tess's life; but also because, like the Marlott scene that follows, it helps to shape and complete the other really essential part of her life, her union with Alec. Indeed in a sense Hardy's tale really ends, not on Stonehenge, or with the stiffly literary 'President of the Immortals' passage, but with Tess's very simple but telling statement to Angel: 'He has won me back to him.' For all the chance or wayward impulses in the story, and perhaps in nature itself, that bring these two together once again, Alec represents a much truer impulse in Tess's life than Angel does. It is not merely that Angel is a paper tiger; Hardy's statement of him, even at its best, leaves Alec, and the side of Tess that answers instinctively to Alec's flesh and blood qualities, the dominant impulse in the book.

Hardy's is a truly original mind (much more so, certainly, than most of his own public statements would allow). What is even more interesting is the combination of this originality with a vein of scepticism that he shares with a lot of other nineteenth- and early twentieth-century writers, each of them, granted all differences of origin and outlook, essentially English middle-class. Conrad is one obvious example here. George Eliot, with her leanings towards a sort of transcendentalism that Hardy would simply have shrugged away as irrelevant, is a more significant comparison. Lydgate's aspirations, and Dorothea's, would hardly have seemed interesting to Hardy. None the less, he would I think have read the following passage, surely very characteristic of some of George Eliot's most basic impulses and feelings, with sympathy and understanding:

Mr and Mrs Casaubon, returning from the wedding journey, arrived at Lowick Manor in the middle of January. A light snow was falling as they descended at the door, and in the morning ... she saw the long avenue of limes lifting their trunks from a white earth, and spreading white branches against the dun and motionless sky. The distant flat shrank in uniform whiteness and low-hanging uniformity of cloud. ...

Meanwhile there was the snow and the low arch of dun vapour – there was the stifling oppression of that gentlewoman's world, where everything was done for her and none asked for her aid – where the sense of connection with a manifold pregnant existence had to be kept up painfully as an inward vision. ... Her blooming full-pulsed youth stood there in a moral imprisonment which made itself one with the chill, colourless, narrowed landscape, with the shrunken furniture, the never-read books, and the ghostly stag in a pale fantastic world that seemed to be vanishing from the daylight. (*Middlemarch*, ch. xxviii)

Of course, Hardy would not have – could not have –written this himself. George Eliot has incorporated into English certain continental, theoretical turns of phrase and thought that Hardy, for all his occasional liking for words like 'siliceous', 'cataclysmal horrors', 'terraqueous distortions', would have rejected. He would never have talked about 'the sense of connection with a manifold pregnant existence', or even about 'the gentlewoman's oppressive liberty'. Neither, if it comes to that, would most other nineteenth-century novelists in English. But in all this difference between the two there is also a constancy, an Anglo-Saxon scepticism that sees the world as containing at once the possibilities here cast up by George Eliot's 'sense of connection', and, disconnected from this but co-existent with it, a nearly tragic oppression, disjunction. Neither Dorothea nor George Eliot sees any sense in the 'shrunken furniture', the unlit transparencies; both, however, sense that the outlook on the 'snow and the low arch of dun vapour' has a necessary fitness and rightness, irrationally co-present with real, and probably unredeemable, miserableness. There is even a low-key beauty in the scene, and it is one Hardy would have recognised and welcomed as quite unsurprising in such a context of despair as Dorothea's life presents at this moment.

10 Henry James: *The Ambassadors*

For the reasons just discussed, Hardy is in many ways a very modern novelist indeed. For all his country settings, and for all he brings certain instinctual drives more strongly and openly into play than most earlier novelists had done, he is not nearly so cut off from the succeeding century as, for instance, James's rather patronising phrase, 'the good little Thomas Hardy', would imply. What Hardy can do, often much more sharply than many twentieth-century writers, is mix the strongly natural forces so evident in his best scenes with a highly sophisticated and modern awareness of the oddness – sometimes the downright injustice – of the circumstances surrounding many people's lives. If some of these 'circumstances' are age-old, and not to be changed by any agency, human or divine, Hardy's noting of this fact – at his best, alert and interested, rather than despairing – is very much in tune with characteristically English middle-class reactions in this century and the last.

Nevertheless, the novel does make certain moves in the early years of this century that were not open to Hardy, and probably not to any English writer at the time when Hardy finished his career as a novelist in the mid-1890s. In particular, there is a sense in which it is both inevitable and right that, still within the tradition of the English middle-class novel from Jane Austen onwards, it is the expatriates and near contemporaries, James and Conrad, who most firmly and most successfully push the frontiers of fiction beyond England and (thinking more especially of James's case) beyond America. Of course this is not simply a matter of geography, any more than it had been, within America earlier, for Melville. But the geography of fiction matters, and it matters more particularly perhaps to James than it does even to Conrad. Conrad, in his phenomenally successful adoption of English language and customs from his early twenties onwards, must have been helped at every point by the very sophistication of European manners and outlook that James most notably lacked. Thus despite some notoriously difficult passages in Conrad, where his remarkable ear for English deserts him momentarily, he is never tempted towards the kind of over-sophistication that spoils some of the later James. Yet, in the end, I think it is precisely this over-sophistication that can point us back to James's real strength, and to the qualities that he added, writing very much *as* an American, to the natively English novel.

The qualities that I have in mind here are certainly new to England, though related ones had been satirised by Dickens, and recorded much more approvingly in Trollope's fairly brief characterisation of Isabel Boncassen. What James makes much more natively English is a certain directness and freshness of approach that one sees at its best, perhaps, in Strether, complicated though some of his reactions are, and at its worst in either the (relatively few) sentimental passages of *The Ambassadors,* or the passages which are really the other side of the same coin: a New World eagerness and unsophistication that is so very aware of its own youth that it is trying too hard, or too literal-mindedly, to outdo Europe at its own game. There are times when James seems very like some of the weaker Elizabethan sonneteers, desperately trying to prove that English can be just as cultivated (or, as it often turns out, just as empty-minded) as the courtly languages of Europe. Fortunately for the English novel there are a great many more sections, particularly in *The Ambassadors,* when James, like the greater Elizabethans, relies instead on native strengths, though of course in his case these are American, not English, and he therefore has to fight the harder to make them what they are in the end, and despite the setting and characterisation: a new dimension to the English novel.

I want to concentrate on *The Ambassadors* for most of this chapter, partly because I think it is the best of the late James novels, but partly too because it is thoroughly characteristic. In particular, it brings together two of the problems that preoccupied James from the beginning of his career as a writer. One of these, which I want to discuss more fully later on in terms of Strether's involvement in the clash of Parisian and American values, is the problem of what future, if any, there can be for one of the finer Jamesian characters who is also very much part of, indeed in some sense a product of, coarser, American middle-class values such as those of the Pococks and Mrs Newsome, or the American banker (and Strether's own contemporary) Waymarsh. It is a problem very like the one George Eliot's Lydgate faces, but in *The Ambassadors* James has chosen a still more finely tuned character, and one who might be expected to have still less in common with the world around him than Lydgate has, or thinks he has.

The other problem, which comes to be very closely associated with the dilemma facing Strether when he has to decide whether or not to reject the coarser Woollett outlooks in favour of Parisian and European ones, is the problem I have already mentioned of a writer whose base is that of an almost permanently young civilisation (young in spirit, that is, even more than in years) when he moves abroad and clearly wants his novels to become part of an English-European, rather than a New England-American, tradition. James had of course been quite conscious from early on of the difficulties that would face him in such a situation, but for a long time this conscious awareness does not seem to have prevented the recurrence of precisely the naïveties he himself foresaw. Thus despite his own very accurate diagnosis in the early 1870s of the 'complex fate' of being an American – 'one of the responsibilities it entails is fighting against a superstitious valuation of Europe' – some of his statements later on about the superiority of Europe continue to be alarmingly naïve, particularly for a man who was also claiming that the art of novel-writing needed the denser world of an older civilisation to flourish on and in. The most famous, or infamous, of these is the list he makes in his critical biography of Hawthorne of the 'items of high civilization' he finds lacking in American life:

> No sovereign, no court, no personal loyalty, no aristocracy, no church, no clergy, no army, no diplomatic service, no country gentlemen, no palaces, no castles, nor manors, nor old country-houses, nor parsonages, nor thatched cottages nor ivied ruins; no cathedrals, nor abbeys, nor little Norman churches; nor great Universities nor public schools – no Oxford, nor Eton, nor Harrow; no literature, no novels, no museums, no pictures, no political society, no sporting class – no Epsom nor Ascot! (*Hawthorne*, ed. Tanner (1967) p. 55)

The comic exaggeration here is not of a kind that can dispel the obvious naïvety and sentimentality about England. Admittedly, there is some evidence that, in the years immediately following, James began to rethink some of his views about Europe and America (see Tanner (ed.), pp. 16–21); and of course the best of his early novels present America itself as far more impressive than anything in this quotation would imply. Notoriously, however, this train of thinking was upset and deranged by his trip back to America in the early years of the century, and *The American Scene* (1907), though full of very sure-footed diagnoses of the 'modern deluge' of American money and business, returns to a sentimentalist's view of the contrast between this and England. For instance, what makes New England shabby and lacking in 'appearance' is, amongst other things, 'the suppression of the two great factors of the familiar English landscape, the squire and the parson'. James may be right about New England, but he has obviously not heard Joseph Arch on either of these two figures as they appeared to an agricultural labourer in England in the nineteenth century; nor has he listened to Cobbett, stomping about rural England in Jane Austen's time and later.

Clearly these passages in James represent an embarrassing naïvety, both about Europe generally and about America's relationships with England and the continent. Yet the odd thing is that the man who could write this way about the superiority of the old world as late as 1907, had, in 1903, given us the Pocock family so admirably taking Strether and Paris by storm. Obviously the Pococks are not the centre of action or attention in *The Ambassadors* – Strether is clearly that, and I think one of James's strongest and finest characters – but neither are they simply the figures of fun, the paper tigers, one might have expected from the writer of the Hawthorne essay or much of *The American Scene. The Ambassadors* would be a lesser book if it had not included – as indeed it does, and with a comedy that is very far from dismissive – Jim's vulgar innuendo about Strether and the Paris 'Varieties' ('Oh, you old wretch!'); or Sarah 'dressed in a splendour of crimson which affected Strether as the sound of a fall through a skylight', or Mamie's 'quiet dignity', which James renders, in Chapter III of Book x, as so inextricably part of the girl's excruciating Americanness: 'she was bland, she was bridal . . . and she had a mature manner of bending a little, as to encourage and reward, while she held neatly together in front of her a pair of strikingly polished hands . . .'

It is a commonplace that the 'International Theme' in James's fiction yields both naïveties and subtleties of fine, or at times superfine, consciousness. What people seem to find harder to grant, but what is I think much more significant still, is the sense in which James's continuing naïvety about both Europe and America can yield also a very telling strength. The sentimentality in that passage from the Hawthorne essay about thatched cottages and little Norman churches is debilitating, as is the exaggerated praise of English squires and parsons; but both these weaknesses come from the same side of James's character and upbringing that gives us the Pococks in Paris, and that can, in the better parts of *The American Scene,* discuss the whole question of American middle-class businessmen and their wives in I think much more *open* ways than any natively English novelist – even Hardy – had so far dared or thought to discuss the place of women generally in society. Dramatising the peculiar position and consciousness of women had of course been a major preoccupation and triumph of English novelists from Richardson onwards; but James's attack is different, and at its best it has, for all the local complications of phrasing, a refreshing directness and simplicity about it that is a welcome and necessary addition to English writing generally.

His chapter on Washington in *The American Scene* itself, for instance, includes this extract:

From the moment it is adequately borne in mind that the business-man, in the United States, may, with no matter what dim struggles, gropings, yearnings, never hope to be anything *but* a business-man, the size of the field he so abdicates is measured. . . . It lies there waiting, pleading from all its pores, to be occupied – the lonely waste, the boundless gaping void of 'society'. . . . Here it is then that the world he lives in accepts its doom and becomes, by his default, subject and plastic to his mate; his default having made, all around him, the unexampled opportunity of the woman – which she would have been an incredible fool not to pounce upon. It needs little contact with American life to perceive how she *has* pounced, and how, outside business, she has made it over in her image. She has been, up to now ... in peerless possession, and is occupied in developing and extending her wonderful conquest, which she appreciates to the last inch of its extent. (*The American Scene* (George Bell, 1907), pp. 345–6).

This diagnosis is practically a repetition in comic-theoretical terms of the scene in Book VIII, Chapter XVIII of *The Ambassadors* that gives us Jim Pocock's arrival with Sarah and Mamie in Paris, and Strether's reflections on them: 'What none the less came home to him, however, at this hour, was that society over there, of which Sarah and Mamie – and in a more eminent way, Mrs Newsome herself – were specimens, was essentially a society of women, and that poor Jim wasn't in it.' There is, however, a crucial difference here, and one which registers a better and more interesting awareness than even the best of the writing in *The American Scene*. Despite the sting in the tail of *The Ambassadors* quotation ('... poor Jim wasn't in it'), it becomes clear that James *likes* Jim's simple vulgarity and openness very much, and, though obviously he knows that a constant diet of Jim in Paris would be a bit trying, both he and Strether welcome this breath of freshness in the sophisticated Parisian air. Jim can welcome Paris in a way no Parisian (nor even, probably, any English person) could; and so with Sarah's contrasting detestation of the whole place, and Waymarsh's deep suspicions of it, superadded, the novel takes on almost a new dimension at this point:

> He gurgled his joy as they rolled through the happy streets; he declared that his trip was a regular windfall, and that he wasn't there, he was eager to remark, to hang back from anything; he didn't quite know what Sally had come for, but *he* had come for a good time. . . .
> 'You mean you wouldn't in Chad's place — ?'
> 'Give up this to go back and boss the advertising!' Poor Jim, with his arms folded and his little legs out in the open fiacre, drank in the sparkling Paris noon . . .

Certainly there is no sentimentality about Paris here, and the fresh note that even 'poor Jim' can bring to the scene is both well rendered by James and, I think, a portent of a more general freshness of approach that, for all its complications, James's fiction brings from the other side of the Atlantic.

On the other hand Strether's role in this confrontation between Paris and Woollett, though it too is rendered for the most part in aptly and firmly comic tones, obviously cuts closer to the bone with James than anything affecting either Waymarsh, or the Pococks, or even Chad himself. Indeed, one of the criticisms most often made of James is that he does this sort of thing almost wilfully: he chooses, that is to say, the hardest circumstances and the bleakest futures precisely for his most sensitive and intelligent characters. Obviously there is some truth in this accusation. Strether is forced to return, at the end of this novel, to the greyness of Woollett, and it is his own honesty and clear-sightedness that has made him see, and therefore act on, the absolute necessity of abandoning not merely Paris itself, but also both the rather devious, and the perfectly genuine, freedoms it offers. So much might make it seem that James had set up the entire story simply in order to make his hero (who in this novel is obviously very close to James himself) suffer the more by presenting him with a dilemma that his own best qualities make unavoidable.

In the end, I do not myself think that this is a fair criticism of James. If it is, it should certainly be made also of a majority of European, and indeed American, novelists and dramatists. It is hard to think of many who do not see at least some degree of suffering as following quite naturally on the possession of any unusual sensitivity or intelligence. But all depends, in such cases, on the span of a novelist's attention, and it seems to me that James, in *The Ambassadors* particularly, proves himself to be one of the least inclined of all modern writers to isolate, and therefore to sentimentalise, the sufferings (or, as in some cases, the apotheosis) of a few selected individuals. He spreads his net much more widely than this, and therefore we see Strether, who is certainly the focus of attention in the whole book, actively taking part in the circumstances that surround him instead of just suffering passively whatever blows that fate, or an increasingly material civilisation, may care to heap on his head.

This is why the American–European confrontation is so important in the novel, and why it is so important to see that James is not rendering America as inertly or unrelievedly brash and vulgar. He does this sometimes, in *The Ambassadors* as well as in others of his books (though in such cases the result is more often an idealisation of Europe than a direct caricaturing of American outlooks and people); for the most part, his concerns are much more forward-looking than this, and allow Strether's admittedly acute and personally rendered tragedy to be part of a general American invasion of Europe which, though it will not have added much to Strether's own life, or to the lives of Madame de Vionnet and the self-exiled Americans who stay in Paris, makes a good part of James's own New World openness and directness a permanent possibility for Europe generally; and, if we think in terms of his whole career, a permanent acquisition for English fiction. Admittedly, putting the issues at stake in this way may sound a bit heartless – almost as if the fate of a few people doesn't matter so long as the novel in general can benefit from the blood-transfusion which the more energetic American middle-class outlook of the Pococks, Waymarsh, and even Strether in his quieter and more

refined way, brings with it. In practice, as I hope the following consideration of some key scenes from *The Ambassadors* will show, James himself
manages to be not in the least heartless about it all, but on the contrary
very keenly aware of the consequences to particular people of this
upheaval in both American and European values.

First in this connection, and for all the very real dangers that James's
venturing to Paris carries with it, there is I think no doubt about the
quality of those early scenes in *The Ambassadors* in which Strether lands
in England and, with Waymarsh and Maria Gostrey variously confronting
him, explores Chester and London. In particular, one of the most telling
things in these scenes – a portent, almost, of what Jamesian comedy can
and will do in some of the more demanding encounters later on – is
James's rendering of Waymarsh. In most respects Waymarsh is indeed
an occasion for comedy, rather than reassurance or stability, in the novel.
He is about Strether's own age (they must both be close to James's own
sixty years at the time of writing *The Ambassadors*), but he has very little
of Strether's sensitivity, and is in addition clearly saddled with all the
limitations of the men James describes in *The American Scene* and more
besides:

> He shook his mane; he fixed, with his admirable eyes, his auditor or
> his observer; he wore no glasses and had a way, partly formidable,
> yet also partly encouraging, as from a representative to a constituent,
> of looking very hard at those who approached him. He met you as if
> you had knocked and he had bidden you enter (Book I, ch. II)

We are reminded several times of Waymarsh's state of nerves, and that
during his legal and business career he has driven himself so hard that he
has only just escaped a nervous breakdown. Consistently, James treats
him as a figure of fun, seen by Maria and Strether as subject to fits of
'the sacred rage', made to wait for hours in Miss Barrace's carriage so she
can identify it the more quickly amongst the others waiting outside the
Paris shops, and characterised by her as 'Sitting Bull' (or, as Strether puts
it, 'Waymarsh had always more or less the air of sitting at the door of his
tent . . .'): 'I show him Paris – show him everything, and he never turns
a hair. He's like the Indian chief one reads about, who, when he comes
up to Washington to see the Great Father, stands wrapped in his blanket
and gives no sign.' (Miss Barrace in Book v, ch. x.)

Yet, from the beginning onwards, this comedy is clearly of a kind that
allows Waymarsh a very distinctive presence, and one that neither Strether
nor James dismisses lightly. Strether playfully agrees with Maria Gostrey,
in Chester, that he is afraid of Waymarsh's impending arrival: so indeed
he might be, because Waymarsh, for all his nerves, his sleepless nights,
and his terror of European 'society' (Strether imagines it as like the Cath-
olic Church for Waymarsh, 'that was to say the enemy, the monster of

bulging eyes and far-reaching quivering groping tentacles' with Maria a 'Jesuit in petticoats, a representative of the recruiting interests . . .') – for all this, Waymarsh has succeeded in ways that Strether must admire, at least in the sense that they are clearly beyond the grasp of a man who could be for so long content as Mrs Newsome's editor.

And it is because of his intense, narrow devotion – a little bit of which Strether himself does share, though exercising it in very different ways – that Waymarsh has succeeded. In the end, what drives Waymarsh to his 'sudden grim dash' to the jeweller's on the other side of the street in Chester, deserting Maria and Strether without a word of explanation, is an impulse of single-mindedness garnered from his past life; and it is also, interestingly, an impulse not at all disconnected from that much more painfully decided and conscious action of Strether's later on in deciding to go back to Woollett. Waymarsh's 'sacred rage' is to do something 'different', that is, something different from the England and Europe he hates but is fascinated by: Strether goes back 'To be right', and because he cannot bear to have got anything for himself from the affair with Chad and Madame de Vionnet, or even from his relationship with Maria in Europe.

So that, in admittedly widely differing ways, Europe is the villain for both Waymarsh and Strether. Woollett may be grim, but it has a rock-like certainty and predictability impossible at any rate in France; and the novel gives us Waymarsh's famous command comically but quite certainly not frivolously: 'Look here Strether. Quit this.' The interesting thing is that, for all his far greater sensitivity, and for all he has learnt during his stay, Strether does, in the end, exactly what Waymarsh has commanded. And he does it for reasons that would have Woollett's, and I think to a very large extent James's own, backing.

So far, and thinking in terms of scenes like these early ones in England together with others like them later on that group together Waymarsh, Strether, Miss Barrace, the terrifyingly adamant Sarah Pocock and others, we have a novel which is both very sure-footed, and also sufficiently similar to native English fiction to blend quite easily with it, while at the same time introducing certain new strains that may (or may not, depending of course on James's handling of them) be a valuable and welcome addition. The ways in which James's novel is adapted to, and indeed grows out of, earlier novels in English are clear, and have been well documented. In particular, there is the easy and natural blend of comic and serious writing in the putting of those questions that so dominate Strether's stay in Europe. Is Waymarsh's suspicion of Europe and all its doings justified? Or is it simply a comic misjudging, a distrust natural enough to a newcomer with his background but actually quite unfounded? Will Strether be right, finally, in disobeying Mrs Newsome's instructions and telling Chad he must stay with Madame de Vionnet? Such questions, for all the differences their national origin carries with it, can be matched easily by others (for instance, those that Lydgate faces when he has to choose between Tyke and Farebrother) constantly posed in the native English novel, and which also turn on a nice blending of the serious and the comic.

On the other hand, there is at least one note that is apparent even early on in *The Ambassadors* (for instance, in the way Maria can so openly accost Strether and so easily adopt him), and that is new to English fiction, at least outside the comparatively brief 'American' encounters in Trollope's *The Duke's Children*. This note of perfectly natural and open simplicity is certainly well and easily rendered by James in the opening scenes, but it does become a bit more difficult and demanding when, later on, it has to bulk much more largely and variously in the complicated business of Strether's dealings with the 'ambassadors' on the one hand, and Marie de Vionnet on the other. Because, as *The Ambassadors* develops, it becomes more and more clear that many of James's own deepest impulses are both more simple and more straightforward than, for instance, those in any of the great Jane Austen or George Eliot novels, to name only the closest comparisons from among the native English and European writers James himself admired. By this I do not mean that either Jane Austen or George Eliot is devious by comparison, or anything less than honest; but rather, that the American novelist has more of his emotional capital invested in Strether's scrupulous honesty (as he has also in Nanda's, Mr Longdon's, Maisie's in the 'English' novels) than Jane Austen has or needs to have in, say, Emma's, or George Eliot in Lydgate's, Dorothea's, Gwendolen's. (Where George Eliot does base a characterisation on unassailable moral rectitude the result is often a crippling sentimentality of the Mordecai or Mirah kind.)

Personally I think that the difficulties this leads to in the late James (some over-writing, some sentimentality about Paris) are not nearly as great, and certainly not as crippling, as is often assumed. Admittedly he does over-compensate in places, and so produce writing that is dismayingly close to Dr Leavis's description of 'an effect of disproportionate "doing" – of a technique the subtleties and elaborations of which are not sufficiently controlled by a feeling for value and significance in living.' Or again, there is the related difficulty of James's sentimental description of the artist Gloriani in Book v, Chapter x, untinged at this first meeting by any irony either from Strether or from the author:

He was to see again repeatedly, in remembrance, the medal-like Italian face, in which every line was an artist's own. . . . Was what it had told him or what it had asked him the greater of the mysteries? Was it the most special flare, unequalled, supreme, of the esthetic torch, lighting that wondrous world for ever, or was it above all the long straight shaft sunk by a personal acuteness that life had seasoned to steel? . . . The deep human expertness in Gloriani's charming smile –

oh the terrible life behind it! – was flashed upon him as a test of his stuff.

Of course in practice, Strether does not (fortunately for him and for us!) continue to worship the 'artist' in anything like this way. James recovers ground and perspective very quickly in Chapter XI with the justly famous passage that makes the emptiness of Gloriani's 'terrible life' perfectly clear: 'Then there was something in the great world covertly tigerish, which came to him across the lawn and in the charming air, as a waft from the jungle. Yet it made him admire most of the two, made him envy, the glossy male tiger, magnificently marked.'

But both the irony of this, and the flat condemnation of Gloriani's 'charming hollow civility' on their subsequent meeting in Book VI, are quite detached from the banalities – James's I think, rather than just Strether's – of the first garden-party scene. That passage is one of the places in the novel that shows very clearly the dangers attendant on James's background – indeed an American swallowed by Paris and the artist world hook, line and sinker.

On the other hand, it was James himself, writing about George Eliot's *Middlemarch*, who made the perfectly simple but true point that every great artist shows the defects of his qualities. Perhaps it will not be impertinent to apply this to James himself, though turning it round in order to claim that some at least of *his* very best qualities stem from the same simplicity of outlook that occasionally betrays him in the face of what he sees as a complex and intimidating European civilisation: he has the qualities of his defects. If this is so, then both the charge against James of an over-written prose that lacks an answering substance or core of 'living'; and the rather similar charge that, in so far as the book has any substance, it is concentrated too much in the sufferings of his highly intelligent élite (mainly Strether and Madame de Vionnet), can be answered. And I myself think that they are answered, particularly as the later scenes in *The Ambassadors* draw together to show, certainly the keenness of the dilemma facing Strether, but also that this is a dilemma brought about by the collision (historically inevitable, perhaps) between two cultures. It is not a fate imposed by James on one or two of his characters simply because they are more sensitive than the rest, and therefore more inclined passively to suffer whatever may happen to them.

The element of essential simplicity in the 'complex fate' being worked out here comes to a head in the 'Lambinet' river scene and the confrontations that follow between Strether, Madame de Vionnet, Chad and, finally, Maria Gostrey. Before this point in the novel, however, Strether has first to be shown as the one American of them all who just possibly might – though not in the least to his own advantage – glimpse some possibility of bringing the raw directness of Woollett, and the experienced duplicity of Paris, into closer contact with each other. Two scenes that concentrate a large part of the novel's potential in this regard are the confrontation between Strether and Chad after the opera, and the later scene – in its genuinely charming way, equally a 'confrontation' – between Strether and Madame de Vionnet at lunch beside the Seine. The first, from Book IV, Chapter VIII, starts with this exchange:

> 'Mother writes,' said Chad, 'a lovely letter.'
>
> Strether, before the closed porte cochère, fixed him a moment. 'It's more, my boy, than *you* do! But our suppositions don't matter,' he added, 'if you're actually not entangled.'
>
> Chad's pride seemed none the less a little touched. 'I never *was* that – let me insist. I always had my own way.' With which he pursued: 'And I have it at present.'
>
> 'Then what are you here for? What has kept you,' Strether asked, 'if you *have* been able to leave?'
>
> It made Chad, after a stare, throw himself back. 'Do you think one's kept only by women?' His surprise and his verbal emphasis rang out so clear in the still street that Strether winced till he remembered the safety of their English speech. 'Is that,' the young man demanded, 'what they think at Woollett?' At the good faith in the question Strether had changed colour. ... He had appeared stupidly to misrepresent what they thought at Woollett; but before he had time to rectify Chad again was upon him. 'I must say then you show a low mind!'

One of the things that helps to make Strether's position in this book so interesting and so demanding is that his is an intelligence not faced with the paper tiger that Mr Longdon, for instance, finds in Van. Obviously Chad is shallow and unscrupulous. His own phrase here – 'I always had my own way' – is quietly but very effectively highlighted by the contrasting personality of Strether. But he has enough charm and interest to make clear the depth of the entanglement that Marie de Vionnet is in; and certainly he has a lot of what the more passive personality of Vanderbank lacks: an active self-interest and cunning that makes his presence a real issue, and that justifies the famous reflection from Strether that follows in the next paragraph: 'Chad had at any rate pulled his visitor up; he had even pulled up his admirable mother; he had absolutely, by a turn of the wrist and a jerk of the far-flung noose, pulled up, in a bunch, Woollett browsing in its pride.'

That last picture of Woollett 'pulled up, in a bunch ...' is splendidly comic writing, and absolutely typical of the way the best of the novel works in intimate and personal situations such as this one. In particular, the very simple pictorial element in the image of Woollett 'browsing in its pride', and pulled up by Chad's jerk of the noose, crystallises the way in which the novel can build on Strether's imagination, but in such a way as to take in also people and scenes that are distant, even alien, to him.

Certainly there is no hint here of the terrible artistry of the first Gloriani passage overwhelming Strether, or of any tendency on James's part to isolate him and his 'sufferings' from the active world – American and Parisian – around him. On the contrary, what we have is a wryly simple image that is nevertheless quite flexible and complicated enough to recall something potentially vicious in Chad, recognise also the aptness of the charge against Woollett, and at the same time value Woollett's 'browsing' as indeed a 'pride' (in all senses of the word) that cannot simply be dismissed.

The second scene, between Strether and Madame de Vionnet at *déjeuner* in the café by the Seine (Book VII, Chapter XVI), is once again strikingly simple, both in its pictorial outline, with the 'shining barge-burdened Seine' outside and Strether's consequent delight in 'the mere way the bright clean ordered water-side life came in at the open window', and in the irony that so quickly and lightly juxtaposes this outlook on Paris, Madame de Vionnet's by now fairly certain banishment from any life that will involve Chad, and the rock-like certainty of the figure of Mrs Newsome in Woollett:

> 'I'm not in trouble yet,' he at last smiled. 'I'm not in trouble now.'
> 'Well, I'm always so. But that you sufficiently know.' She was a woman who, between courses, could be graceful with her elbows on the table. It was a posture unknown to Mrs Newsome, but it was easy for a *femme du monde*.

This is the scene that follows immediately from the much more threatening one of Madame de Vionnet 'discovered' by Strether virtually alone in Notre Dame. The quick change of key is as remarkable as the simplicity of the pictorial element in both, and is a reminder that, if James's straightforwardness is sometimes understressed by readers and critics, his famous 'complexity' is still a real issue and, in part at least, essential to the role that Strether must play out before the novel can bring Europe to realise an American presence (or, as far at least as Strether himself is concerned, absence). Sadly enough, it is Madame de Vionnet's own future that is as much at stake here as Strether's; and so it is these two who finally embody the confrontation between the ambivalence of Europe and the stubborn certainty of Woollett.

The trouble between the two of them comes to a head late in the novel when, in Book XI, Chad and Madame de Vionnet upset Strether's 'Lambinet' river landscape, literally by rowing into it. This scene certainly has its dangers for James himself, as well as for the characters: he has chosen, as I think he perfectly well knows here, precisely the sort of too ordered and too perfect a French landscape that an American might well choose to encapsulate his ideal of French art and French country life. 'What he saw was exactly the right thing – a boat advancing round the bend and containing a man who held the paddles and a lady, at the stern, with a pink parasol. It was suddenly as if these figures, or something like them, had been wanted in the picture . . .' (Book XI, ch. XXI)

But it is the irony – again, a perfectly simple and obvious irony – behind phrases like 'exactly right' and 'these figures . . . had been wanted' that gives backbone to what might otherwise have been a dangerously idyllic retreat for Strether and for the book, a mere conjuring of French landscapes that offer a contrast to and escape from the difficulties of actual living. As it is, the boat and the figures in it are indeed a perfection of the Lambinet picture-landscape; but they are also 'exactly the right thing' in another sense, that is they are needed to perfect the whole drive of the story to this point, and so actually *ruin* the Lambinet picture effect. Because this is the moment in the book when Strether must see and face openly what he has been trying to pretend to himself for so long might not be behind Maria's tactful silence and Little Bilham's protective, gentlemanly lie of Book IV, Chapter IX: '"Why isn't he free if he's good?" Little Bilham looked him full in the face. "Because it's a virtuous attachment."'

Of course it is not just the adultery that, in terms of the book as a whole, worries Strether. Indeed it is not even primarily that, but rather the hesitation caught as the boat, without Chad turning round, pauses a fraction, and Strether realises that Madame de Vionnet is 'quickly and intensely debating with Chad the risk of betrayal. He saw they would show nothing if they could feel sure he hadn't made them out . . .' This, and still more the dinner and train journey afterwards, with Madame de Vionnet quite obviously dressed for a return to their hotel upstream rather than the chilly evening trip back to Paris, show not so much an American caught in the toils of European duplicity – after all, there can be no pretending on either side that the true facts aren't obvious, and so if this is European cunning it is certainly not fooling anybody – not so much this, then, as the final and absolute impossibility, at least for these people, of trying to blend or unite American and Parisian living, however sophisticated in their different ways each of the two cultures may be. On the river, one essential note in this realisation is finely caught in the Jamesian comedy of Strether's elephantine hat-waving at the two of them. It is a last hope that he might prevent further attempts at hide-and-seek, and it has just the right note of lightly stressed desperation at the sheer unlikeliness, after that long history of equivocation by Chad and Marie de Vionnet, that this could possibly come off:

It seemed to him [Strether] again . . . that he had but one thing to do – to settle their common question by some sign of surprise and joy. He thereupon gave large play to these things, agitating his hat and stick and loudly calling out – a demonstration that brought him relief as soon as he had seen it answered. The boat, in mid-stream, still went a little wild – which seemed natural, however, while Chad

turned round, half springing up ... Our friend went down to the
water under this odd impression as of violence averted – the violence
of their having 'cut' him, out there in the eye of nature, on the assumption that he wouldn't know it. He awaited them with a face from which
he was conscious of not being able quite to banish this idea that they
would have gone on, not seeing and not knowing, missing their
dinner and disappointing their hostess, had he himself taken a line to
match. (Book xi, ch. xxxi)

I imagine James is not for a moment supposing that such embarrassing
attempts at pretending something hasn't happened might not occur in
America and England too. What worries Strether, and James, about this
scene and the dreadful train journey back to Paris is the possibility
of a whole world where thinly veiled pretence can be accepted as completely natural, almost as much a part of the normal social order of events
as the reduction of Jeanne de Vionnet's marriage to an arrangement, 'a
move in a game'. Or – since putting it this way might be to understress
a little too much the book's subtlety, and the number of different possibilities it throws up – perhaps one should say that what faces Strether
increasingly clearly from now on is the knowledge that, though he
himself can hardly any longer ignore the fact that, as he puts it, 'there had
been simply a *lie* in the charming affair – a lie on which one could now,
detached and deliberate, perfectly put one's finger'; though this is so,
as well as Chad he has himself been educated by Paris and Madame de
Vionnet, and changed very much for the better. There is clearly no
future for him in staying in Paris, because he would not at all be safe in
the haven Maria promises, but on the contrary exposed not only to his
own sense of the wrongness of this for a man of his type but, as he points
out, to her sense of it too; and in addition therefore he would be quite
useless to Marie de Vionnet as something to cling to – 'a source of safety
she had tested' – when Chad, as he clearly will, finally leaves her. On the
other hand, what, of his new knowledge and life, can possibly be trans-
ported back to Woollett, let alone take root there?

'Nothing at all, or virtually nothing' is, in round terms, the answer the
novel finally gives to this question. But it does not give its 'answer' in
quite such a flatly condemnatory tone of voice as this would suggest;
nor, in consequence, does it condemn Europe and America to the perpetual isolation from each other that Strether's withdrawal, and the bleak-
ness of Madame de Vionnet's future, would entail if these were the only
circumstances in James's mind here at the end. One sign that they are not
is there in the wryly comic tone of the excellent scene at the beginning of
Book xii, when Strether posts his reply to Madame de Vionnet's invitation, and reflects on the influence of the terrifying *Postes et Télégraphes*
on an elderly American in Paris making an assignation with an already
compromised married woman:

... the little prompt Paris women, arranging, pretexting goodness knows what, driving the dreadful needle-pointed public pen at the dreadful sand-strewn public table: implements that symbolized for Strether's too interpretative innocence something more acute in manner, more sinister in morals, more fierce in the national life. After he had put in his paper he had ranged himself, he was really amused to think, on the side of the fierce, the sinister, the acute. He was carrying on a correspondence, across the great city, quite in the key of the *Postes et Télégraphes* in general ...

During the day of waiting that follows we see Strether absolutely idle in Paris, not even going to see Maria Gostrey after all, and allowing himself the last indulgence of imagining an unforeseen return by the Pococks, who might then find him lounging about, eating ice-creams and drinking lemonade, apparently totally regardless of any Woollett obligations or principles of conduct whatever. Strether has decided to waste the day entirely.

Of course, Strether has not in the least forgotten his Woollett affiliations and principles, but what this very funny scene has made possible is a degree of relaxation – a glimpse of possibilities other than those demanded by the stern Woollett code of action – that affects to some extent even the rather terrible scene with Madame de Vionnet that follows immediately. Because what strikes Strether first of all in this later scene, and what the novel allows him to reflect on with remarkable freedom and relaxation, given the circumstances, is that Madame de Vionnet is completely unperturbed by the embarrassment of their earlier meeting on the river. Whatever does worry her, it is clearly not that:

> He perceived soon enough at least that, however reasonable she might be, she wasn't vulgarly confused, and it herewith pressed upon him that their eminent 'lie', Chad's and hers, was simply after all such an inevitable tribute to good taste as he couldn't have wished them not to render ... (Book XII, ch. XXXII)

Here, once again, is a world of appearance which is more real, and more natural, than anything Mrs Newsome's imagination would make it out to be: a form of disguise attempting to cover a secret and probably guilty reality underneath. Madame de Vionnet can make 'appearance' a perfectly natural way of living, and one which she feels no need or impulse whatever to apologise for.

And so, in the very finely turned ambivalence of Strether's musings at this point in the scene, James allows the two worlds – in the end, quite irreconcilable – to come as close together as they possibly can without some sort of mutual harm or even destruction resulting. Thus the double negatives of Strether's description of the 'tribute ... he couldn't have wished them not to render' yield a perfectly real and continuing 'trust' in

Madame de Vionnet which, however, then needs the quickly ambivalent sentence added: 'That is he could trust her to make deception right.'

Up to now, the novel's sense of the ambivalence and freedom possible to comedy has dominated the scene. But *The Ambassadors* is indeed a book founded at least as much on a straightforward directness of impulse as on any of the various forms of sophistication – American as well as Parisian – it also uses. It is therefore right that what precipitates, and to a very large extent controls, the crisis and events that follow is a very simple reaction of Strether's: 'He presently found himself taking a long look from her, and the next thing he knew he had uttered all his thought. "You're afraid for your life!"' There follows the scene where – perhaps for the only time in the book? – there is no distinction left between what Madame de Vionnet is and what she appears to be. It is a scene that, given earlier exaggerations about her 'youth', and given too some perhaps tell-tale turns of phrase even here ('the finest and subtlest creature, the happiest apparition, it had been given him, in all his years, to meet . . .'), might easily have turned to a softer sentimentality. As it is, and backed by the sheer amount of persistent self-honesty that James has managed to include in Strether's character, his writing in the only openly emotional scene he allows himself in the whole book – if we except, that is, the scenes of Sarah Pocock's equally genuine indignation and anger – is direct, uncomplicated and simply leaving the for once unambiguous facts to tell their own tale:

> It drew out her long look, and he soon enough saw why. A spasm came into her face, the tears she had already been unable to hide overflowed at first in silence, and then, as the sound suddenly comes from a child, quickened to gasps, to sobs. She sat and covered her face with her hands, giving up all attempt at a manner. 'It's how you see me, it's how you see me' – she caught her breath with it – 'and it's as I *am*, and as I must take myself, and of course it's no matter.' Her emotion was at first so incoherent that he could only stand there at a loss, stand with his sense of having upset her, though of having done it by the truth. . . . She was older for him to-night, visibly less exempt from the touch of time; but she was as much as ever the finest and subtlest creature, the happiest apparition, it had been given him, in all his years, to meet: and yet he could see her there as vulgarly troubled, in very truth, as a maidservant crying for her young man. The only thing was that she judged herself as the maidservant wouldn't; the weakness of which wisdom too, the dishonour of which judgement, seemed but to sink her lower. (Book XII, ch. XXXIII)

The last thing the book does is present this very fine scene as any vindication of Woollett principles (the Scarlet Woman getting her just deserts); nevertheless it is Strether's brash American honesty that has forced what he here calls 'the truth' into the open. Admittedly, his version of truth still isn't the whole thing. Immediately after this, Marie de Vionnet brushes aside Chad as a person with a contempt that Strether, even at the end, when he is convinced of Chad's falseness, would not venture: '"... Oh from him – !" Positively, strangely, bitterly, as it seemed to Strether, she gave "him", for the moment, away.' And then she adds, in her continental and unpredictable way, another comment still more unusually – for her – direct, and also probably more bleakly self-critical than any that even Mrs Newsome could command if ever she could be imagined in similar circumstances:

'We bore you – that's where we are. And we may well – for what we've cost you. All you can do *now* is not to think at all. And I who should have liked to seem to you – well, sublime!'
He could only, after a moment, re-echo Miss Barrace. 'You're wonderful!'
'I'm old and abject and hideous' – she went on as without hearing him. 'Abject above all. Or old above all. It's when one's old that it's worst . . .'

But if it is Marie de Vionnet's presence and vision of the future that commands this particular exchange, it is still Strether's remark, and Strether's presence, that has forced this in some ways uncharacteristically brutal honesty out of her; and the whole scene, besides being impressive in itself, adds tremendously to the rightness of what follows, his decision to go back to Woollett. The novel could easily have ended with a comically self-aware Strether abandoning his scruples and, without placing any more reliance in the future than he has anyway, accepting Maria Gostrey's candid invitation. As it is, James's own scruples triumph, and Strether's replies to Maria's question 'What then do you go home to?' are a completely convincing blend of his own psychological need to *feel* 'in the right', and the novel's sense of something needing to *be* 'right', almost in an absolute sense:

'There's nothing, you know, I wouldn't do for you.'
'Oh yes – I know.'
'There's nothing,' she repeated, 'in all the world.'
'I know. I know. But all the same I must go.' He had got it at last. 'To be right.'
'To be right?'
She had echoed it in vague deprecation, but he felt it already clear for her. 'That, you see, is my only logic. Not, out of the whole affair, to have got anything for myself.'

A few lines after this the novel ends with Strether's comically despairing but unstressed 'Then there we are!'; but just before it does so, a comment of Maria's sums up the essential simplicity behind this indeed "difficult" James character and novel: 'So then she had to take it, though still with her defeated protest. "It isn't so much your *being* 'right' – it's your horrible sharp eye for what makes you so."'

That James brings new and valuable qualities *to* English fiction (rather than just learning from it or from 'the Europeans' generally) seems to me undeniable. And this is especially true of *The Ambassadors*, for all it is a novel concerned at least as much with the shock of discovering un-bridgeable gulfs between Europe and America as with anything the two may have in common.

It is also in some ways a newer and fresher book than *The Awkward Age*. Nanda's future is not merely bleak, as Strether's is too; it is also – unlike his – rather sadly defeated, and to some extent this note of sad resignation limits the range and outlook of what is in other ways a very fine novel. One of the most remarkable things about *The Ambassadors* is the air of active and interested curiosity that Strether, and for the most part the book as a whole, manage in the face of events that are just as divisive, and just as threatening, as the ones that surround Nanda's and Mrs Brook's self-imposed exile.

And if the note of resilient comedy so struck has its affiliations with similar ones in native English fiction, part at least of its base in *The Ambassadors* is new. The whole book has an openness, and a scrupulous but also remarkably cheerful honesty of purpose about it that seems the peculiar property of the Americans. Except for Chad (whose career, appropriately enough, is to be in advertising), each of them shows this quality. Even Sarah's furious and rather silly indignation, and Way-marsh's deep suspicion, are, like Jim's sheer delight in Paris, perfectly free and unreserved. Together (and with most of the expatriates included in this), the Americans provide a remarkably sure and solid basis for James's culmination to his story: the very particular kind of American, middle-class honesty of purpose that forces the most intelligent of them all, Strether, back to Woollett at the end.

11 Conrad's Trust in Life: *Nostromo*

For all the exotic settings of many of his books, Conrad does not, I think, extend the frontiers of the English novel quite as far as James at his best does. To a large extent this is simply because he does not need to. Conrad is, after all, an experienced (and even at times duplicitous) European himself.

Indeed, that has been the core of the difficulty a great many readers have found with him. Certainly the most telling of the criticisms that have been and still are being made of his work, and in particular of *Nostromo*, have one thing in common: a feeling that Conrad himself is subject to a debilitating scepticism or despair very like that he shows assailing Martin Decoud and Emilia Gould. Such criticisms take the emptiness and sterility that these people, in their very different ways, see in modern life as invading the very fabric and texture of the novel itself, limiting, and perhaps in the end crippling, its more imaginative impulses. D. H. Lawrence's sweeping denunciation of all of Conrad sums up a general feeling about *Nostromo*: 'Why this giving in before you start, that pervades all Conrad and such folks ... the Writers Among the Ruins. I can't forgive Conrad for being so sad and for giving in.'

Dr Leavis's assessment of the novel is more challenging still, because his criticism goes together with what must surely be the finest account anyone has given of the characteristic Conradian strengths as they appear in *Nostromo* and other tales. For instance Dr Leavis singles out, as one of the book's strongest points, Conrad's account of Decoud's last days on the Great Isabel and the 'significant power' with which Conrad in those scenes renders the scepticism that in the end, Leavis feels, threatens the achievement of the novel as a whole. His conclusion is that ' . . . for all the rich variety of the interest and the tightness of the pattern, the reverberation of *Nostromo* has something hollow about it; with the colour and life there is a suggestion of a certain emptiness.' A little later he goes on to describe what he feels to be missing in *Nostromo* as the kind of 'self-sufficient day-to-dayness of living Conrad can convey, when writing from within the Merchant Service, where clearly he has known it'. 'For life in the Merchant Service there is no equivalent in *Nostromo* – no intimate sense conveyed of the day-by-day continuities of social living.' (*The Great Tradition* (1948) pp. 200–1)

A part answer to this criticism would be simply that the very terms of *Nostromo*, the setting and action of the tale, take it so far beyond life in the merchant service that no equivalent for that is either relevant or even conceivable in Costaguana. Indeed, Conrad himself makes this point clearly and well in his presentation of Captain Mitchell. In 'Typhoon', published in 1902, he had shown Captain MacWhirr as thoroughly and impressively in command of his world. There is no hesitation or touch of sentimentality in Conrad's depicting of the shipboard world and the storm that MacWhirr so effortlessly and unthinkingly dominates. In *Nostromo* (1904), the elements of the action are so varied that neither a single person, nor even a code of conduct, could possibly command them in the sense that MacWhirr commands his ship. And Conrad demonstrates this by placing 'Fussy Joe's' personal qualities (very similar to MacWhirr's) as simply one strongly contrasting element amongst lots of others. On the occasion of Mitchell's defiance of Sotillo, for instance, he puts the point explicitly:

> The old sailor, with all his small weaknesses and absurdities, was constitutionally incapable of entertaining for any length of time a fear of his personal safety. It was not so much firmness of soul as the lack of a certain kind of imagination – the kind whose undue development caused intense suffering to Señor Hirsch . . . (Part III, ch. 2)

On the other hand, this still leaves at least part of Dr Leavis's criticism unanswered. If it is clear that neither Fussy Joe, nor the profession he represents, can pull the world of *Nostromo* together, who, or what, can? Any answer to this question would I think have to grant some of Leavis's doubts. In particular, it seems pretty clear that the emptily operatic quality of the part of the tale giving us Nostromo's visits to the girls on the island, and finally his death at Viola's hands, is no accident. The writing in these scenes is often clumsily symbolic, at the end simply melodramatic; and these weaknesses are much more than stylistic slips on Conrad's part. There are times, clearly, when he is unable any longer to face the loneliness and despair he himself has so vividly portrayed in Decoud's death and in Mrs Gould's realisation that 'material interest' has left her no family, and indeed virtually no personal, life at all. The knowledge Conrad has shown elsewhere in the book of the ways in which business and technology, on an international scale, can and must engage with private lives here collapses into anguish of a sentimental, because purely personal, kind:

> 'It is I who loved you,' she whispered, with a face as set and white as marble in the moonlight . . .

She stood silent and still, collecting her strength to throw all her fidelity, her pain, bewilderment, and despair into one great cry.

'Never! Gian' Battista!'

Dr Monygham, pulling round in the police–galley, heard the name pass over his head . . . . In that true cry of undying passion that seemed to ring aloud from Punta Mala to Azuera and away to the bright line of the horizon, overhung by a big white cloud shining like a mass of solid silver, the genius of the magnificent Capataz de Cargadores dominated the dark gulf containing his conquests of treasure and love.

This is Conrad at his very worst, and it is the greatest pity that the novel has to end on such a note. Personally, however, I feel that the book as a whole is less touched by this kind of desperately muddled and melo-dramatic symbolism than, say, *The Rainbow* or even *Women in Love* is touched by Lawrence's often exaggerated defiance of the constricting tendencies he sees in modern life. In neither writer can one find 'day-by-day continuities of social living' quite as solidly and impressively rendered as George Eliot, in particular, rendered them in *Middlemarch*, some thirty years before Conrad began his novel. But in *Nostromo* there does seem to me something that answers to another, slightly different demand of Leavis's, namely the one he formulates as 'that kind of self-sufficient day-to-dayness of living' so clearly present in Conrad's merchant marine world. I do not mean that life in Costaguana is at all like life on board ship, any more than it is like the solidly middle-class world of Middlemarch. Never-theless, there seems to me a sanity and sense in Conrad's writing in *Nostromo* that compares with the best of George Eliot, and that is the result of his realisation that neither the unstable political future of Costa-guana, nor even the despair of Decoud and Mrs Gould, will destroy the sheer reliability of ordinary daily existence.

One of the clearest manifestations of a resilient and buoyant sanity in Conrad is the prose of that scene where Captain Mitchell, surrounded by looting, torture and the unpredictability of political revolution, yells indignantly that his watch has been stolen. I don't mean so much that the quality of 'day-to-dayness' and ordinary sustaining living in this scene comes from Mitchell himself, or even from his concern for the chrono-meter given him by a grateful insurance company, though all this helps. It is rather that Conrad – and it *is* Conrad in this novel, not the shadow-boxing Marlow-Conrad – can write about events like these with such an extraordinarily assured, crisp comedy. If the absurdity of existence worries Conrad – and often enough it clearly does – he has mastered the worry thoroughly and completely in this scene. The whole sequence is absurd – more so still in the parts of it that show Hirsh dangling from the rope tying his hands behind his back – but it is quite impossible to detect any disabling worry in a writer who can show us, in prose of this kind, one

of his main characters handled so unceremoniously by the sheer chance of a
bandit's suspicious fears:

> In the clamour of voices and the rattle of arms, Captain Mitchell made
> himself heard imperfectly: 'By heavens! the fellow has stolen my watch.'
> The engineer-in-chief on the staircase resisted the pressure long
> enough to shout, 'What? What did you say?'
> 'My chronometer!' Captain Mitchell yelled violently at the very
> moment of being thrust head foremost through a small door into a sort
> of cell, perfectly black, and so narrow that he fetched up against the
> opposite wall. (Part III, chapter 2)

That is from Chapter 2 of the third book, 'The Lighthouse'. In Chapter
5 of the same book we get a scene that perhaps tests Conrad more because not only is the steadying bulk of Captain Mitchell absent here, but
Conrad's writing has to reflect much more directly on the ridiculousness
of Sulacan events and politics generally (if indeed you call them 'politics'
at all at this stage: it is the entry into Sulaco of Pedrito Montero and his
meeting with the totally ridiculous National Guard leader, Gamacho). The
over-insistence of one or two passages in this sequence is evidence that the
absurdity of it all does indeed dismay him a little and come close to
unsettling that steadily comic glance with which he took in the Mitchell
scenes. Conrad's personal bitterness nearly overcomes him in the repeated
ironic insistences: 'the easy massacre of an unsuspecting enemy evoked no
feelings but those of gladness, pride. . . . Not perhaps that primitive men
were more faithless than their descendants of to-day . . .'; 'the great
guerillo, the famous Pedrito . . .'; 'Señor Fuentes . . . a true friend of the
people'. On the other hand, and despite the situation here (with the
brief stability of the Ribierist regime ended and the town in the hands of
Gamacho's looters, who will be driven out only by Montero's guerrillas),
these signs of unease on Conrad's part are brief and insignificant, even in
this surely very testing chapter. In the chapter as a whole, Conrad's
writing draws easily, unobtrusively on his own sense for the dependably
real, the predictable presence of small, steadying details: 'the little black-
coated person of Señor Fuentes'; the heat and glare of the Plaza, with
Gamacho, his coat flung off, sleeves turned up high above the elbows
addressing the crowd and pausing every moment 'to wipe his streaming
face with his bare forearm . . .'
It might look like stretching the ordinary meaning of words a bit to
claim that, in such a scene, any details could call up and impart the solid
steadiness of ordinary life, the 'self-sufficient day-to-dayness of living':

> On his left hand, Gamacho, big and hot, wiping his hairy wet face,
> uncovered a set of yellow fangs in a grin of stupid hilarity . . . . In the
> intervals, over the swarming Plaza brooded a heavy silence, in which the
> mouth of the orator went on opening and shutting, and detached

phrases – 'The happiness of the people,' 'Sons of the country,' 'The entire world, *el mundo entiero*' – reached even the packed steps of the cathedral with a feeble clear ring, thin as the buzzing of a mosquito. But the orator struck his breast; he seemed to prance between his two supporters. (Part III, chapter 5)

But it is, I think, precisely a stretching of the limits of the ordinary that Conrad manages here. In summary outline, Gamacho's stupidity is merely bizarre, and Pedrito's disappointment at the wrecked Intendencia – 'We are not barbarians,' he said' – merely pathetic. In Conrad's actual prose, the scene is not merely believable, but interesting and imaginatively solid. Characteristically, there is no religion, metaphysic, or political philosophy here that Conrad finds he can put a moment's faith in; what he can and does do is cull support from details like that of Gamacho 'wiping his hairy wet face . . . ', even the absolute rightness of his yellow fangs and their 'grin of stupid hilarity'. For these reasons the irony of the whole scene is confident as much as, or more than, simply cynical. In particular, and after some dryly European irony at the expense of the National Guards – it might almost be Decoud speaking – the chapter concludes with a picture, quite unlike any Decoud would characteristically have given us, of Gamacho lying at home, dead drunk. Montero has by now decided the Guards must be got rid of or they will do more damage than they are worth, so he simply orders his cavalry to charge them:

> The National Guards of Sulaco were surprised by this proceeding. But they were not indignant. No Costaguanero had ever learned to question the eccentricities of a military force. They were part of the natural order of things. This must be, they concluded, some kind of administrative measure, no doubt. (Part III, chapter 5)

So much is indeed the tone of the Paris boulevardier, taking in some fresh piece of bizarre behaviour that Sulaco and the universe have turned up for his amusement. The total significance of the scene, however, is brought to a head in the last lines of the chapter that follow immediately. Here Conrad's comedy both deepens and relaxes beyond the range of mere sophistication. The sheer facts of Sulacan life are rendered in all their vulgarity but without the slightest sign either of revulsion, or of the over-finicky nature so well caught in Decoud's dislike of the instruments he is forced to use.

> But the motive of it escaped their unaided intelligence, and their chief and orator, Gamacho, Commandante of the National Guard, was lying drunk and asleep in the bosom of his family. His bare feet were upturned in the shadows repulsively, in the manner of a corpse. His eloquent mouth had dropped open. His youngest daughter, scratching her head with one hand, with the other waved a green bough over his scorched and peeling face.

The same kind of writing, and related kinds, support to a considerable extent the main characters in the story and the governing events: mainly the winning of silver that brings prosperity, but also the threat of deeper and further confusion, to everybody in Sulaco. That picture of Gamacho asleep in the bosom of his family is not the sort of brilliant but detachable fantasy, with no more than a loosely thematic connection with the rest of the novel, that you sometimes get in Dickens. Here the resilience in Conrad's writing that is evident in his vision of Gamacho, completely at home in slovenly carelessness, carries over to quite opposite manifestations of Sulacan life such as the over-fastidious regulation and care of the Gould household. It is the same comic intelligence that gives us Gamacho, or the much more horrifying comedy of Hirsch being tortured, that introduces also that parrot into the corridor of the Casa Gould:

> 'Of course,' he said to his wife.... [Holroyd] may have to give in, or he may have to die to-morrow, but the great silver and iron interests shall [*sic*] survive, and some day shall get hold of Costaguana along with the rest of the world.'
> They had stopped near the cage. The parrot, catching the sound of a word belonging to his vocabulary, was moved to interfere. Parrots are very human.
> 'Viva Costaguana!' he shrieked, with intense self-assertion, and, instantly ruffling up his feathers, assumed an air of puffed-up somnolence behind the glittering wires. (Part I, ch. 6)

Indeed, for a writer with such a grimly sustained purpose ('The Silver of the Mine' symbolism occasionally gets a shade literal-minded, particularly where Nostromo's own musings are in question), Conrad can show a remarkable flexibility and a surprisingly relaxed comic play. A case in point, though not directly concerning any of the main characters, is Sotillo's stupid major putting out the binnacle light:

> 'Aha! I have unmasked you,' he cried triumphantly. 'You are tearing your hair from despair at my acuteness. Am I a child to believe that a light in that brass box can show you where the harbour is?...' Other officers ... tried to calm his indignation, repeating persuasively, 'No, no! This is an appliance of the mariners, major. This is no treachery.' The captain of the transport flung himself downwards on the bridge, and refused to rise. 'Put an end to me at once,' he repeated in a stifled voice. (Part II, ch. 8)

On the other hand, and naturally enough, this particular degree of easy relaxation is comparatively rare in *Nostromo* and in Conrad generally. And when we consider in more detail the role of the Goulds, Decoud, Monygham – Nostromo I regard as impressively rendered for the most part, but, despite the title and original inspiration as recorded by Conrad himself, essentially peripheral – when we look at these people, the difficulties increase. Conrad seems driven to exile all his main characters, in this novel particularly, in an isolation more complete and more unsurmountable than that facing any other set of people in an English novel to this date (1904). Decoud's sense of his loneliness and of the futility of things as he experiences them just before his suicide is the extreme case, but it is also the culmination of his life, and it bears a distressing resemblance to, in particular, Mrs Gould's feelings at the end of the novel, surrounded by her wealth and prosperity:

> There was something inherent in the necessities of successful action which carried with it the moral degradation of the idea. She saw the San Tomé mountain hanging over the Campo, over the whole land, feared, hated, wealthy; more soulless than any tyrant, more pitiless and autocratic than the worst Government; ready to crush innumerable lives in the expansion of its greatness . . . . An immense desolation, the dread of her own continued life, descended upon the first lady of Sulaco. With a prophetic vision she saw herself surviving alone the degradation of her young ideal of life, of love, of work – all alone in the Treasure House of the World. The profound, blind, suffering expression of a painful dream settled on her face with its closed eyes. In the indistinct voice of an unlucky sleeper, lying passive in the grip of a merciless nightmare, she stammered out aimlessly the words –
> 'Material interest.' (Part III, ch. 11)

The question of how completely, thoughout the book, Conrad himself shares this despair of Mrs Gould's is raised very sharply indeed by the context in which we meet this passage. It comes in the chapter immediately following the painfully vivid detail of Martin Decoud's suicide on the Golfo Placido.

> On the tenth day, after a night spent without even dozing off once . . . . the solitude appeared like a great void, and the silence of the gulf like a tense, thin cord to which he hung suspended by both hands . . . . Only towards the evening, in the comparative relief of coolness, he began to wish that this cord would snap . . . .
>
> The dawn from behind the mountains put a gleam into his unwinking eyes. After a clear daybreak the sun appeared splendidly above the peaks of the range. The great gulf burst into a glitter all around the boat; and in this glory of merciless solitude the silence appeared again before him, stretched taut like a dark, thin string.
>
> His eyes looked at it while, without haste, he shifted his seat from the thwart to the gunwale. They looked at it fixedly, while his hand, feeling about his waist, unbuttoned the flap of the leather case, drew the revolver, cocked it, brought it forward pointing at his breast, pulled the trigger, and, with convulsive force, sent the still-smoking weapon hurtling through the air. His eyes looked at it while he fell forward and

hung with his breast on the gunwale and the fingers of his right hand
hooked under the thwart. They looked –
'It is done,' he stammered out, in a sudden flow of blood. (Part III, ch. 10)

It is a terrible indictment, not just of 'material interest', but of life itself,
and the fact that Decoud's fumbling at his waist is only just saved by the
steadiness of the prose from a touch of the gratuitous, of horror for its own
sake, is perhaps an added indication of how close Conrad himself is at this
moment to feeling as Decoud does about the beautiful, meaningless void
around him. After this, Mrs Gould's still more grating loneliness (she is
clearly certain that *her* life must continue), surrounded not by emptiness
but by immense power and wealth, seems to range Conrad very much on
their side, as if he could not actively participate in the believable, solid life
that he has created around these people.

But if one has to admit that there is a part of Conrad (just as there was a
part of Swift, for instance) that shies away from life, as if it will inevitably
be stifling or corrupting for any of his fully imagined characters, one has
also to allow a part of him – personally I think much the stronger and more
dominant part in *Nostromo* – that not merely accepts modern life, as it
were grudgingly, but that is actively interested in it and prepared to trust
it. The central surviving figures in this regard at the end of the tale, and
therefore the crucial test of Conrad's resources, are Charles and Emilia
Gould and Dr Monygham. There are others, of course, that are relevant
and that indeed help essentially in building the novel's attack on the void
that otherwise, Conrad clearly fears, modern living might turn out to be.
But the statuesque Father Corbelàn, or even old Viola, impressive though
they certainly are, do not occupy such testing positions as the Goulds and
Monygham. Neither is vulnerable, or even exposed to the conditions of
modern life, in the way these central figures, together with Decoud, are
throughout the novel.

Conrad's triumph with Charles and Emilia Gould is that he keeps both
of them strongly linked to the wider world of business and politics
throughout. Obviously, as Mrs Gould's reflections on 'material interest'
and her husband's obsession with the mine show, each is locked within his
or her own personal life, unable to share anything at all except, as Conrad
says in Chapter 4 of Part I, in public: 'Their confidential intercourse fell,
not in moments of privacy, but precisely in public, when the quick meeting of their glances would comment upon some fresh turn of events.' This
I think is a very shrewd stroke of Conrad's. If he had drawn either or both
of the Goulds as fugitive throughout – avoiding public contact with each
other and with strangers as much as they avoid intimate relationships – we
would have had a novel that could scarcely engage at all with the larger
conditions of modern life, but that felt these only as something completely
alien. Perhaps Lawrence's Gerald Crich, who shares a good deal with
Charles Gould, comes close to this condition, and of course novels since

Lawrence abound in completely alienated characters, 'outsiders' for whom the world is indeed an absurd joke.

It is that for Decoud – or would be, if it weren't for his passion for the rather unlikely Antonia Avellanos – but it is not for either of the Goulds. At the bottom of Emilia's fear of the silver mine is the knowledge that its power makes all too much sense in her life; and Charles's initial reaction to the Sulacan corruption he knows he must use is more positive still:

> It seemed to him too contemptible for hot anger even. He made use of it with a cold fearless scorn, manifested rather than concealed by the forms of stony courtesy which did away with much of the ignominy of the situation. At bottom, perhaps, he suffered from it, for he was not a man of cowardly illusions, but he refused to discuss the ethical view with his wife. (Part II, ch. 1)

Indeed, Charles Gould's scorn for the forces opposing him is fiercer and more tenacious than Gerald Crich's. Both are defeated, on the personal plane, by the material interest they wrestle to subdue, but unlike Gerald, Charles will not give up. He hangs on to the very point when Montero has led him out to be shot and Padre Romàn, following Don Pépé's instructions, will dynamite the mine. As Monygham says, 'I imagine the old padre blowing up systematically the San Tomé mine, uttering a pious exclamation at every bang, and taking handfuls of snuff between the explosions.' And the dynamiting, had it happened, would have been no more than a temporary set-back for the material interests that now rule the western province. As Gould knows perfectly well, and indeed as Holroyd says in so many words, the international resources backing San Tomé are practically inexhaustible. If necessary, the silver can wait where it is in the mountain until conditions are more propitious.

Given this essentially purposeful context, Gould's obsession with the mine enables the novel, instead of merely documenting the effect on individual human lives of outside, alien circumstances inimical to creative and personal life, to use the sterile marriage itself to reach out actively into the threatening world of business and affairs. Throughout his novels, Conrad's men are mostly bachelors, either in fact or, even when actually married, by strong inclination combined with the necessities of the kind of life (usually shipboard) that they choose to lead. In this Conrad may be extreme, but he is certainly not unique. In fact, he is only one of a great many nineteenth- and twentieth-century writers – poets as well as novelists – for whom the notion of marriage is either impossible, or irrelevant to literature, or relevant only in that it contains the seeds of inevitable failure. Written out at length, such a list would make a startling and shining exception of Jane Austen, but there would be very few others.

But all depends, not so much on the simple fact of sterility in the Gould marriage, or even on the contrast at the end with the fertile Basilio, 'grown fat and sleek', playing in the garden with his youngest child (III, 11), as on the alertness and the fairness with which Conrad diagnoses the total situation – from the international financiers and engineers down to the Casa Gould itself – and apportions promise and blame between the individuals threatened and the circumstances threatening them. Sometimes, as perhaps in the rather heavily obvious contrast with Basilio, or the repeated symbolism of the inhumanity of the silver, he seems on the edge of opening up a dichotomy as futile as any of Dickens's: society is totally villainous, and people have only their own individual impulses and sentiments to rely on for spiritual nourishment and sustenance. But mostly in this novel he uses even the Gould marriage as a way of juxtaposing and dramatising both the threat and the promise of the material wealth ready to pour into Sulaco from England, America, France and – since whatever we think of the wretched Hirsch, we believe him where money is concerned – Germany too.

A foothold of promise in the 'material interest' that threatens Mrs Gould is doubly important for Conrad because, if this is totally lacking, he, and the novel, will be the more dangerously poised over those metaphysical gulfs that frighten Decoud. As with the metaphysical doubts, there is no credo one can quote from the novel as evidence that Conrad has triumphed in this regard. Every line of the book shows that he believes in none such. There are, however, scenes where a more complicated marshalling of resources takes place, and I would like now to quote from one of these, the departure of Barrios to fight Montero (Part II, Chapter 4), as typical of the way in which Conrad prepares, in the first half of the novel, for the still greater assaults on his own belief in the possibility of existence that are launched later on with Decoud's suicide, Mrs Gould's near-despair, and the threat of still further revolutions in Costaguana. In this scene, as indeed in so many others, Conrad puts the Goulds, Decoud and Monygham at the centre of an extraordinary variety of conflicting, enmeshed possibilities. Certainly there is no sense of their being merely reflectors of the general hopelessness of things.

Barrios owes his appointment as a Ribierist commander at least partly to the Goulds' influence but partly also to the fact of his 'established political honesty'. Though said to be as unlucky in the field as at gambling, he will not go in for buying and selling victories. So much might seem in itself unlikely, indeed close to a sentimentality, given the Costaguana Conrad has described for us to date: Charles Gould's 'cold, fearless scorn' of the habitual, instinctive mode of corruption around him has been already well documented by this stage of the novel, and we have also had from the very beginning the knowledge of Ribiera's pathetic defeat (in point of actual time, he stumbles over the mountains soon after Barrios sails). In context, however, the Conrad irony applies to Barrios too, and with an appropriate touch of wry sympathy:

General Barrios, in a shabby blue tunic and white peg-top trousers falling upon strange red boots, kept his head uncovered and stooped slightly, propping himself up with a thick stick. No! He had earned enough military glory to satiate any man, he insisted to Mrs Gould, trying at the same time to put an air of gallantry into his attitude. A few jetty hairs hung sparsely from his upper lip, he had a salient nose, a thin, long jaw, and a black silk patch over one eye. His other eye, small and deep-set, twinkled erratically in all directions, aimlessly affable. (Part II, ch. 4)

To Decoud, Barrios is 'an ignorant, boastful Indio', no less ridiculous than the threatening barbarian Montero. To Mrs Gould, who doesn't know him personally at all, he and his soldiers are simply objects of dismay: 'Mrs Gould heroically concealed her dismay at the appearance of men and events so remote from her racial conventions, dismay too deep to be uttered in words even to her husband. She understood his voiceless reserve better now.' (Part II, ch. 4) But Conrad's view is clearly different from both of theirs. Again, as with Gamacho, he notes details of the whole scene with interest and with none of Decoud's revulsion; and he goes on to establish Barrios in a setting and life that is not merely believable, but rendered with a tolerant irony that establishes a trust in the continuance, the very texture and feel, of this life that is to Decoud merely absurd, to Mrs Gould unreal, and to her husband something to be coldly used and controlled. In this spirit Conrad tells us that 'the faction Barrios joined needed to fear no political betrayal. He was too much of a real soldier for the ignoble traffic of buying and selling victories'; and immediately goes on to explain, with no bitterness to contradict or undermine the professional honesty attributed to Barrios, that there is however another reason for his appointment:

After the triumph of the Ribierists he had obtained the reputedly lucrative Occidental command, mainly through the exertions of his creditors (the Sta. Marta shopkeepers, all great politicians), who moved heaven and earth in his interest publicly, and privately besieged Señor Moraga, the influential agent of the San Tomé mine, with exaggerated lamentations that if the general were passed over, 'We shall all be ruined.' (Part II, ch. 4)

Just after this, as Barrios is leaving, we get Mrs Gould's and Decoud's reactions to him; but we also get a scene that weaves together Conrad's interest and belief in both the intense idealisms of the Casa Gould, and the ordinary, everyday, grass-roots facts of life, here focused on Barrios's departure and the speech he makes:

His impulse had been to be very civil on parting to a woman who did not wobble in the saddle, and happened to be the wife of a personality very important to a man always short of money. He even pushed his attentions so far as to desire the aide-de-camp at his side (a thick-set, short captain with a Tartar physiognomy) to bring along a corporal with a file of men in front of the carriage, lest the crowd . . . should 'incommode the mules of the señora.' Then, turning to the small knot of silent Europeans looking on within earshot, he raised his voice protectingly –

'Señores, have no apprehension. Go on quietly making your Ferro Carril – your railways, your telegraphs. Your— There's enough wealth in Costaguana to pay for everything – or else you would not be here. Ha! ha! Don't mind this little picardía of my friend Montero . . . Fear nothing, develop the country, work, work!'

The little group of engineers received this exhortation without a word, and after waving his hand at them loftily, he addressed himself again to Mrs Gould –

'That is what Don José says we must do. Be enterprising! Work! Grow rich! To put Montero in a cage is my work; and when that insignificant piece of business is done, then, as Don José wishes us, we shall grow rich one and all, like so many Englishmen, because it is money that saves a country, and—'

But a young officer in a very new uniform, hurrying up from the direction of the jetty, interrupted his interpretation of Señor Avellanos's ideals . . . (Part II, ch. 4)

The irony here seems to me akin to George Eliot's when she gives us Mr Brooke's utterly mindless talk about 'political economy', learning, 'thought', and all those other things young women do not understand and that we must not 'take too far'. It is clear that neither Mr Brooke nor Barrios understands the larger issues and ideals that, say, Charles Gould, Decoud, Monygham are pursuing (or, in the other book, Lydgate, Dorothea, even, in his way, Casaubon); what both Eliot's and Conrad's tolerant and far-reaching irony makes clear, however, is that the larger issues can have no substance and life outside or beyond the sheer muddle of, in the *Nostromo* scene, Barrios's departure. More positively, it is precisely in the physical detail of scenes like this – the 'woman who did not wobble in the saddle', the 'thick-set, short captain', the recognition, ironic certainly but also correct enough, that 'There's enough wealth in Costaguana to pay for everything' – that Conrad, like George Eliot before him, founds his trust in life, in the day-to-day business of living.

'Go on quietly making your Ferro Carril – your railways . . . ' That, of course, is precisely what must happen, sooner or later, in this rich province, and Barrios's careless acceptance of the inevitable is as essential to any real progress in this direction as Charles Gould's idealism – more so, in fact, because more simply human, and therefore more significant of a hope that can be set against Mrs Gould's despair and Monygham's grim prediction later on:

> 'There is no peace and no rest in the development of material interests.
> They have their law, and their justice. But it is founded on expediency,
> and is inhuman . . . . Mrs Gould, the time approaches when all that the
> Gould Concession stands for shall weigh as heavily upon the people as
> the barbarism, cruelty, and misrule of a few years back.' (Part III, ch. 11)

Monygham is very impressive indeed throughout, and his views, at any
rate on the Gould marriage, are clearly very close to Conrad's own.
Nevertheless, his views on 'rectitude' and 'the continuity and the force
that can be found only in a moral principle' carry with them a certain
stiffness and inflexibility that show the easy-going morality of the Occidental Province in a better, much more fruitful light. Barrios's completely
un-English – indeed, un-European – nature is one focusing example of
this, as is also the security and naturalness of the physical details Conrad so
easily surrounds him with. In the chapter from Part II when he leaves to
fight Montero these are developed further, not in terms of Barrios himself,
but in terms of Conrad's own subtly unspecific rendering of the combined
inevitability, menace, and promise of Charles Gould's creations, the
telegraph and the railway:

> The carriage rolled noiselessly on the soft track, the shadows fell long
> on the dusty little plain interspersed with dark bushes, mounds of
> turned-up earth, low wooden buildings with iron roofs of the Railway
> Company; the sparse row of telegraph poles strode obliquely clear of
> the town, bearing a single, almost invisible wire far into the great
> campo – like a slender, vibrating feeler of that progress waiting out-
> side for a moment of peace to enter and twine itself about the weary heart
> of the land. (Part II, ch. 4)

The act of 'twining itself about the weary heart of the land' carries a clear
and unmistakable ambivalence that comes to mind again at the end of the
novel when Mrs Gould and Monygham look with such despair on the
nature and significance of 'material interest'. But in this chapter, the scene
as a whole shows in addition a strong confidence in the independence,
almost the self-reliance of physical detail (the railway building, the turned-
up earth, the telegraph poles striding clear), and a probing interest even
in the thin wire stretching out into the country. The scene and the chapter
end with the party returning from the harbour startled by the noise of
their carriage wheels 'traversed by a strange, piercing shriek', a locomotive
returning with material trucks from the campo. The questioning, interested writing that gives us the noise of the trucks pulling up, the 'tumult
of blows and shaken fetters under the vault of the gate', has a bit of Dickens's
earlier interest in the sheer power of man's creation of the railway, and
some too of Lawrence's mixed alarm and fascination. Certainly it is not at
this point the writing of a Dr Monygham, a Mrs Gould, or even a Decoud.
It has far too much willing interest in the new phenomena, the telegraph

and the railway, to fit any of these personalities completely. But neither, on the other hand, is it anything like the coldly utilitarian idealism of Charles Gould.

In these ways, and in numbers of scenes like this one, the Goulds' lives and their enterprise act in the novel as a foothold into the world outside themselves, though this is a world that neither Charles nor Emilia can fully share or take part in. Perhaps the acid test of Conrad's real interest in the activity and sweep of that world (beyond the circle of pain and loneliness in which we leave Emilia Gould near the end of the novel) is his treatment of the recurrent scenes of physical pain, and the apprehension of physical pain, that the action, and the stories related from Guzman Bento's time, bring up. There are a number of such scenes in the novel, ranging from the report of Father Beron's quite horrible torturing of Monygham, to the much more lightly done admission from Captain Mitchell himself: ' "These gentlemen," he would say, staring with great solemnity, "had to run like rabbits, sir. I ran like a rabbit myself. Certain forms of death are – er – distasteful to a – a – er – respectable man." ' (Part 1 ch. 2)

That I think is excellently done by Conrad. It is not so much that he is seeing here that, under certain circumstances, any man may run like a rabbit (though, if the man is a Captain Mitchell, with some imperturbable, pompous dignity none the less); the larger significance of the passage, and of the way Mitchell tells it, is that it is told with such remarkable sanity and calm. And in context, the sanity and calm are Conrad's own, as much as Mitchell's. That context is one of the most extended confrontations in all of Conrad between various forms of Western civilisation on the one hand, and the untamed, and possibly untameable, on the other. I think myself that the confrontation is taken much further, and dealt with more securely, than it is even in 'Heart of Darkness', and one local sign of this superiority is that the moments of testing reality are given a much more physical, tangible presence than whatever it is Conrad tries to sum up in Kurtz's famous ejaculation, 'The horror!, the horror!' There are better moments than this in 'Heart of Darkness' – the tellingly simple detail of Marlow's feeling his shoe damp and looking down to find it full of the helmsman's blood is one – but what is remarkable about *Nostromo* is the confidence with which we are brought back again and again to the presence of pain and fear. The manifestations of these are remarkably various, and it is a sign of Conrad's confidence that they are so, and that each can be given a proper, and physical, location (Hirsch hung by the arms, the captain of Sotillo's transport flinging himself flat on the deck, Sotillo himself scrambling booted and spurred into a hammock with a pretended fever and a genuine rattling of teeth). But perhaps the scenes that focus best of all the significance, for Conrad himself, of the apprehension and presence of pain are those involving Doctor Monygham.

It is partly that we know Monygham better, and care more for him, than we do for the minor characters like Sotillo and Hirsch. More than this, though, Monygham is the most resilient of all the major figures in the book. As well as his strong, though perhaps rather stiffly held, belief in 'moral principle', he has a sardonic wit that is more adaptable, and can meet more challenges even than Charles Gould's rock-like constancy to his one ideal. And yet Conrad presents even Monygham as having been broken down by simple, unendurable physical pain. The man directly responsible is Father Beron, Guzman Bento's torturer, and he is given us as the polar opposite of the ascetic 'chaplain of bandits', Father Corbelàn (who incidentally is finally called to Rome and made Cardinal-Arch-bishop as a counter to Holroyd's protestant missionaries). Father Beron is described as a 'big, round-shouldered man, with an unclean-looking, overgrown tonsure on the top of his flat head, of a dingy, yellow com-plexion, softly fat, with greasy stains all down the front of his lieutenant's uniform, and a small cross embroidered in white cotton on his left breast.' This is taking fact to the very edge of melodrama, but even the added detail in the next sentence anchors the torture in believable fact by sticking to the physicality of the man: 'He had a heavy nose and a pendulant lip.' Father Beron's method is to listen impatiently to a prisoner's declarations of innocence and then 'take him outside for a while'. 'When the prisoner returned he was ready to make a full confession, Father Beron would declare, leaning forward with that dull, surfeited look which can be seen in the eyes of gluttonous persons after a heavy meal.' (Part III, ch. 4)

In Dr Monygham's case, it is perhaps as much a fear of what such a man *may* do, as the pain of what he is actually doing, that completes the torture; nevertheless, Conrad's account of Mongyham's subjugation, and its effect on his future conduct and character, hinges on sheer physical pain:

> The doctor had been a very stubborn prisoner, and, as a natural con-sequence . . . his subjugation had been very crushing and very complete. That is why the limp in his walk, the twist of his shoulders, the scars on his cheeks were so pronounced. His confessions, when they came at last, were very complete, too. Sometimes on the nights when he walked the floor, he wondered, grinding his teeth with shame and rage, at the fertility of his imagination when stimulated by a sort of pain which makes truth, honour, self-respect, and life itself matters of little moment.
>
> And he could not forget Father Beron with his monotonous phrase, 'Will you confess now?' reaching him in an awful iteration and lucidity of meaning through the delirious incoherence of unbearable pain. (Part III, ch. 4)

It is the memory of this breakdown that, in harness with his strongly idealistic nature, governs Monygham's conduct throughout the tale. Above all there is the knowledge of his inability to face the now dead but still frightening Beron: 'the sickening certitude prevented Dr Monyg-

ham from looking anybody in the face.' An idealism reduced to this pitch
is or can be a dangerous ingredient for a novelist to handle, particularly
when, as here, the character's natural loyalty, and ultimately love, fix on a
woman who is married and who, for a man like Monygham, is therefore
impossibly distant, however kind and friendly she may be. The elements
of the story could easily have dissolved either into a sentimental nostalgia
(indeed they come close to this when the sight of Mrs Gould on her
return from abroad 'suggested ideas of adoration, of kissing the hem of
her robe'), or into a general helplessness affecting not just Monygham
himself but the cast of the novel as a whole and its very writing.

In point of fact, what happens is a much tougher strain of writing –
tougher than any that even George Eliot, for instance, can muster with
respect to Lydgate's defeat – and one that takes its keynote from Conrad's
presentation and discussion of Monygham's physical breakdown. Bento
dies of apoplexy and Dr Monygham is unexpectedly released from prison:
'As he dragged himself past the guard-room door, one of the soldiers,
lolling outside, moved by some obscure impulse, leaped forward with a
strange laugh and rammed a broken old straw hat on his head.'

Conrad leaves the nature of the 'obscure impulse' tactfully unstressed
and unspecific, but the soldier's act is a clear local sign that his novelist's
eye is on the externals of the situation as well as on the character's inward
state. As a result we have a picture of Dr Monygham that is 'absurd'
in a much stronger way than any that could have been rendered through
Decoud's eye alone, telling though his comments are in a different way:
'Decoud ... leaning his back on the balustrade, shouted into the room with
all the strength of his lungs, "Gran' bestia!" ' That act of Decoud's,
during the balcony scene with Antonia in Part II, Chapter 5, has always
struck me as one of his finest moments; it is a defiantly open, gallant
proclamation of radical scepticism. However, Conrad's own tone on the
ridiculousness of events is, as it needs to be, both more penetrating and
tougher-minded:

> And Dr Monygham, after having tottered, continued on his way.
> He advanced one stick, then one maimed foot, then the other stick;
> the other foot followed only a very short distance along the ground,
> toilfully ... and yet his legs under the hanging angles of the poncho
> appeared no thicker than the two sticks in his hands. A ceaseless trembl-
> ing agitated his bent body, all his wasted limbs, his bony head, the
> conical, ragged crown of the sombrero, whose ample flat brim rested on
> his shoulders. (Part III, ch. 4)

It is the comically alive strength given here to Dr Monygham 'continuing
on his way' that enables the following discussion of his sense of his own
unfitness, and of his devotion to Mrs Gould, to avoid any of the sentimentality that, naturally enough, tends to invade the character's own
private feelings.

A rule of conduct resting mainly on severe rejections is necessarily simple. Dr Monygham's view of what it behoved him to do was severe; it was an ideal view, in so much that it was the imaginative exaggeration of a correct feeling. It was also, in its force, influence, and persistency, the view of an eminently loyal nature.

There was a great fund of loyalty in Dr Monygham's nature. He had settled it all on Mrs Gould's head. He believed her worthy of every devotion. (Part III, ch. 4)

Even some of George Eliot's writing on the defeated Lydgate would suffer, I think, by comparison:

Perhaps if he had been strong enough to persist in his determination to be the more because she was less, that evening might have had a better issue. If his energy could have borne down that check, he might still have wrought on Rosamond's vision and will. We cannot be sure that any natures, however inflexible or peculiar, will resist this effect from a more massive being than their own . . . . But poor Lydgate had a throbbing pain within him, and his energy had fallen short of its task. (*Middlemarch*, ch. *LXXV*)

Though George Eliot and Conrad share some tendencies to sentimentalise situations like this; and though George Eliot has stronger passages of writing and ones that easily conquer her tendency at the end of this passage to indulge the 'throbbing pain within him'; though both these things are true, in the last resort Conrad's treatment of Monygham's 'fund of loyalty' is finer then George Eliot's virtual admission that she has chosen as her hero a man who has 'fallen short of his task'. All depends on the tone in which an author may be driven to admit such a fact. To take the crucial example, Shakespeare's heroes 'fall short of their task' in a dozen ways, only a very few of which (Hamlet's perhaps?) invade the texture of the plays themselves. Others, that in summary form might look sentimental, are in practice not so:

You must bear with me.
Pray you now, forget and forgive: I am old and foolish.

If no novelist can match this scene from *King Lear*, neither can any other dramatist or poet, and the reason they cannot is something that can only be caught from the authority and rightness of Shakespeare's language *in* such a situation. But Conrad's language when he is envisaging scenes of loss, torture, pain is remarkable, and stays so even if and when the comparison is Shakespeare. In *Nostromo*, Dr Monygham is the focal point of such scenes, because he suffers most, or at least he does if we take 'suffering' to mean an amalgam of physical pain and intellectual torment. What most distinguishes Conrad, though, is his ability to extend the strength of Dr Monygham's personal resilience throughout the novel generally. It is not so much Monygham's own personal life and example that are at issue here, though these, as they emerge in his sardonic comments on local events, are impressive enough. For instance, when the engineer-in-chief of the railway demands how on earth Sotillo will ever dare to look any of his friends in the face again, it is Monygham who replies, 'He'll no doubt begin by shooting some of them to get over the first awkwardness.' More significant still, however, than this personal strength and adaptability of Monygham's own is the sense in which he focuses an ability of Conrad's that permeates all the most testing scenes of the novel. Comedy, pain, fear are constantly mingled in *Nostromo* – literally dozens of scenes come to mind – but perhaps the most telling, as an example of the spreading beyond the major characters of a toughness of mind prepared to take on the extremes of physical and mental pain, are the scenes involving the German hide-merchant, Hirsch.

Hirsch is the man who cannot bear the notion of Montero because rebellion will mean loss of money: 'There were hides there, rotting, with no profit to anybody – rotting where they had been dropped by men called away to attend the urgent necessities of political revolutions' (Part II, ch. 5). It is almost impossible to count the number of idealists – political, metaphysical, social, personal – in this novel, but Hirsch is one. He is not *just* interested in money (though he is that – obsessed by it, in fact); he's also, as here, affronted by the very notion that anything could interfere with getting profit from hides. In some sense, he cares less about whose the profit is than that there should be one, for somebody. In this way, Conrad hints at links between Hirsch and some of the major characters (most obviously, Gould).

One thing, however, distinguishes Hirsch from the rest; he is indeed, as Nostromo puts it, 'a miracle of fear', the one character in the novel whose 'imagination' carries him so far beyond the solid ordinariness of Captain Mitchell that, from the time of his hiding in the lighter to his death, he is literally crazed by fear. Once the possibility of buying hides is swamped by physical danger, there is nothing left in Hirsch himself to remind us directly either of Monygham, or of anyone else in the book. Hirsch is the extreme case, the man whose greed for material possessions is matched only by his fear of the consequences of action. For all this though, in the actual writing that gives us his torture and death there is once again a toughness, a mixture of absurd comedy and absolute seriousness, that reminds us of the Conradian strengths focused so often in Monygham's sardonic wit:

Already a rope, whose one end was fastened to Señor Hirsch's wrists, had been thrown over a beam, and three soldiers held the other end, waiting. He made no answer. His heavy lower lip hung stupidly. Sotillo made a sign. Hirsch was jerked up off his feet, and a yell of despair and agony burst out in the room, filled the passage of the great buildings, rent the air outside . . .

Sotillo, followed by the soldiers, had left the room. The sentry on the landing presented arms. Hirsch went on screaming all alone behind the half-closed jalousies while the sunshine, reflected from the water of the harbour, made an ever-running ripple of light high up on the wall. He screamed with uplifted eyebrows and a wide-open mouth – incredibly wide, black, enormous, full of teeth – comical. (Part III, ch. 9)

If writing like this is aware, as it manifestly is, of fear, loneliness, physical pain, it nevertheless presents these, as facts of modern life, with a strength and – the word is virtually Conrad's and Dr Monygham's own property – resilience few can match. Certainly it is hard to think of any modern novelist who can so successfully run the risk of taking metaphysical doubts to the point where they become so unmistakably a matter of the character's, and the reader's, apprehension of physical pain and distortion: 'uplifted eyebrows and a wide open mouth – incredibly wide, black, enormous, full of teeth – comical.'

Conrad's writing generally in *Nostromo* extends beyond the bounds of Captain Mitchell's excellent but unimaginative sanity, and beyond the bounds too of anything Conrad himself could have inherited from the 'code' of the merchant marine. What Conrad, the Polish immigrant, has absorbed is some more general 'Englishness' than this. Indeed, and for all his exotic settings and his driving people like Monygham and Hirsch to the very extremes of human endurance, he is in some ways more in touch with the native sense of middle-class, 'Middlemarch' England than even Henry James was. And he never doubts its viability as radically as D. H. Lawrence, the Nottingham miner's son, seems at some points to doubt, not merely middle-class England, but life itself.

12 D. H. Lawrence: *Sons and Lovers, Women in Love*

A persistent criticism of *Women in Love* has been that it is the climax of a literary career expressing distrust in, and finally disgust with, modern life. I do not myself believe this to be true, any more than I believe parallel charges against Conrad to be true, but some of those who do would add that it is not just 'modern' life, or our mechanistic civilisation, that Lawrence distrusts, but humanity itself. Thus Gerald's delight in choking Gudrun – 'The pure zest of satisfaction filled his soul. He was watching the unconsciousness come into her swollen face, watching the eyes roll back. How ugly she was!' – is mirrored in, for instance, 'The Prussian Officer', in Paul Morel's treatment of Miriam, and in the twisted view of love that many of Lawrence's stories seem to entail. On this reading the whole business is summed up in Birkin's *contemptus mundi*; which, moreover, is literally 'contempt' since it appears to look forward to nothing beyond the mechanistic, quasi-Darwinian hope that the 'creative mystery' will throw up new and 'higher' forms of life, superseding the now worn-out notion of humanity:

> 'The whole idea is dead. Humanity itself is dryrotten, really. There are myriads of human beings hanging on the bush – and they look very nice and rosy, your healthy young men and women. But they are apples of Sodom, as a matter of fact, Dead Sea Fruit, gall-apples. It isn't true that they have any significance – their insides are full of bitter, corrupt ash.' (*Women in Love*, ch. XI)

There is no doubt that Lawrence was indeed tempted by a deep distrust in human life; and moreover it is precisely this insecurity that is behind the over-insistent, precious note in his worst prose:

> She closed her hands over the full, rounded body of his loins, as he stooped over her, she seemed to touch the quick of the mystery of darkness that was bodily him. She seemed to faint beneath, and he seemed

to faint, stooping over her. It was a perfect passing away for both of them, and at the same time the most intolerable accession into being, the marvellous fullness of immediate gratification, overwhelming, out-flooding from the source of the deepest life-force, the darkest, deepest, strangest life-source of the human body, at the back and base of the loins . . . .

> They were glad, and they could forget perfectly. They laughed and went to the meal provided. There was a venison pasty, of all things . . .
> (*Women in Love*. ch. XXIII)

To say that that is embarrassingly bad is to put it mildly. Worse, the bathos of it cannot possibly be dismissed as a mere lapse of 'style' or 'artistry'. It is Lawrence's distrust in life that leads him to this flailing about, and to the desperate search for a 'mystery' that will end all uncertainties. At such moments in *Women in Love* (and even more frequently in *The Rainbow*), Lawrence commits what is perhaps a still worse and more betraying 'stylistic' failure, the outward form of which is a disastrous uncertainty as to who is speaking, novelist or character, and therefore as to how much belief we can have in what is said or felt. Of course, a novelist or drama-tist must always be faced with this problem: if I give the character or *persona* I have created the autonomy he naturally demands, how far can I then believe in, or endorse, what he says? For instance, is the *novel* committed in any way to those disastrous dance movements the sisters like? (' "Do you mind if I do Dalcroze to that tune, Hurtler?" she asked in a curious muted tone, scarce moving her lips.') Or to any of Hermione's trance-like states? At his best Lawrence dramatises this problem brilliantly; at his worst, he simply allows his own prose to follow whatever moment-to-moment feelings Ursula or Birkin or whoever may have. Thus in 'Moony' (on the whole I think a very good chapter), we get prose that follows in the wake of Birkin's stiff, and ultimately authoritarian, meditations to the point where all the obvious questions are forgotten and the character's internal monologue reads as if it were *un*questioningly the author's own:

> There remained this way, this awful African process, to be fulfilled. It would be done differently by the white races. The white races, having the Arctic north behind them, the vast abstraction of ice and snow, would fulfil a mystery of ice-destructive knowledge, snow-abstract annihilation. Whereas the West Africans, controlled by the burning death-abstraction of the Sahara, had been fulfilled in sun-destruction, the putrescent mystery of sun-rays. (*Women in Love*, ch. XIX)

This veering about from the excesses of one character or state of feeling to the excesses of another (generally its opposite) is unfortunately character-istic of much of Lawrence's writing, and pretty clearly it is activated by a recurrent despair about the future, not just of modern society, but also of the human race. It results, too, in precisely the kind of authoritarian writing that Lawrence has (in part rightly) been accused of. Faced with a desperate metaphysical uncertainty of this kind, a writer will clearly be tempted to invoke some ultimate authority, and in Lawrence's case this comes in the form of the nebulously 'strange' and 'mysterious' forces he tends sometimes to invoke, though disguising his own participation in the deal by attributing the resultant, usually pretty hectic, prose to a Birkin or (in her less ironic moments) an Ursula. Gudrun, too, is made to participate at times, conveniently forgetting the questioning she submits herself to in the most impressive of the scenes with Gerald, for instance under the colliery arch and when he walks into her house and bedroom after his father's death.

The worst that can be said against Lawrence is indeed the worst: he takes more risks than most writers, and so he is driven to extreme states in order to try and repair the damage these have done. It should be added here that taking risks of this kind in writing is fairly obviously a twentieth-century activity, and others who have done the same – Yeats, Joyce, Eliot – have also, together with Lawrence, been driven to rely occasionally on authoritarian impulses that tend to subdue the questioning demands of the present by relying on ultimate 'mysteries' they prefer not to – or dare not – question.

The crucial case in any assessment of Lawrence himself, or in any adverse criticism of him, is *Women in Love*. But the beginnings of a possible answer to basic criticisms of his novels, and of his view of modern life, seem to me best sought in a consideration of some aspects of *Sons and Lovers*: in particular, the part Walter Morel has to play there. In his account of Lawrence, Eliseo Vivas, in his book *D. H. Lawrence: The Failure and Triumph of Art* (1960), is worried by scenes like the Morels' kitchen fight in Chapter 1 of *Sons and Lovers*. Vivas admires the 'immediacy' of the writing in this scene, but then – and here he is representative of the majority of Lawrence's critics – he attacks the scene on two grounds. First, he complains that the 'experience of being dragged into the quarrel is anything but pleasant and it induces in the reader ugly and frustrated emotions which he could well do without.' Second – and this is a very common complaint about *Sons and Lovers* – he feels Lawrence is unfairly a partisan in the fight: '. . . Lawrence himself is on the side of the young wife against the drunken husband . . . Lawrence here is not merely presenting a quarrel but is doing more, he is probably justifying a private grudge of his own.' By this, I take it, Vivas means that Lawrence is indulging a grudge against his own father.

Both these objections seem to me to be based on a crucial misreading – a misreading not just of this scene but of *Sons and Lovers* as a whole and, through this, of Lawrence's whole position with regard to modern society. As I read them, this and allied scenes seem to me to present Walter Morel as a very impressive man. It is not just that Lawrence, as everyone agrees,

can render the scenes in the mining village very well. The writing goes far
beyond mere realism to find, along with the brutishness in this working-
class culture – almost part of it, in fact – a directness and physicality, a
blind honesty of feeling that is or can be a sustaining force beyond the
grasp of either Paul or Mrs Morel. In the novel this is, admittedly, a *blind*
honesty and energy – that is Lawrence's criticism of it – but the point of
the whole novel, or one of the main points, is that it nevertheless offers
something that a cultivated, highly sophisticated life cannot. Lawrence is
not on Mrs Morel's side unequivocally. Certainly, her way of living tends
towards an essential refinement and an educated intelligence beyond the
miner's range – this is, of course, developed in later novels in terms of
Birkin, Ursula, Gudrun and others. But one of the main points made by
Sons and Lovers is Lawrence's strong sense of the loss consequent upon this
gain. Morel's personality, his physical presence felt in the very texture of the
writing, show a powerful energy that strives against sophisticated and
civilised living. His is the basic physicality in man that must, whatever the
cost and whatever the outcome, resist any attempt at refinement:

> 'Good gracious,' she cried, 'coming home in his drunkenness!'
> 'Comin' home in his what?' he snarled, his hat over his eye.
> Suddenly her blood rose in a jet.
> 'Say you're *not* drunk!' she flashed.
> She had put down her saucepan, and was stirring the sugar into the
> beer. He dropped his two hands heavily on the table, and thrust his face
> forward at her.
> ' "Say you're not drunk," ' he repeated. 'Why, nobody but a nasty
> little bitch like you 'ud ' ave such a thought.'

This is indeed – Vivas is right – an ugly scene, and Morel is ugly in it:

> He came up to her, his red face, with its bloodshot eyes, thrust forward,
> and gripped her arms . . . . Coming slightly to himself, panting, he
> pushed her roughly to the outer door, and thrust her forth, slotting the
> bolt behind her with a bang. Then he went back into the kitchen,
> dropped into his armchair, his head, bursting full of blood, sinking
> between his knees. (*Sons and Lovers*, ch. 1)

But these are not emotions which a reader 'could well do without'. The
scene is radically unsettling because it is cast in extremely personal terms –
what great novel is not, at points? – and they cut pretty close to the bone.
But an essential part of this unsettling quality is, quite simply, the tragedy of
the man. His dignity, and the dignity of the life that produced him, is there
in the scene in Chapter VIII where he undresses and – as Paul could never
do – washes himself in the scullery and in front of the kitchen fire
with a consciousness of himself that is entirely unembarrassing because it
is unaffected. More impressively still, it is there in the scenes where he hears
of William's death and helps bring the coffin into the cottage:

Morel walked on a few strides, then leaned up against a truck side, his hand over his eyes. He was not crying. Paul stood looking round, waiting. On the weighing-machine, a truck trundled slowly. Paul saw everything, except his father leaning against the truck as if he were tired. (*Sons and Lovers*, ch. VI)

Paul's consciousness in these scenes is one of the key things about them; but another is an element of which he is only partly aware, sometimes not at all. The novel presents Walter as Paul's enemy, but also as representing, taking part in, a whole way of life that is both simpler and stronger than his, because less enquiring, less self-conscious:

Paul saw drops of sweat fall from his father's brow. Six men were in the room – six coatless men, with yielding, struggling limbs, filling the room and knocking against the furniture. The coffin veered, and was gently lowered on to the chairs. The sweat fell from Morel's face on its boards. (*Sons and Lovers*, ch. VI) .

In these scenes after William's death – at the pit-head and in the cottage – Walter is almost completely inarticulate, but they belong to him rather than to anybody else, and the spare directness of the writing focuses on him consistently.

It is precisely the unsophisticated dignity about the man that produces – because it *has* to – the sensual outbursts in scenes like the kitchen fight. In everything he is and does, Walter embodies a way of life that is valuable but also extremely vulnerable, and vulnerable in particular to Paul's needling intelligence and sensitivity. Even in the kitchen scene, however, one is surely aware that the nature and interests of a man like Paul could easily combine to produce a refinement of cruelty that Walter is quite incapable of. Walter's cruelty is physical and immediate, brutish. Paul's more menacing cruelty later on is the product of a sensitive, reflecting intelligence, and the book shows Lawrence's deep concern that Paul's treatment of Miriam, for instance, or of his mother, is – has to be – far less human than Walter's reactions to his wife ever were.

The treatment of Baxter Dawes in *Sons and Lovers* is another crucial case, and, when put together with the treatment of Walter Morel, it forces one to the conclusion that even Lawrence's own statement, 'I shan't write in the same manner as *Sons and Lovers* again', may be slightly misleading. He did not, of course, write in the same manner again, but there is surely a sense in which the distinctively working-class culture of Morel, Dawes, Clara, the Nottingham factory, together with the ways in which this culture and these people faced a new situation, is both important in its own right and remained important to Lawrence throughout his life. Dawes himself might seem an insignificant example, but in context he is not. Like Morel, Dawes is presented as a man defeated and humbled by Paul's sophistication (compare the scene where, in front of the other miners in the kitchen, Morel has to ask his son to count the butties' money for them). But like Morel too, Baxter has something about him that is instinctively surer, more self-contained, than anything or anybody in the more sophisticated later generation. Clara sees this, and it leads her to a realisation that Dawes loved her in a way that Paul never could. There is a real truth in her emotional outburst, 'He loved me a thousand times better than you ever did . . . . He did! At any rate, he did respect me, and that's what you don't do.' In Paul she detects, correctly, a chilling reserve of critical intelligence, 'a sort of detached criticism of herself, a coldness' that fights off real respect. Baxter is more open. He can be, and is, brutal, but the resilience in the writing that gives us his brutality, or the brutality in the Morels' kitchen fight, is, if not exactly the men's own, then something with which they, rather than Paul or Mrs Morel, are immediately and instinctively in touch. It is this *instinctive* strength, too, that enables both Walter and Baxter Dawes to 'own themselves beaten', and Lawrence's rendering of their final defeat is in no sense patronising or vindictive:

> Dawes had been driven to the extremity of life, until he was afraid. He could go to the brink of death, he could lie on the edge and look in. Then, cowed, afraid, he had to crawl back, and like a beggar take what offered. There was a certain nobility in it. As Clara saw, he owned himself beaten, and he wanted to be taken back whether or not. (*Sons and Lovers*, ch. XIV)

Women in Love offers no direct comparison with *Sons and Lovers*. The life figured in Walter Morel and Baxter Dawes is still relevant to Lawrence's concerns here – for instance it has a distinct impact on Ursula and Gudrun in the opening pages, and then later on as they see the labourers after the Arab mare incident, and later still as Gudrun thinks of the colliers when she is with Gerald under the railway bridge – but it is far off now, no longer available as a way of life that the major characters can either take part in or react strongly against. Nevertheless it seems to me that Gerald, the new colliery owner, is taken wrongly by most readers in something the same way as Walter Morel, and the very different life that he embodies, is taken wrongly. The two cases are related, if I am right about them, in that Lawrence's real interests and insights are more broadly based in modern life than they would be given any reading that concentrated on, say, Birkin's rejection of civilisation and the sort of 'Benthamism' espoused by Skrebensky.

Because Gerald is not a Skrebensky at all. It is not just that Gerald is a person and Skrebensky, often, a mere symbol. Almost every key scene that features Gerald – the Arab mare, the water party, the rabbit, 'Gladiatorial', the final death in the snow – has reserves of power and strength that cannot possibly be described as merely negative or corrupting. There is more to him, and about him, than merely the 'go' that first strikes the sisters (for example in the scene in 'Diver' where Gudrun gives the admittedly telling criticism of Gerald, 'The unfortunate thing is, where does his *go* go to, what becomes of it?'). And there is more to him than can adequately be described by seeing him as the centre for an adverse diagnosis, however keen and intelligent, of modern life. He is indeed, as Dr Leavis has shown, *the* centre for such a diagnosis; but in and around him there is in addition a force – the vague word will have to do for the moment – that escapes the diagnosis; that is not, in the very last analysis, susceptible to it.

If one asks, for instance, what it is that makes that final scene of Gerald's death so impressive, it is very hard to give an answer – much harder than it would be if Gerald's purpose in life, or lack of purpose, could be defined as Skrebensky's can. The actual breakdown of Skrebensky in front of Ursula is movingly rendered; but the issues at stake there, of his failure as a person and the related failure of his Benthamite philosophy of life, are relatively easy to grasp. This is not:

> He was weak, but he did not want to rest, he wanted to go on and on, to the end. Never again to stay, till he came to the end, that was all the desire that remained to him. So he drifted on and on, unconscious, and weak, not thinking of anything, so long as he could keep in action.
> The twilight spread a weird, unearthly light overhead, bluish-rose in colour, the cold blue night sank on the snow. In the valley below, behind, in the great bed of snow, were two small figures; Gudrun dropped on her knees, like one executed, and Loerke sitting propped near her. That was all. (*Women in Love*, ch. xxx)

In the first place it is odd, but I think utterly convincing, that the scene as a whole should begin with that dryly witty remark of Loerke's as Gerald is desperately choking Gudrun (it follows the picture of Gudrun's ugly swollen face with the eyes rolled back): 'Monsieur! ... Quand vous aurez fini – ' It is this dry detachment of Loerke's – not in itself particularly admirable – that stops Gerald. And then, in that very sure change of key as Gerald goes off, one realises that this scene might be as much an opening out of possibilities as a shutting down (though obviously it is that too). Gudrun, Gerald, Loerke – they all three of them resist definition, more strongly as a matter of fact than Birkin does. As far as Gerald is concerned, what we have here is a sense of his movement as at once a 'drifting' (his connections with the world and Gudrun and the mines have been snapped completely), and also a movement that is strongly individual, in a sense purposeful.

During the course of the novel the question of what strong attraction it is that binds Birkin to Gerald is kept tactfully unspecific ('Gladiatorial', for instance, explores the possibilities in physical contact between the two men without ever becoming summarisable as a chapter on 'homosexuality'). And here too, at the end, the question is left open, even while one central point is being made unambiguously clear: Gerald is, and has been all along, a centre for Birkin. Gerald has long ago shown that something in him cannot accept Birkin's *Blutbrüderschaft*; but even after this rejection, his presence in the book has been such as to offer stability to Birkin. His physical strength and skill, as in the tobogganing scenes just before his death, are one manifestation of this for Birkin, as they are also for Gudrun (Gerald is 'one perfect line of force . . . '); so even is his power as an industrial magnate:

> She [Gudrun] knew that if he were confronted with any problem, any hard actual difficulty, he would overcome it. If he laid hold of any idea, he would carry it through. He had the faculty of making order out of confusion. Only let him grip hold of a situation, and he would bring to pass an inevitable conclusion. (*Women in Love*, ch. xxix)

The criticisms of this force of 'will' are instantly felt and made by Gudrun, as they are by Birkin. But the force of even their criticisms spends itself before it has completely comprehended – let alone annulled – the 'perfect line of force' that Gerald can be. This is the real explanation for Birkin's stunned dismay at Gerald's death. Or to put the whole issue another way round: for all that has to be said against him, Gerald remains, up to and including the scene of his death, an implicit criticism of Birkin – especially that is, of Birkin's deliberate choice in throwing the world away. I am not sure that the novel stresses this criticism of Birkin quite strongly enough, but it is, surely, more strongly made in terms of Gerald's abilities and his physical presence than in anything Ursula says in her early mocking irony at Birkin's expense. Hers is a negative position; Gerald's is not, or not entirely.

The part he plays in the snow scene at the end is certainly far from ineffectual or negative. Nor is his death entirely a matter of any 'tragic' loss of potential. The 'cold blue night', the great bed of snow, the 'fallen masses of rock and veins of snow slashing in and about the blackness of rock, veins of snow slashing vaguely in and about the blackness of rock' – all this, so far from merely symbolising 'negation', is tangibly, physically present. Its presence is that of something at once compellingly ordered, and at the same time threateningly disordered ('veins of snow slashing in and about the blackness of rock'). And it belongs to Gerald, as of right. Indeed, all the snow scenes throughout 'Continental' and 'Snowed Up' are too strongly present to be either a mere antithesis of the African darkness, or a mere illustration or dramatisation of Gerald's personality. They effect a bewildering release of energies in everybody, as in the Schuhplatteln. But they are also something in the cosmos with which Gerald, above all, and with him Gudrun, are quite positively in touch:

> The passion came up in him, stroke after stroke, like the ringing of a bronze bell, so strong and unflawed and indomitable. His knees tightened to bronze as he hung above her soft face . . . He felt strong as winter,

his hands were living metal, invincible and not to be turned aside. His heart rang like a bell clanging inside him. (*Women in Love*, ch. xxix)

The danger of this state in Gerald is registered immediately in Gudrun's withdrawal, and later in the horror she feels when she sees his reflection in the mirror and cannot turn round to face him. But there is also here a still remaining sense that his energy is illimitable – something that could never, for instance, be contained or placed by any ironic vision like Loerke's – and it is this that makes his 'drifting' walk at the end a purposeful one. Though having said that, one has immediately to admit that the closing scene of Gerald's life is dominated by a quite terrifying sense of emptiness and loss. The novel cannot be summarised or schematised:

He had come to the hollow basin of snow, surrounded by sheer slopes and precipices, out of which rose a track that brought one to the top of the mountain. But he wandered unconsciously, till he slipped and fell down, and as he fell something broke in his soul, and immediately he went to sleep. (*Women in Love*, ch. xxx)

It is no criticism of earlier English novelists, or even of Lawrence's own contemporaries – Conrad, Joyce, E. M. Forster – that none of them could have envisaged that scene of Gerald's death. Emily Brontë – her rendering of Heathcliff's absorption with death is the clearest parallel – could not have done so, unless perhaps the circumstances under which she wrote had been utterly different from what they were. The contrast between Lawrence and other writers is useful here mainly in that it may help to illustrate, or draw attention to, the weight Lawrence is placing on Gerald and the way Gerald lives his life. Much of the novel's uniqueness is invested in Gerald. His death is the culmination of a series of scenes, particularly those from 'Coal Dust' (Chapter ix) onwards, which provide the main drive and purpose for Lawrence's whole vision of modern life and the scope that individuals may have in it.

'Coal Dust', as the title signifies, is the chapter in the book that most specifically remembers the world evoked in *Sons and Lovers*. It starts, however, with the scene, quite unlike anything in *Sons and Lovers*, of Gerald on his Arab mare facing the train at the railway crossing. This is often taken as overtly symbolic (Gerald's mechanical 'will' subduing emotion and the flesh); but in fact the significance of the scene is quite other than this. In the first place it begins, with compelling ease, by evoking the significance of the simple facts of industrial England. This, certainly, is something that has its place and that will not be subdued either by Birkin's contempt for it or by the tragedy of Gerald's ultimate failure to transcend it.

Going home from school in the afternoon, the Brangwen girls descended the hill between the picturesque cottages of Willey Green till they came to the railway crossing. There they found the gate shut, because the colliery train was rumbling nearer. They could hear the small locomotive panting hoarsely as it advanced with caution between the embankments. The one-legged man in the little signal-hut by the road stared out from his security, like a crab from a snail-shell. (*Women in Love*, ch. ix)

The scene has its due importance; it remains meaningful throughout the chapter because there is nothing strained or wilful or vindictive in the prose that renders the 'shut' gate and the colliery train. Indeed, one of the essential facts about the whole chapter is that it is not only the animalism of the horse, but this industrialism too that Gerald is fighting, *and* fighting more impressively than Birkin ever does. It is he, Gerald, who registers its importance, and it is in and through Gerald that Lawrence shows that this is something that cannot simply be condemned out of hand, in Birkin's way, or run away from. The train, for instance, has its own autonomy. It refuses to be reduced to the easy terms of a symbol of mechanical civilisation and so dismissed as inimical to humanity. It is too much a necessary fact of humanity's own creation. Ugly though it is, it is indeed a creation, a thing to be reckoned with, and Lawrence, through the man and the horse confronting it, knows this:

> The noise was released, the little locomotive with her clanking steel connecting-rod emerged on the highroad, clanking sharply. The mare rebounded like a drop of water from hot iron, Ursula and Gudrun pressed back into the hedge, in fear. But Gerald was heavy on the mare, and forced her back. It seemed as if he sank into her magnetically, and could thrust her back against herself.
> 'The fool!' cried Ursula loudly. 'Why doesn't he ride away till it's gone by?'
> Gudrun was looking at him with black-dilated, spellbound eyes. But he sat glistening and obstinate, forcing the wheeling mare, which spun and swerved like a wind, and yet could not get out of the grasp of his will, nor escape from the mad clamour of terror that resounded through her, as the trucks thumped slowly, heavily, horrifying, one after the other, one pursuing the other, over the rails of the crossing. (*Women in Love*, ch. ix)

By the same token the horse, too, is more than a symbolic extension of Gerald's body. Despite the phrase ' . . . almost as if she were part of his own physique', the real meaning of the scene is that the horse, though obviously it answers a physical need of Gerald's (something that, like the train, he feels he must conquer), is beyond him, an animal that is simply different from mankind. Ursula is absolutely right in her protest: 'But why does he do it? . . . Why does he? Does he think he's grand, when he's bullied a creature ten times as sensitive as himself?' She is right, this is indeed a bullying of something other than himself. The horse, like the rabbit later on, has its own strongly physical existence and its sensitivity. Throughout the scene Gerald is facing things that are far more challenging than any simple extension of his own personality could be. The 'otherness' of a horse, like the 'otherness' of the explosive, blindly animalistic rabbit, is one of these things; another is the fact that man's ugly creations, like the train, the mines, the colliery town that so strongly attracts and repels Gudrun, cannot *simply* be dismissed as ugly and repulsive, much as Birkin, and even Gerald in some frames of mind, would like to do so. These, too, have now their necessary importance and autonomy.

From here on in the novel there are, certainly, weak moments. In 'Water Party', the next key scene, the directness and spareness of Lawrence's prose dissolves at times into the bathos of 'the perfect fire that burned in all his joints', the empty flailing about of

> Then he clambered into the boat. Oh, and the beauty of the subjection of his loins, white and dimly luminous as he climbed over the side of the boat, made her want to die, to die. The beauty of his dim and luminous loins as he climbed into the boat, his back rounded and soft – ah, this was too much for her, too final a vision. (*Women in Love*, ch. xiv)

This is hysterical writing, taking refuge in a mere wash of feeling that is so insistent as to be hardly feeling at all. Lawrence's attention is so laxly applied (or, if you prefer it, so fixedly) to some of these passages that he even gets local detail distractingly wrong. He has obviously forgotten, for instance, that you don't 'row' a canoe with a 'paddle', let alone have the passenger seated in the back facing the rower (paddler?). For all this, the best even of this scene is certainly strong enough to make it a nodal point in the development of that tense expectancy in the Gerald – Gudrun relationship that culminates in his walking to death in the snow. Here in 'Water Party', starting with Gudrun's facing the Highland cattle, giving Gerald 'the first blow', and then continuing to the scene where the two sit with the space between them isolated in the canoe, we get the first crucial exploration of the ways in which Gerald's commitment to death includes a tensed strength. To put it – as the novel does increasingly from here on – in more personal terms: Gerald's strength satisfies Gudrun, even though he cannot finally satisfy her. We know even now that there is a point beyond which he cannot go, except to death, but his strength – physical, sexual, and in his own suppressed way, spiritual – makes this point indeed a sticking-place, a dominant fact in the life of the novel.

Lawrence is obviously an experimental writer, and he takes the risks that his experimentalism involves, like the weak bits of 'Water Party' and the even weaker bits in 'Excurse'. But reading the whole section following 'Water Party' (and indeed almost all of the book), the inescapable impression is that the writing has a spareness, a toughness and stripped-down quality that *The Rainbow*, good as it is, lacks. The more radical of the two novels is actually the more sustained and direct. Thinking in terms of *The*

Rainbow one would expect the excesses of 'Water Party' to recur – they are not, after all, 'lapses of style', but excesses that Lawrence was driven to, under the circumstances as he saw them – but in fact there is only one other key point, nine chapters later in 'Excurse', where hysteria intervenes cripplingly. For the most part, the writing in the rest of the novel is firm, metaphorically assured, observantly witty:

> And then quite suddenly [the rabbit] settled down, hobbled among the grass, and sat considering, its nose twitching like a bit of fluff in the wind. After having considered for a few minutes, a soft bunch with a black, open eye which perhaps was looking at them, perhaps was not, it hobbled calmly forward and began to nibble the grass with the mean motion of a rabbit's quick eating.
>
> 'It's mad,' said Gudrun. 'It is most decidedly mad.' (*Women in Love*, ch. xviii)

This is after the rabbit has subsided from its fury, and the change of tone is absolutely right. The 'black and white tempest' of the rabbit, and of Gerald brutally subduing the rabbit, is a driving force within the novel; and one of the clearest manifestations of the sureness with which Lawrence has envisaged this sensual energy is the change of tone from the nakedly physical scenes earlier, when Gudrun's wrists are scored by the rabbit's claws, to this mocking evocation of the creature at the end, 'considering'. – Lawrence has recognised, as he did in the Arab mare scene, a terrifying immanence in physical facts, in the sheer physicality of the whole natural world. But in this novel in particular, the recognition is so collected and so firm that the evocation of the flesh is direct, substantial (only rarely hysterical); and the changes of tone registering another viewpoint (either disturbedly metaphysical like that of the next chapter, 'Moony', or ironic as here at the end of the rabbit scene) are consistently sure.

I think the reason for this sureness and substantiality is that, whereas in *The Rainbow* Lawrence tended to see modern civilization largely as a threat, here he has envisaged it in a different way. It is still a threat, of course. but for all the criticisms the novel itself makes of Gerald and Gerald's way of life – or ways of life, since they are certainly various – he is also seen consistently as a stabilising force. He is a centre against which Birkin's free enquiry is played off: until Gerald's death, when the prospect that faces Birkin is rendered, I think with absolute frankness on Lawrence's part, as dismayingly problematical. Gerald's 'will' dominating the horse, brutally subduing the rabbit, diving for his sister, wrestling with Birkin – the manifestations of it are intensely rendered as well as various – is not merely 'understood' by Lawrence, but in some ways, and granted all the criticisms and qualifications, allowed its full value – almost, indeed, endorsed. Gerald did face the train and, at whatever cost, subdue the mare; and only Gerald, in the novel, could or would have done so. I am not suggesting that Gerald, or even Lawrence, is fully conscious of this role; only that it is there, and that its relevance to the modern world is of an active and positive kind.

Gerald Crich and Walter Morel: you could hardly pick two 'characters' less alike. But, as Dr Leavis has shown, more is at stake than any question of 'characterisation', and the ways in which each of these men manifests a contained, baffled strength prove Lawrence's trust in life to be more widely and more truly based than any concentration on a Birkin philosophy of life could possibly do. As I have said, I think that both novels are currently misread, in so far as what these two men *are* is underestimated by most readers and critics. I also think that the *final* dimension Gerald has is underplayed even by Dr Leavis. Dr Leavis's book *D. H. Lawrence: Novelist* (1955), seems to me unquestionably the major work on Lawrence so far. It is broadly based (as, for instance, in the discussion of *The Rainbow* and George Eliot); and it opens up possibilities that are closed to those who read Lawrence's major work either as 'pure art' or as something to which pre-formed 'criteria of judgment' may be applied. It is also – contrary to popular opinion – admirably frank and direct on Lawrence's deficiencies. The whole discussion of *Kangaroo* and *Aaron's Rod*, for instance, brings these into the open; and on the 'Egyptian Pharaoh' passage in *Women in Love* Dr Leavis has this to say:

> I see here a fault of which I could find worse examples in *Women in Love*, though it is a fault that I do not now see as bulking so large in the book as I used to see it. It seems to me that in these places Lawrence betrays by an insistent and over-emphatic explicitness, running at times to something one can only call jargon, that he is uncertain – uncertain of the value of what he offers; uncertain whether he really holds it. (p. 148)

That seems to me clear and to the point. One might worry a bit about what the 'worse examples' would turn out to be, but I do not think they would be such as to alter this judgement materially.

   Where I find Leavis's account less than adequate is in his discussion of the significance of Gerald in *Women in Love*. Throughout his book, Leavis stresses the importance of Lawrence's 'diagnostic' intelligence. Obviously he had to do so, and there can be no question that he was right in doing so. But the very act of showing this quality in Lawrence raises a further difficulty: the diagnosis of modern life, particularly as it is presented in *Women in Love*, is so shattering that it leaves nothing much left for us to live by or in. Birkin and Ursula, as Dr Leavis has pointed out, are not a 'norm' that we, or Lawrence, can place securely and confidently against the terrifying failure of a Gerald. Indeed, considered in any detail at all, Birkin's way of life is simply not viable for anybody but himself and Ursula (and Lawrence leaves even their future a very open question at the end of the novel).

   Leavis stresses all these difficulties, and in addition shows that Birkin's life enacts an exploratory process, not a simple-minded affirmation or prescription. None the less, the cumulative tendency of his argument is to grant Birkin and Ursula a positive role denied to Gerald and Gudrun. For all the difficulties that face them, Birkin and Ursula are seen as testing out 'the need for some norm for the relations between men and women other than what Gerald and Gudrun enact'. They certainly do represent normative possibilities, and I would not for a moment deny the positive spirit in which the Birkin – Ursula relationship is shown. What I doubt is the implication that Gerald's life must in consequence be placed against Birkin's as essentially the negative one of the two. In some sections of his chapter Leavis himself seems to suggest that there are ways in which Gerald could be seen as strongly in touch with deeper sources of life, but the general tenor of his argument does not allow these suggestions the weight they should surely have:

> Lawrence's preoccupation with relating the overt expressions of personal life to the impersonal depths goes with his power of presenting in the disorder of the individual psyche the large movement of civilization. It is because it gives so much, and gives the unexpected, that *Women in Love* has been judged to give less than the reader has the right to demand. (pp. 191–2)

It is a question of what a term like 'the large movement of civilisation' encompasses. Clearly it encompasses a lot, and Lawrence is seen all along by Leavis as trusting both deep instinctive life-forces and the 'tradition' he revivifies in, for instance, *The Rainbow*. But I think that in *Women in Love* he also puts his trust quite specifically in contemporary life, contemporary civilization – to the point, indeed, where his criticisms of it are truly radical because couched in his firmest prose and nowhere misdirected towards men of straw such as Skrebensky.

Leavis's account is the one that has shown both the significance of Gerald's case and the 'potency' with which Lawrence invests it. His remark – actually applied to the presentation of Hermione – 'she becomes for us a potent specific presence', seems to me very significant. One might easily use the phrase 'a potent specific presence' about Birkin too; but there is surely a sense in which, of all the characters in the novel, Gerald should have a prior claim, and this even in the teeth of the impotent 'will' that finally breaks him. Because in the last resort, not only a good deal of the novel's extraordinary range and density, but also its stability, is founded on Gerald's life and death. At all points, his is indeed a 'potent specific presence'. I would myself add: far more assuredly so than Birkin's is, essential though Birkin is to the exploratory spirit in which the whole book is written.

13 Conclusion

The ending of *Women in Love* is indeed impressive, because the questions it puts are very honest ones, and honestly *questions*, not, for the most part, statements masquerading as questions, or long passages from Birkin that need satiric comments from Ursula to redeem them from being simply Lawrentian propaganda. Nevertheless, it is Birkin's mind that is dominant there at the end; and certainly his own impulse is still to think, not in terms of any broad set of relationships between people, but rather in terms of some particular individual who may supplement his own individual relationship with Ursula. Clearly what he wants is a 'marriage' that might include a man too, but hardly 'men' or 'mankind'. And, equally clearly, Lawrence sympathises with this impulse towards a post-Romantic, élitist life, with an artist-figure dominating the scene.

A marriage, or life, of this kind, if it were put into practice from day to day over anything like the span of an adult life-time, would be practically a denial of all that the English novel has hitherto stood for: to reject all but a few very special individuals is to reject life itself, and to side with the very worst impulses in Romanticism against the hard practicalities that the best English novelists, at least from Richardson onwards, have backed. Indeed, there is a clear sense in which the nineteenth-century novel is at odds, not only with Romanticism, but with contemporary poetry too; and this battle develops even within the corpus of a twentieth-century novelist like Lawrence, sometimes to the point where whole passages of a given work are devoted to self-congratulatory prose-poems: writing that *pretends* to be interested in other people, but actually is merely using them as pawns in a game, or manifestations of a controlling 'self' that in the end eats all it sees.

On the other hand, in his best work Lawrence also makes it clear – albeit a little grudgingly sometimes – that Birkin's and Ursula's giving up the world of teaching and schools, and Gerald's giving up industry, however necessary this may be for them personally, is no answer to the continued and demanding presence of the world. Something of this realisation on Lawrence's part is there for instance in the railway-crossing scene, and in the way Gerald's strength at that point is not merely locked within himself, as the considerably diminished strength of introverted and alienated figures so often is in later literature, but meets that of the animal, and also that of the solidly real train, the crossing, the whole detail of surrounding countryside, including the workmen who jeer at Ursula and Gudrun afterwards. And beyond commanding scenes like this of the crossing, or 'Rabbit', or Gerald with Gudrun after his father's death – all scenes that share something of the generalising quality of symbol, but without the fixity and inertness of most symbols – beyond these, there are lots of smaller, less obvious suggestions of the permanence and worth of worldly things that combat Birkin's vision of mankind dying out, or being limited effectively to one or two special people of transcendent vision and authority. The Lawrence of *Women in Love* cannot people his world as easily or as prolifically as earlier novelists could. For instance, there are few, if any, of the foolish or limited but somehow solidly permanent George Eliot figures like Mr Brook and Celia, Mrs Cadwallader, Chettam, and so on. But he can still sketch in very vividly indeed the irony of Loerke's best moments ('Quand vous aurez fini', to Gerald choking Gudrun); the strange pair who take Ursula's present of the chair in the market place; Mrs Crich facing Birkin at the wedding-party; and the picture of Gerald dancing the Schuhplatteln near the end of the novel, and being mocked by Gudrun afterwards for his triumph (quite unconscious on Gerald's part) with the German Professor's daughter.

Lawrence's best work, therefore, seems to me much more stable than the extremes of 'modernism' (or individualism) that Lukács, and others after him, have quite rightly complained of; and this precisely because it takes part willingly and actively in the very world – it is basically a middle-class world – that the 'salvator mundi' part of him wanted to reject or talk down to. He was right, of course, to reject a good many things in the middle-class England that he saw and dramatised in the major novels and stories. So indeed were a lot of other people, fifty or more years earlier than Lawrence, who foresaw that the rise of a middle-class democracy (whether in Tocqueville's America, or in the England of people as different as Carlyle, J. S. Mill, Morris) would entail the consequent dangers of a 'tyranny of the majority'; and, going with this, the dangers too of an ever-growing public administration that might indeed lessen notorious inequalities of income and opportunity, but that would also be subject to a stiffening of the sinews – a tendency to outgrow its own strength, and therefore to stifle the very opportunities it was designed to liberate and make more freely available to all. Lawrence saw all this, and, in consequence, he hated democracy more fully and completely than anyone, including even writers like Yeats, Joyce, Eliot, has managed to do in this century. His distinction is that, more than most other creative writers, he has indeed trusted the tale, rather than the teller. His best work trusts an impulse within himself that pits a twentieth-century individualism of the Birkin kind against middle-class collectivism, but manages to do so without in any sense rejecting the stability that that collectivism, for all Birkin's suspicions of it, can maintain.

Clearly, Lawrence did initiate changes in the English novel, and so in English sensibility generally. For instance, he was much more successful than either Virginia Woolf or James Joyce in freeing the novel from what might have become a too strict adherence to the stories of particular people locked within their own environmental pattern. 'Tell Arnold Bennett that all rules of construction hold good only for novels which are copies of other novels. A book which is not a copy of other books has its own construction, and what he calls faults, he being an old imitator, I call characteristics.'[1] Yet he is more of a gradualist than some of his own pronouncements would indicate. I do not believe, myself, that he ever did abandon completely 'the old stable *ego* of the character'.[2] It persists (fortunately) in characters like Gerald, Gudrun, Ursula, even Birkin; just as similar stubborn realities persist in the day-to-day details of the novel itself. If his language is never tempted to the experiments Joyce and his followers have indulged, this is because his working-class/middle-class background continues to mean much more to him than he is ever willing consciously to allow. There *is* a 'story' in *Women in Love*, for instance, and it is couched partly in terms that any nineteenth-century novelist, used to telling stories about ordinary people in ordinary language, would clearly have recognised and responded to. Coal, and soot, and diamond are quite clearly distinct in Lawrence's best fiction, and the fact that they may all be carbon elementally is relatively insignificant.

Lawrence placed no bomb under English fiction. Surgery, yes (though one might prefer some more constructive metaphor for what he did);[3] but nineteenth-century, middle-class certainties are still the mainstay of the best English novels – indeed, of the best of English literature generally – just as they were the mainstay of his own writing, even after *Sons and Lovers*. This is why his innovations are likely to stay, where those of the later Joyce, for instance, reducing language itself to a mere wash of feeling and a quite directionless, 'train-of-association' thinking, will not. If God is not mocked, neither, for a long time yet, will nineteenth-century England be mocked. Clearly it had its own instabilities – one need only recall the appalling conditions under which most of England's population then lived, as also the frustrations and fears at still more permanent injustices and dislocations that most of the novelists record – but at least some of these instabilities were fruitful, rather than debilitating. Not very much of nineteenth-century poetry after Keats has survived (unless one counts the thin end of Romanticism that continues to direct modern poets to talk about the 'self' in preference to the world about them); and there was virtually no drama in England, or even Ireland, with any basis at all in modern living. But the novel has certainly survived, and it will continue to do so as long as what gave it birth, a flourishing middle-class England, survives.

That, of course, is very much in question. But then it always was, and personally I doubt that the symptoms recently of fear, unrest, even outright rebellion are any more marked than they were in the England of a hundred and thirty years ago. Certainly the famous predictions made then by Engels and Marx, for all the remarkable insight that singles both men out and that makes many of their comments closely relevant to a study of literature, have not proved true, and are clearly very unlikely to do so, at least in any of the forms originally announced. What seems much more likely is a continuation of the relatively gradual changes in living that have marked both this century and the last; and with these, of course, there will be changes also in literature and in the novel. One very healthy sign in this regard is that English drama is clearly no longer the sleeping partner it was for so long, including virtually the whole of the period when the novel was taking shape, form and substance. If this continues, we can I think look forward to the continuance also of a widely and strongly based literature, and one that flourishes on precisely the contradictions and clashes that the early Blake imagined, and that marked the progress of nineteeth-century middle-class life generally in England.

Notes

CHAPTER I

1 For figures on literacy see: J. W. Dodds, *The Age of Paradox* (Gollancz, 1953), esp. pp. 128ff.; R. K. Webb, *The British Working Class Reader, 1790–1848* (Allen and Unwin, 1955); R. D. Altick, *The English Common Reader* (Chicago, 1957); E. P. Thompson, *The Making of the English Working Class* (Pelican ed., 1968) pp. 783–94.
2 George Lukács, *Essays on Thomas Mann* (Merlin Press, 1964) p. 94.
3 George Lukács, *The Historical Novel* (Merlin Press, 1962) p. 33.
4 D. H. Lawrence, *Selected Literary Criticism*, ed. Anthony Beal (Heinemann, 1955) p. 115.
5 Restoration comedy is perhaps one exception to this sweeping generalisation. But I do not myself see any more, at least until the end of the nineteenth century. See my book, *A Study of Elizabethan and Jacobean Tragedy* (Cambridge University Press, 1964), especially concluding chapter.
6 On the working class generally, and its attitudes to the Radical leaders and others of the middle class, see E. P. Thompson's excellent book, *The Making of the English Working Class* (Gollancz, 1963; Pelican, 1968). Thompson puts the beginnings of working-class alienation earlier than most (i.e. in the 1790s). Asa Briggs notes that the term 'middle class' did not come into general usage until the 1830s: 'Middle-Class Consciousness in English Politics', *Past and Present* (April, 1956) pp. 65–74.
7 R. J. White, *Waterloo to Peterloo* (Heinemann, 1957) p. 153
8 Thompson, *Making of the English Working Class* (Pelican ed.) p. 203. Thompson's discussion of the state of the country in this period is very revealing. In addition, F. O. Darvall notes that, by the summer of 1812, the government had felt it necessary to build up a force of 12,000 troops distributed between Leicester and York. There were also local militia, 'watch and ward' groups, yeomanry: *Popular Disturbances and Public Order in Regency England* (O.U.P., 1934) pp. 115–17.
9 E. J. Hobsbawm, *Labouring Men* (Weidenfeld and Nicolson, 1964) p. 24; and cf. Thompson, *Making of the English Working Class*. The period of the First Reform Bill is, of course, the one covered in *Middlemarch*, q.v. below, Chapter 7.
10 Beatrice Webb, *My Apprenticeship* (1926) pp. 274–6. Of course, a great many others of the essayists, like Arnold, comment on industrial and working-class matters (though even Arnold's very bitter comments on working-class behaviour during the Hyde Park riots are not, I think, reflected directly in any of his major poems: See *Culture and Anarchy*, ed. Dover Wilson (C.U.P., 1950) p. 105.
11 Charles Booth, *Life and Labour of the People* (1897) IX, p. 441.
12 *My Apprenticeship*, p. 149.

CHAPTER 3

1 From Reuben A. Brower's *The Fields of Light* (Oxford University Press, 1951); the relevant chapter, together with Mark Schorer's essay 'The Humiliation of Emma Woodhouse', is reprinted in the *Twentieth Century Views* collection on Jane Austen, ed. Ian Watt (Prentice-Hall, 1963). The collection also reprints Kettle on *Emma*, the D. W. Harding essay, Lionel Trilling on *Mansfield Park*, and others.
2 From Lionel Trilling, *The Opposing Self*, quoted *Twentieth Century Views*.

CHAPTER 5

1 For some examples, see John W. Dodds, *The Age of Paradox* (Gollancz, 1953); and Margaret Dalziel, *Popular Fiction 100 Years Ago*, (Cohen, 1957).
2 Though this is no extraordinary prescience on Mrs Gaskell's part, since the 'theory' was, in one form or another, common in pre-Marxist England. Margaret Cole credits Robert Owen with formulating the notion 'long before Marx' in her book *Robert Owen of New Lanark* (Batchworth Press, 1953) p. 2. And even *laissez-faire* economists like Ricardo showed a clear and strong feeling for labour as a source of value.
3 Denis de Rougemont, *Passion and Society*, translated by Montgomery Belgion from the earlier version in French (Faber, 1956).
4 In *Ruth* the seduced but innocently pure heroine dies from the saintly act of nursing her rakish lover through typhus.

CHAPTER 6

1 *An Autobiography* (World's Classics ed., 1953) p. 272.
2 Trollope himself came to doubt the viability of novels having 'two absolutely distinct parts', *An Autobiography*, p. 305.
3 Ibid., pp. 120, 134, 274.
4 A. O. J. Cockshut, *Anthony Trollope* (Collins, 1955).

CHAPTER 13

1 Letter to J. B. Pinker, 16 December 1915.
2 Letter to Edward Garnet, 5 June 1914.
3 See D. H. Lawrence, 'Surgery for the Novel – Or a Bomb', *Phoenix* (Heinemann, 1936).

Index